Managing Human Resources

STRATEGIC APPROACH TO WIN

Managing Human Resources

STRATEGIC APPROACH TO WIN

AJIT KUMAR GHOSH
Reader in
Human Resource Management,
Department of Commerce,
University of Burdwan

Manas Publications
New Delhi-110 002 (INDIA)

MANAS PUBLICATIONS
(Publishers, Distributors, Importers & Exporters)
4402/5-A, Ansari Road (Opp. HDFC Bank)
Darya Ganj, New Delhi - 110 002 (India)
Phones: Off.: 011-23260783, 23265523,
Res.: 011-23842660
E-mail: manaspublications@gmail.com
www.manaspublications.in

ISBN: 978-81-7049-149-1 (13 Digits)
81-7049-149-5 (10 Digits)

Rs. 495/-

Designed at
Manas Publications
Printed in India at
HS Offset, Delhi
and published by Mrs Suman Lata for
Manas Publications, 4402/5-A,
Ansari Road (Opp HDFC Bank),
Darya Ganj, New Delhi - 110002 (INDIA)

Contents

Foreward

I was delighted to go through the manuscript of the publication, *Managing Human Resources: Strategic Approach to Win* of Dr. Ajit Kumar Ghosh, who had been a student of the Department of Commerce of this University and subsequently obtained Ph.D. Degree. Dr. Ghosh has been a prolific writer in the area of Human Resource Management and has contributed to different journals of national and international importance. His experience as Senior Manager (Personnel) in a nationalised bank and also in a manufacturing industry has helped him gather practical experience from the field which actually serves as the basis on which theories are built. At present Dr. Ghosh is Reader in Human Resource Management of our University and we are really glad that he has decided to help the newly started course with his vast experience.

In fact, a subject like Human Resource Management is fast changing keeping pace with the changing socio-economic environment of the country and also the attitude of the legislative bodies. The exposure which Dr. Ghosh had during his service career has been given proper shape in his book and I am sure that its readers which will include not only students of Management but also practitioners in the field will benefit much. Further, human behaviour, being the subject, common men will also get good direction in the matter of their attitude towards their wards in giving them proper guidance so as to help them become effective citizens of the country and behave in a rational manner. I am sure that critical appreciation of the book by the concerned persons will be gracefully accepted by Dr. Ghosh for making improvement in future editions.

A.K. Mallik
Vice-Chancellor

Preface

Every human being is born to win, to achieve and to succeed in his activities. But he may not be successful in his operations, he may not be able to win, he may not be able to achieve his goals, if he lacks some qualitative traits essential for the achievement of his mission. These qualitative traits frame his mindset appropriately with positive thought patterns so that he may have a clear perception of the people around him as also the objective set or assignment given to him. The person with a positive mindset may not find it difficult to achieve his goal. This book is designed to reflect different kinds of behavioural activities of human beings with the objective of exploring the qualitative factors and traits a person should possess for the accomplishment of a task and the achievement of goals.

The subject of this book is the manifestation and reflection of the behaviour of human beings, particularly those of people at work. People with different ego-states work together and interact with each other. A series of interactions take place in a situation, whether one is working as a subordinate, as a boss or as a peer; these interactions are manifested in day-to-day activities. Considering the vastness of such behavioural manifestations, it is not possible to incorporate all behavioural activities in one book. The main or important behavioural activities which affect human relations are discussed. The focus of this book is on human behaviour. To understand human behaviour, emphasis has laid on the interaction of people, ego-states, boss-subordinate relationships, leadership and the exploration of the contributing factors for achievement of goals.

This book comprises ten chapters. An in-depth study and objective assessment of the ego-states of persons is made in

Chapter One in order to explore the causative factors of different behaviour by different persons.

As we know, variations in behavioural activities are due to uneven states of ego patterns of individuals and they cannot manifest their activities rationally and judiciously if their adult ego-states are not free from contamination or the influence of others' egos. Detailed discussions in respect of contamination of adult egos as also the mindset of contaminated persons is made in Chapter Two.

Human needs are discussed in Chapter Three. Every human activity and behaviour has a direct relation to a hierarchy of needs the person wants to satiate. The driving force of the person tends to manifest his behaviour according to his needs and requirement. Different types of behaviour are, therefore, reflected in the process of work activities as per the needs of the people.

People behave differently as they have different mindsets, dispositions and thought processes. From such a viewpoint human beings have been categorised into four groups to ascertain their nature, behavioural patterns, qualitative traits and leadership phenomena. All these are discussed in Chapter Four.

The dispositional states of people can affect the smooth functioning of day-to-day activities in a work situation. Human relations get disturbed and a congenial work atmosphere does not exist. Both boss and subordinates do not feel comfortable working together. Such a situation does not prevail where people at work are more or less proportionately ego-balanced, where adult egos of people remain unhurt and uncontaminated (or less hurt and less contaminated) by other ego-states. The behavioural manifestations of such contaminated or uncontaminated bosses and subordinates are discussed in Chapter Five, along with a detailed look at rational methods of tackling situations and activities, with the objective of helping people develop mutual understanding, trust and confidence in one another.

To bring a healthy, conducive and facilitating environment in the organization and also to develop better human relations through interactive processes the importance of the qualitative traits of the boss is well accepted. A detailed study is conducted in Chapter Six which looks at the qualities the boss should possess to create a positive image in the mind of the subordinate to develop mutual understanding, trust and confidence in the workplace.

The role performance of subordinate and his qualitative traits cannot be ignored in the context of establishing healthy human relations. The boss can be successful in his objectives for bringing a healthy climate of human relations if his subordinate interacts in the desired direction. And this is possible when the subordinate possesses requisite qualities for carrying out the interactive processes. The qualitative traits of the subordinate as also organizational milieu are discussed in Chapter Seven.

The boss works as a leader of the team. His style of functioning, mode of tackling issues, approaches, thought processes and perceptions indicate his quality of leadership. Various kinds of leadership are discussed in Chapter Eight in order to find the suitable and appropriate leader for the establishment of sound human relations.

Healthy human relations create a conducive environment for effective operation of one's activities. It helps the individual to proceed uninterruptedly to achieve his goal. It is possible for him to succeed, to win and to achieve if he owns some qualitative traits. The most important and forceful qualitative trait is self-determination, which pushes the driving force of the person to reach the destination. Those desired qualitative traits are examined in Chapter Nine.

A human being can mould his mindset to a great extent, if he sincerely desires, through a process of persistent application and activation of the driving force. A series of HRD hummings (200 in all), which act as influencing agents to motivate the person to manifest his positive behavioural activities, are listed in Chapter Ten.

This book can be used for those who are interested in leadership behaviour, interpersonal relationships and personality theory. Human beings want to fulfil their desires and expectations. They set goals and want to achieve them. But most of them don't achieve all the time. This book will help people to succeed in their operations, to fulfil their missions, to accomplish their assignments and to achieve their targets. It is intended to be of value to those who are engaged in research activities and management practices and also to students, particularly those in management disciplines, parents, teachers and members of clubs and to persons irrespective of caste, creed, religion or profession, who want to develop will-power, to reframe their mindsets, to interact in a positive way, to establish healthy human relations and above all to satisfy their needs.

I have conducted interviews of nearly 500 people from different communities and religions engaged in different occupations and professions in different states, through questionnaire methods and also through interface discussions, in order to know their mindset, ego patterns and thought processes on different issues and have heard their success and failure stories in their activities. All these people deserve thanks for their ungrudging cooperation extended to me in collections of primary data.

I wish to thank Professor Amit Kumar Malik, Vice-Chancellor of Univerity of Burdwan for his constant encouragement, active cooperation and valuable advice and also for writing foreward of the book.

I am thankful to Dr. R.N. Banerjee, former Professor and Sh. P. Das, Professor, Department of Commerce, University of Burdwan for their valuable guidance in the completion of this book.

Thanks are due to Sh. T.V. Lakshminarayanan, Deputy General Manager, Bank of Baroda, Punjab, Chandigarh, Jammu & Kashmir Region and my professional colleagues and bank officials for their encouragement and continued help.

I am also thankful to Sh. Mahender Singh, Sh. K.L. Arora, Sh Kul Bhusan, Sh. Debashis Ganguly, Sh. Pradip Sahu, Sh. L.N. Kumar and Ms Vandana of Bank of Baroda for their cooperation and able assistance in reading the proof.

Thanks are also due to my wife Dr. (Mrs.) Bhabani Ghosh, to my son Nilmadhab Ghosh and to my daughter Ananya Ghosh for their patience, encouragement and considerate co-operation.

Finally, I express my sincere thanks to the publishers, Manas Publications for their untiring effort and support in bringing out this volume.

AJIT KUMAR GHOSH

CHAPTER 1

Causative Aspect of Human Behaviour

THE DYNAMIC CONCEPT OF HUMAN BEHAVIOUR

It is necessary to study human behaviour for an understanding of the needs, aspirations, desires, and motives of human beings, as these tend to decide the kind of drive and activities to be exploited in a particular situation and for a particular assignment. The study of human behaviour should not only be pursued in the work place; it is equally necessary in other fields of activities and organizations. In every form or setting, be it the home, club, hospital, school, college, university, institution or organization which has clear objective and goal, exploration of human behaviour occupies a pivotal position.

If we look back to the past, it becomes crystal clear that humans have manifested changed behavioural patterns from hunting activities to industrial working. Such changed activities were caused due to appropriate stimuli provided to the people at different points of time, stimuli which comprised technological benefits, economic and non-economic measures for the satiation of needs, and environmental factors, all of which acted as the driving force for alienation from the evolutionary behavioural activities.

Human behaviour is not a static form; it remains in its inflexible state until the driving force permits the activation of positive change in behavioural patterns. It may be noted that the driving force is filled with an optimum quantum of positive input of a similar nature to individual desires. The greater the degree of input of such similar nature, the more will be the positive reflection in behavioural patterns. A graphic representation of the behavioural pattern can be shown in the following way:

(Individual behavioural pattern)

=(+) Change in behavioural pattern (if positive input is given as per requirement of individual in terms of nature and quantity) or (–) change or no change for short period in behavioural pattern (if input is contrary to or not as per requirement of individual in terms of nature and quantity).

However, there will be a negative change or no change for some period in the behavioural patterns of the individual if the driving force is equipped with the input which is contrary to, or not as per the requirements of, the individual in terms of nature and quantity.

Static behavioural patterns are of a short duration. A negative behavioural effect is manifested if the unwanted and adverse input continues to pour into the driving force tank. The positive and negative revelations of individual behaviour may be depicted as following graphic.

The driving force starts working as a pusher to achieve a goal when it is filled with the required stimuli and the behavioural effect is reflected in individual performance and activities. If the driving force receives a persistently negative input, it creates a big jolt in the perceptive entity of the individual, which consequently tends to evidence abnormal negative changes in the behavioural pattern. The person concerned may strive his best to withdraw his area of operation and to engage in other activities which may not even be according to his choice and desire. All the functional forces are unable to continue with the present system of activities when negative stimuli accumulate one after another. If there is no possibility of alienation to alternate activity, the individual may exert will power to sustain the negative input without any perceptible manifestation. But this 'silence phase' cannot last long in an unchanged state of supplies of negative stimuli, and may either lead to an aggressive behavioural pattern of activities tending towards a culmination of transaction, or have a compromise tie for not transmitting any negative input so perceived.

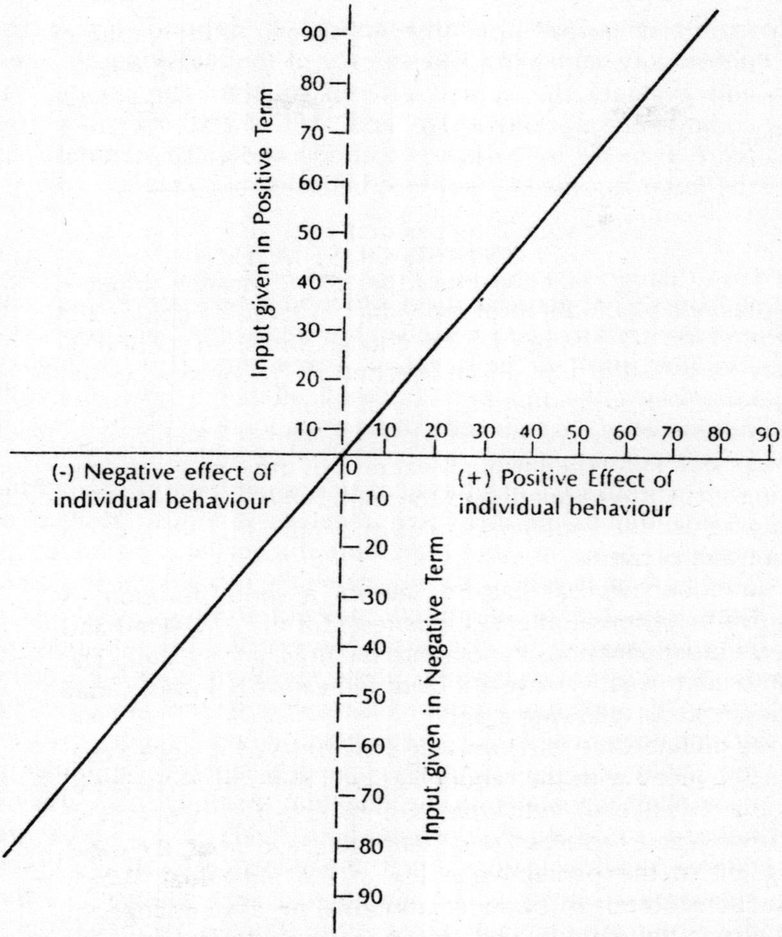

It may so happen that there is no external source available to provide input to the driving force. Under such circumstances, stimuli existing in the internal reservoir system play a vital role in activating the driving force which makes changes in behavioural manifestation depending upon the degree and nature of the stimuli supplied.

Notably, the individual may not exhibit signs and symptoms in behavioural activities immediately after the driving force is poured with stimuli. A period 'to observe and study the phenomena' is given to reflect changes in behaviour. There is no fixed period for observance. It depends upon the potentiality, capability and efficacy of the individual to assess and evaluate the stimuli offered to him. The greater the comprehending knowledge and skill of the individual, the more accurate his or her perception about the stimulus, and the faster the manifestation of behavioural changes.

GENESIS OF STIMULI

It may so happen that in a situation where more then one stimulus (positive and negative) are transmitted, one particular stimulus (positive or negative), even though it is singular considering the number of stimuli offered, works as a 'role playing actor' to influence the driving force to exhibit change in behavioural pattern.

The individual exhibits activities as per the direction of the driving force and this force receives stimulus, positive or negative, at any point of time. Both the qualities of stimuli, i.e. positive and negative, are not generally received at the same time from the same source; positive stimulus may follow negative stimulus or vice versa. There is also the possibility of continuously supplying one particular stimulus to the driving force. The source of the stimulus may not be the only one. The driving force may secure stimuli from different sources. Hence, the quality of stimuli supplied may not necessarily be similar to each other. Variations in the quantum of stimuli may also be noticed. In a situation where both qualities of stimuli are offered, the driving force directs the individual to manifest such behavioural activity which is dominant as a stimulant. If the driving force is dominated by positive stimulus, the behavioural reaction becomes positive. The reaction is the reverse if the driving force is dominated by negative stimulus. This can be graphically represented as follows:

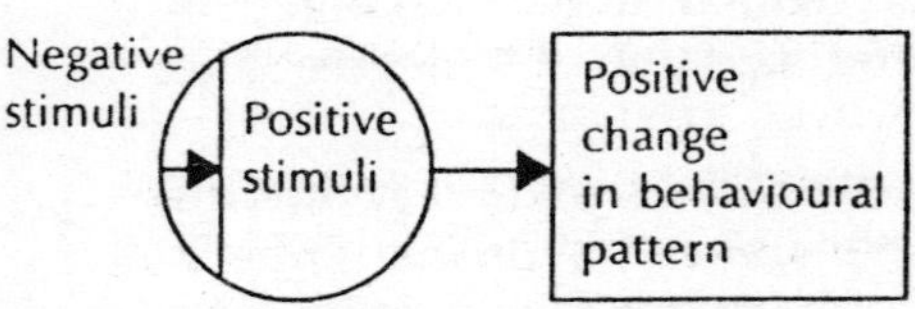

Driving force dominated by positive stimuli

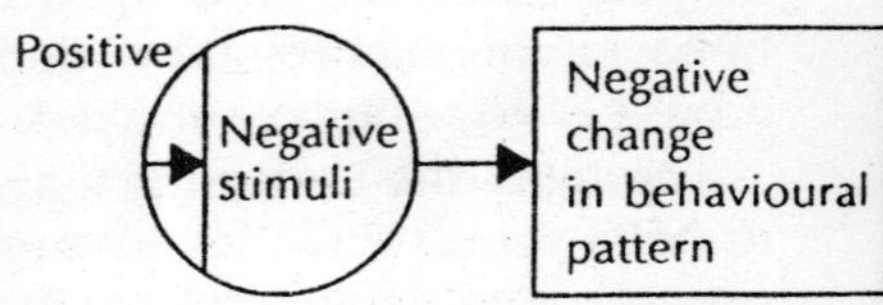

Driving force dominated by negative stimuli

It may so happen that, in a situation where more than one stimulus (positive/negative) is transmitted, one particular stimulus (positive or negative), even though it is singular, considering the number of stimuli offered works as a 'role playing actor' to influence the driving force to exhibit change in behavioural pattern. This 'role playing actor' continues to dominate the driving force so long as it is bestowed with such authority. The other homogenic stimulating input, which may be large in number and size, remains in a passive state within the driving force so long as the controlling power rests with the 'role playing actor'. But as soon as the 'role playing actor' loses its power of control because of a change in situation, the other opposite stimulator (either positive or negative) becomes active to influence the driving force to manifest the behavioural activities. From amongst the homogenic nature of stimulators, a particular stimulator becomes more powerful than the others and tends to exercise its authority to influence the driving force. Under such a situation this stimulus occupies the position as a 'role playing actor'. It is, therefore, evidenced that a single stimulus possesses the power to dominate the driving force at any point of time.

In some cases, supplier of stimuli transmits input (positive/negative) to the driving force with some motive for satiation of his vested interest. The recipient of the stimuli may or may not be aware of the inherent reason for providing such input immediately on receipt. But subsequently, when the individual continues to receive the same input from the same source which he does not expect, he can perceive the genesis of the supplies. If the input received is of a positive nature and the receiver does not merit it considering his capability, skill and situational demand, calculated and pre-projected behavioural activities are noticed. The concerned individual likes to remain in the foothold of the stimuli supplier and, to ensure persistent supply of positive input, he establishes an informal nexus. As he knows his strengths, weaknesses and limitations, for apparently manifesting positive behavioural activities and performance, he develops team work and strives to enhance his image as a productive performer. He exhibits positive behavioural reaction with possibly non-productive performance till he gets positive stimulus from the transmitter, who holds control over the driving force. If the positive stimulus is provided by the single supplier and other inputs are negative in nature, the behavioural pattern of the individual shows negative indications immediately after replacement of the positive dominator by a negative dominator. But there may be less variation or no variation at all in terms of performance and the behavioural activities provided. However, situational variables prevalent during the tenure of exercising influence by the positive stimulator are exploited by the individual with a foresighted approach. The active role-playing period of such an individual is more or less short, if otherwise not able to obtain some pusher for providing positive input, after the expiry of the tenure of the dominating positive stimulus.

Under the circumstances, when the 'role playing actor' remains out of power to provide positive input to the individual and the concerned person fails to procure a substitute to supply positive stimulus, the following possible and probable activities are noticed:

i. The individual for some period keeps himself passive to observe and study the 'phenomena'
ii. He makes an all-out effort in a systematic and strategic manner to establish superficial rapport with the present negative stimulus supplier in a bid to obtain breathing time to project the next course of activities.
iii. He surrenders to the input provider with a view to gaining positive stimuli at any value for the sustenance of his entity as a so-called performer.
iv. He strives for withdrawal from the present state of position and, in case of a failure to achieve his desired goal, he quits the position.

When the negative stimulus is transmitted by the person with ulterior motive, for satisfaction of his contaminated ego, and the recipient perceives the input as a motivated and concocted phenomena considering his different qualitative perspective, a state of fear psychosis is developed in the mind of the individual. The input supplier sends the stimuli keeping in view that a proper response cannot be effectuated. The supplier's intention is to perpetuate cross transactions with the stimuli taker and, in the process, he initiates steps to throw the individual from the present position. If he fails to succeed in his aim, he resorts to necessary measures to condemn the activities of the respondent and to retain him in the same position with vested stigma till the tenure of his dominating period. The process of ruining the potentiality of the individual through the supply of negative stimuli is new to the situation and does not have adequate exposure to excel in handling the problem. In some cases, the stimuli provider gives cognisance to race, caste, creed, religion, qualifications, experience and connection of the recipient before he supplies negative input. Moreover, the input supplier may fail to give proper judgement as to the quality of input to be provided if his ego pattern is not optimally structured. A person with contaminated adult egos, by either the child ego or parent ego, may not evince rational judgement and may become susceptible to the vagaries of the situation. The person with a balanced ego structure may rarely get involved in vindictive deals to provide such negative stimuli to the individual, as his adult ego remains open for objective assessment and evaluation of one's potentiality vis-à-vis performance. However, when negative stimulus is provided ignoring efficiency, capacity and the qualitative traits of the individual, the following activities are likely to be manifested in terms of performance and behavioural reactions.

i. Since the stimuli taker is aware of the origin of the negative input provided by the supplier, he may not exhibit any reaction for some period after he gets stimuli. He allows sometime to the stimuli provider to rethink and reassess the course of action taken to erode the individual's potential faculty.
ii. After the observation period is over, if the individual notices no change in the degree and quality of stimuli, he may try to develop an understanding with the nexus group, with the objective to give an exact perception about himself, so that the proper stimulus is supplied.
iii. If the individual does not succeed in establishing ties with the informal group or gets similar stimuli, he may feel shaky and insecure.
iv. He may try to switch over from the present position if possible, otherwise he bears with the negative stimuli for the period he can sustain. Thereafter, a change in the behavioural pattern is evidenced and the individual may react immediately in a negative way.

v. Since the individual does not get positive strokes even in a situation when he treats himself as a best performer, his mental faculty subsequently faces obstacles in its functioning. Personal growth and development gets deterred as the input giver never acknowledges the individual's contribution.

vi. With the repeated and frequent receipt of negative stimuli not warranted by the individual's action, the stimuli taker may have an altogether different perception of the stimuli supplier. Some of the assumptions about such a stimuli provider are given hereunder:

1. The individual considers the stimuli giver as the one who stands in the way of his development and growth.
2. The stimuli giver is biased and irrational.
3. He is a fault-finding personality.
4. His career path remains a blocked activity so long as the stimuli provider holds the power of domination.
5. He is meant for some persons who form the nexus group.
6. His contaminated adult ego can never function impartially. Hence, rational and judicious activity cannot be expected.
7. He keeps on praising and enhancing the image of the people who belong to his informal group and are basically non-performers.
8. He is a great destroyer of career development and takes recourse to vindictive activities.
9. He initiates necessary measures to humiliate.
10. He nurtures his own persons in such a way that any of his nexus group is not put into difficulties in his absence.
11. He is an authoritarian, and also a facilitator, pusher and pathfinder for the persons of the nexus group formed by him.

The person who supplies negative stimuli to individuals without judging whether they really need it, or without considering their activities and qualitative dimensions, may not be acceptable to the people and the milieu to which he belongs. Such a person initiates his activities for the accomplishment of any assignment in a negative way. He considers his people as non-performers, having no desire, needs and aspirations, and to activate the driving force he feels negative input is required. The stimuli provider wants to achieve his goal by awarding punishment, reprimanding, abusing, coercing and resorting to demotivating measures. Though for short periods he may succeed in fulfilling his target, he may be a non-performer in the long run under the same conditions and situations. This 'negative stimuli supplier mostly for all' does not have a proportionate and balanced ego structure and because of his having a contaminated adult ego, he cannot differentiate between performer and non-performer. His adult ego cannot assess any person, situation and environment objectively and rationally. He is a weak and stubborn personality, and has a preconceived image and idea about the people around him. He is unreliable, indecisive, and flexible in his decision-making process and a time-killer in judgement. He shirks responsibility towards others and does not hesitate to divert blame to them at the opportune time. He is self-centred and never surrenders or sacrifices an inch to the benefit of others. He is conscious and particular about his rights and privileges but delays the sanction of perquisites to others who raise relevant queries. He spends much time on trifling issues which can be performed by a subordinate. He does not make any cost-benefit analysis for the facilities given to him, if these are selected according to his choice. The 'negative stimuli supplier mostly for all' is a power-seeker, authority crazy. He imposes his authoritarian approach in each and every situation and does not consider its propriety or its suitability of application. He bases his activity approach on 'theory X', which demands completion of the job through the exercise of authority, directive and close supervision. He pretends to be the person believing in the motivational concept and, to create his such so-called image amongst the people, he outwardly participates on some ritual games. He forms a very small informal group with some persons who feed him with information in respect of inter-personal relations, interactions of people and the assumptions of people about him. This 'small group' also tries to build up a positive and people-oriented image about him by the citation of stray incidents of his intentional action. The other members of the small group, as per directives and stipulated understanding, bring up the activities of this negative stimuli supplier at the appropriate forum and initiate necessary measures to convince people about his changed attitudinal behaviour.

Such a negative stimuli supplier is reluctant to delegate authority. He concentrates activities of all areas of operation under his own control and demands his credit when the goal is achieved. But in case there is a failure to meet a target, or if anything goes wrong, he identifies the accountable person and in each and every case he prepares a background paper in such a manner that only the persons in concerned areas of operation are responsible. In regard to his power, he does not share with anybody. He even does not hesitate to ignore any sort of imposition made by the superior, if, due to such imposition, his authority is shared.

Since the adult ego of such a negative input provider cannot function freely because of its contamination either by the child ego or the parent ego (mostly the critical parent ego), he is fond of analysing and detecting critical aspects of the performance of his people in the presence of others. He finds pleasure in the critical evaluation and assessment of others and feels proud and satisfied in communicating such evaluations to others, whether connected or unconnected with the assignment. He criticizes people whether they are performers or non-performers and seldom appreciates people for excellent performance. He creates a holocaust on small issues and makes others know about such issues with the intention of freeing himself from the episodes. He is impatient, hurried and wants to complete the job in no time without looking to any perspective concerning the assignment and he fails to reflect perfection, accuracy and quality in his performance. He thinks highly of himself and considers others, regardless of experience, qualification and expertise as non-achievers, non-performers and unsuitable for the assignment. A very negligible number of persons, who too are members of the 'small group' formed and patronized by him, are declared to be performers. He cannot tolerate his contemporaries, especially when their performance and activities are appreciated, and if they are considered to be winners of awards for excellent performance. He chalks out a list of his achievements in his own way and transmits them through his small group to a different hierarchical set up, including to his people. This is done to develop a better image about his work ability and performance amongst the people at large.

The negative stimuli supplier lacks courage, confidence and the ingredients necessary to tackle any sensitive issue solely and independently. He is dependent on his people for the accomplishment of such tasks but never treats them as trustworthy, barring a few exceptions. He fears to take bold steps to bring any change in the situation and prefers to continue with the present system. He wants to get on with people who are subdued, docile, tolerant, patient, introverted, and non-focal. He feels comfortable to work with such qualities of people as they are amenable to any situation. He initiates necessary adjustments to get the people around him according to his choice and liking as he cannot exercise his full control over people who are argumentative. He likes to remain with the job and so devotes much more time on the job than as usually required. He finds satisfaction in inconveniencing people. On rare occasions, he indicates his happiness when someone achieves something or is given an award for excellent performance.

He meets people, identifies their area of activities, interacts with them and, through the authoritarian approach, indicates accountability and transparency for the accomplishment of a job. He never thinks of the need to establish congenial interpersonal relations through mutual understanding and trust, as a measure to help achieve the goals. If he talks about co-operation, assistance and help in an appeal to the people for fulfilling the targeted goal, it is absolutely an outward act to delude the people and to raise his image as a people-oriented team leader.

This 'all-the-time negative input supplier' may have some ulterior motives to supply negative inputs to the individual. It does not matter to the negative stimulus provider whether the supply is rational and proportionate to the individual's need, desire, activity and ability. Since the input transmitter forms biased perceptions about the individual, he supplies input with the intention to humiliate the individual for his 'earlier activities'. The ultimate objective of the stimulus supplier is to create a situation so that the individual withdraws from the existing position or surrenders to the supplier. Even after adopting such measures, if the individual does not come to the terms of the negative stimulus supplier, he has to face direct confrontation with the stimulus provider, who strives to initiate steps to make the individual ineffective and to identify him as non-performer and a non-achiever. Such a negative stimulus transmitter cannot tolerate any sort of action of the individual and so condemns the individual in some other way for his activities. He remains unhappy with the individual and makes the individual understand that due to his 'previous activities' he has to suffer the consequences. A continuous supply of negative stimuli for a prolonged period increases aggressiveness, hostility and dangerous inter-personal relations between the stimulus supplier and the respondent and the resultant effect is withdrawal by either or both of them from the present area of activity. The main differentiating area between this kind of negative stimulus supplier and other negative stimulus suppliers is that the former brings early settlement either in the form of compromise or in the form of withdrawal from the present state of activities, whereas the latter's process of activities is comparatively slow and time consuming.

There are some people in society who constantly want to please others, to make them comfortable, to give others things want if they are the authority to provide them, without strict compliance to the norms and rules. The person of this category of people supplies positive stimulus to the individual on most occasions as and when warranted. He never questions himself before he gives anything to others, as to whether the concerned individual deserves it or not. This person appears to be enlightened, liberal and people-oriented. He never gives deep thought to issues whenever they crop up. He takes every issue casually and does not attach due weight to it before disposal. He does not see the issues from the right angle and does not make judicious, rational and objective assessments. He seldom takes any matter negatively. To him everybody is a performer and he merits appreciation, reward and recognition. He is weak in the conceptual approach, dependent on others for decision making, flexible in ideas and thought, with a tendency to succumb to pressure. He lacks the appropriate analytical capability for ascertaining a situation. He is non-assertive and is not prompt and quick in his activities.

The 'all the time positive stimuli-giver' cannot function freely, as his ego pattern does not remain in a balanced state. His adult ego is contaminated either by the nurturing parent ego or by the child ego. This person, in his formative childhood, may have received lots of stimuli with 'dos' and 'don'ts', 'shoulds' and 'should nots' and remained under the protection of somebody. Upon reaching adulthood, this person's adult ego plays back the tape recorded in childhood and wants to supply positive stimulus to each and every person.

He is not a power-seeker. He does not intend to centralize his authority. He is a believer in delegation and distribution of functional power. He gives liberty to people to work independently. He is least bothered about quality of decisions and work performed. He remains happy with the completion of assigned task. So perfection, accuracy and decency do not result in any change in his role behaviour.

He is a peace-purchaser and does not want to be involved in any sort of dispute. He resorts to appeasement tact for the disposal of any issue. He likes to keep everybody happy. He believes in motivational therapy for the achievement of targets and so gives positive stimuli to individuals. He does not differentiate between performer and non-performer and thinks that everybody can be achievers and that the people who are non-achievers at some point and in some situations because of non-availability and non-supply of appropriate inputs, can become achievers at different situations if proper nourishment is given. He assumes that positive stimuli which are provided to individuals will bring attitudinal changes, growth and development, particularly of the people belonging to the non-performance group. Positive stimulus, if given unexpectedly, moulds the ego pattern of the individual, since he has remained in a deprived state for long. The individual then starts manifesting positive behavioural activities. However, the efficacy and effectiveness of positive stimuli, if provided to one and all regardless of the situation and whether deserving or not, loses its efficacy, and the individual may not display behavioural activities appropriately. The respondent may not accept the positive stimulus in the right spirit and direction when he sees the open and abundant supply of stimuli to individuals. The respondent may hold some assumptions about the activities and behavioural style of such a stimulus supplier and may form a distinct perception about the stimulus provider. Some of the assumptions of the stimulus taker are discussed below:

1. The stimulus supplier has no 'say' on any issue. He always depends on others for each and every matter. He cannot go beyond the area prescribed by his people.
2. He is lenient in his role-activity and uses a 'high relationship low task' behavioural style in all situations. He cannot exercise consistency in the decision making process and,

as a result, more or less each and every matter receives the same treatment and behaviour.

3. Since the stimulus provider, in most situations, manifests positive behavioural reactions, he hardly tends to impose punitive measures. Hence a state of lawlessness and disorder is likely to penetrate into the total system.
4. He is a man of weak personality and cannot sustain any pressure for long. He searches out ways and means for 'time-being solutions' as he believes in 'ad-hocism'.
5. He is non-performer and non-achiever in the real sense. Because of his 'high relationship' approach, people interpret the situation differently and do not feel compelled to complete the job assigned to them. A state of non-performance and non-achievement becomes prevalent in the system.

From the foregoing discussion, it is thus apparent that stimuli suppliers exercise their influence on the respondents for appropriate manifestation of activities. They provide stimuli depending on their ego states, motives, and the needs of the driving force situation, mindset and the milieu they pass through. Accordingly, stimulus suppliers are of following types:

1. Mostly-all-the-time negative stimulus supplier (MATTNSS)
2. Mostly-all-the-time positive stimulus supplier (MATTPSS)
3. Negative stimulus supplier with ulterior motives (NSSWUM)
4. Positive stimulus supplier with vested interests (PSSWVI)
5. Need based positive/negative stimulus supplier (NBPNSS)

Each and every stimulus is important to both the stimulus provider and the stimulus receiver. The stimulus receiver responds to the stimulus as per the expectations of the stimulus supplier only when he receives the right stimulus. The stimulus supplier, while providing any stimulus, either positive or negative, should have a thorough cognisance of the activities as mentioned under.

1. Each stimulus should carry some purpose/objective of the provider.
2. The stimulus should be understandable to the receiver, who can then respond appropriately.
3. The stimulus should be relevant.
4. The stimulus should convey some message to do or not to do.

5. It should be given to the right person, at the right place, the right time and in the right situation.

For effective and desired transaction, the stimulus supplier should have a clear and definite perception about the stimulus provided, the respondent and his probable reaction. The perception of the stimulus provider is based on the following assumptions:

1. That the respondent is the appropriate person to whom the stimulus is to be provided.
2. That the respondent is likely to react to the stimulus.
3. That the respondent belongs to the 'small group' formed by the stimulus provider or by any of his associates with some vested motives.(The stimulus provider holds this assumption only in a situation where positive stimuli are required to be provided, with some motive for the satiation of vested interests.
4. That the respondent is the same person about whom information is received through the feedback process.
5. That the behavioural activities of the respondent on earlier occasions, affecting or causing to affect the interest of the persons connected with the stimuli supplier, are intentional and the respondent still continues to have the same perception about the concerned people. (The stimulus provider may hold such assumptions when he intends to transmit' 'negative stimulus with ulterior motives' for the satisfaction of his contaminated ego.)

EXPLORATION OF CAUSATIVE FACTORS FOR DIFFERENT BEHAVIOURAL APPROACHES OF THE STIMULI SUPPLIER

Stimuli offered by the suppliers vary from individual to individual. Some provide mostly positive stimuli or mostly negative stimuli with or without any specific motives, while others provide need-based or nearly need-based stimuli. It is pertinent to mention that the stimuli provider never gives the same kind of stimulus to each and all respondents at different situations and times.

There is, therefore, variation in transmitting stimuli between suppliers. Now naturally, the question arises as to why people behave differently and provide different kinds of stimuli. The reply to the question of the 'why' of behaviour rests with the existence of different ego states of the people providing stimuli to the individuals. To explore the causative factors of such variant behavioural styles, it is therefore pertinent to make an in-depth analysis and objective assessment of ego states of individuals.

EGO STATES

Each and every person, irrespective of age, carries three ego states: the 'Parent', the 'Adult' and the 'Child'. These three states may be proportionate or disproportionate to each other.

Parent Ego

This is that part of the ego state which an individual acquires from his parents and parent substitutes during his entire period of childhood, especially during the formative period of his childhood. The child receives different qualities and natures of stimuli from his parents at different points of time and situations. He generally gets any of the following types of stimuli during the period of his childhood.

i. Mostly all-the-time negative stimulus with or without motive.
ii. Mostly all-the-time positive stimulus with or without specific purpose.
iii. Need based positive/negative stimulus. With the receipt of continuous stimulus from the parents, the child holds some idea with regard to the behavioural patterns of his parents and perceives the parent as any of the following stimuli supplier:
   a. Mostly all the time negative stimuli supplier (MATTNSS)
   b. Negative stimuli supplier with ulterior motive (NSSWUM)
   c. Mostly all the time positive stimuli supplier (MATTPSS)
   d. Positive stimuli supplier with vested interest (PSSWVI)
   e. Need based positive/negative stimuli supplier (NBPNSS)

The stimuli received by the child from his parents during the period from the immature stage to the mature stage (i.e., the period of child development) greatly influence similar manifestations in his activities. The child studies and evaluates each and every stimulus received from his parents and responds accordingly. He also makes comparative analyses of the stimulus received by his playmates/classmates from their parents. He feels unhappy and grieved when he is maltreated, and may see his mates getting nice treatment from their parents. He feels satisfied and proud of being a member of his family when he receives better treatment and behaviour from his parents as compared to the treatment received by his classmates and playmates from their parents.

With the passage of time and the persistent intake of the stimuli, the child develops more or less similar ego patterns in his personality structure. He keeps all such stimuli provided by his parent in terms of advice, admonition, instruction, precaution, warning, abuse, reprimanding, appreciation, etc., in his memory like a tape recorder, and plays it back at the time of necessity in his adult age.

Now, considering different types of stimulus provided by parents and the perception held by the child in regard to parents as stimulus supplier, the parent can be characterized as (a) Critical Parent or (b) Nurturing Parent. Negative stimuli suppliers (viz., MATTNSS and NSSWUM) as mentioned in (a) & (b) above are critical parents while positive stimuli suppliers (viz., MATTPSS and PSSWVI) as above noted in (c) & (d) are nurturing parents. Need based positive/negative stimuli suppliers (NBPNSS) are nurturing parents/critical parents when they supply as per direction of their adult ego in an unbiased manner.

A critical parent makes critical evaluations and assessments of each and every activity and provides stimulus to the child. He supplies negative stimulus through abusing, criticizing, rebuking and reprimanding. He thinks himself supreme in every aspect and considers himself to be the one who knows everything. This type of parent hardly gives positive strokes to the child. He believes in an authoritarian style of behaviour for task accomplishment. With a continuous inflow of negative stimulus from the parent during the development period, the child forms some ideas about his parent which subsequently dominates his own ego pattern.

The nurturing parent always gives advice to the child as what he should or should not do. Such a parent takes excessive care of the child, more than is needed. He seldom allows the child to be exposed to the vagaries of the environment. He sets a list of do's and don'ts, shoulds and shouldn'ts for the child. He provides positive stimulus practically all the time. He gives unwarranted protection, shelter and support to the child. The persistent supply of positive stimulus shapes the child's ego pattern and manifests nurturing parental behaviours in his post-child development period. In a situation where critical and nurturing parents work independently in a balanced state of ego patterns and provide stimuli as per the need of the child, a congenial environment exists in the family system. The child with the receipt of such balanced stimuli develops similar patterns in his parent ego. Such parent evaluates each and every activity, analyses the situation and then provides stimuli.

Adult Ego

This is the most important ego state of the individual. The supply of stimulus, response to stimulus, actions, interactions and all other activities a person is required to pass through during the course of transactions are an integral part of the functional activities of adult ego. The qualitative aspect of activity depends largely on how the adult ego functions. If the adult ego is not under the influence of any other ego state and there is no stint of contamination by other ego state, it can work freely and independently. The activity part of this ego state not affected by any other ego state includes:

i. Collection of data from primary as well as secondary sources.
ii. Storing of data in the data bank.
iii. Processing of data to suit requirements.
iv. Examination, scrutiny and analysis of issues/situation to provide stimulus/respond to stimulus.
v. Objective assessment/evaluation of issues/situation.
vi. Thorough finding and refinding of genesis of issues/situation.
vii. Ascertainment of probable effect of issues.
viii. Application of a rational and judicious decision-making process.
ix. Proper and unbiased judgement.

The adult ego provides rational judgements on issues if it functions on its own. It gives need-based stimulus or responds to stimulus appropriately, as is suited to the environment and requirements, when it has no other ego state to interfere with its activities. But this is not so in reality. Adult ego states in most individuals are contaminated either by the child ego or by the parent ego or by both ego states and, as a result, the adult ego state cannot work effectively and without bias. Under such circumstances, the role playing activity of the adult ego is invariably influenced to function as per the demands of the influencer. If there is more than one influencing agent (ego state), mixed behavioural activities are noticed, but the dominating agent (ego state) retains dominance over other agent (ego states). For instance, if the child ego occupies the dominant position, the adult ego tends to manifest child-like activities and behaviour. The structure of different ego states is shown diagrammatically:

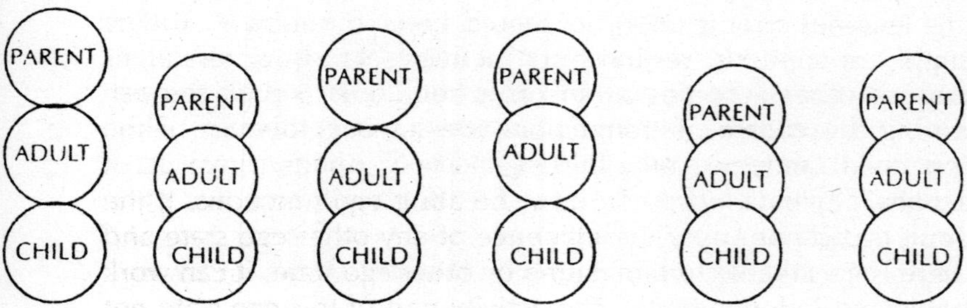

. Balanced Ego State 2. Adult Ego state contaminated by parent ego & child ego 3. Adult Ego state contaminated by child ego 4. Adult Ego state contaminated by parent ego 5. Adult Ego state contaminated by child & parent ego & dominated by parent ego 6. Adult Ego state contaminated by child & parent ego & dominated by child ego

Child Ego

This ego manifests the behavioural activities of a child during the period just after his coming out of the mother's womb till the expiry of childhood. So long as child remains in the mother's womb, he gets influenced by the mother's behaviour—physical, physiological and psychological. He has no activity to manifest on his own. After he is born in the new world in a totally different environment, he experiences varied cultures, activities, milieus and situations, which, on different occasions and at different points of time and in different forms, he receives as stimulus. He expresses his behaviour in terms of emotions, verbal and non-verbal indications, and sentiments which may be a sequel to the stimuli he receives persistently from authority figures. His revelation of behavioural activities occurs due to his possession of inherent spontaneous impulses and experiences through the learning process. He learns from the training received directly from the parents or parent substitute, as also from the activities of such authority personalities. All these he manifests through behavioural activities later on.

The child, therefore, expresses his behavioural activities during his evolutionary period as (i) Natural Child (ii) Trained or adapted child & (iii) Witty child.

Natural Child

This is that part of the child ego which exhibits behavioural functions in a natural way. In other words, a child behaves in the manner that a child he should behave normally. Such a child expresses his behavioural activities to show his anger, aggressiveness, co-operation, affection, love, rebelliousness, emotion, sympathy, accommodativeness and enthusiasm. Thus, the child cries, screams, shouts, quarrels, jumps, runs, plays, laughs, enjoys, embraces, fights, breaks glasses, toys and other objects, splashes water, slams doors, windows, throws balls and anything available to him, sucks on thumbs, chews on blanket, etc.

The child's behavioural activities largely depend on how his parents nurture him during the period of his development. The nature and type of stimulus given to the child, the response of parents, the perception developed by the child towards the parent and parental behavioural style and situational variables contributes considerably to shape the behavioural pattern of the child. If the child gets only positive stimulus containing supportive and relationship indications from parents or parent substitutes, he cannot decide what is right, what is wrong, or what he should do or not do. He gets confused about his role behaviour and so may not react in the proper direction. Since he does not get warnings or commands from parents in regard to the consequences for not obeying or complying with norms/ rules, he becomes adamant. He misinterprets the parental excessive support as sanction and permission to do as he desires. He becomes self-centred. He cannot tolerate to share with others. He tries to dominate persons who come in contact with him. He strives to impose his ideas and opinions on others and he becomes aggressive whenever he fails to achieve. He is respectful to parents, loves and gives high regard to parents but gets hurt at the smallest negative stimulus given by the parents. He exhibits concealed anger and morose behaviour; he stops talking to the negative stimulant provider, keeps himself forcibly aloof from attending family rituals or taking part in family activities. Sometimes he refuses to take food till his anger subsides or is otherwise convinced with explanations given to satisfy his ego. It also happens that such a child screams and manifests his behaviour expressing his feeling at being neglected in the family and starts weeping loudly for some time and then for sometime separates himself from family activities. He stops talking or talks less and forms an idea about the parents on his own. A child who receives supportive and relationship behaviour from both parents and parent substitutes all the time feels that they take unusual care and give extraordinary protection. He becomes much more desperate, disobedient, disloyal to parents only when he cannot exhibit his activities according to his whim and desires or his parents interfere in his whimsical activities. Sometimes when he gets angry, he attempts to leave house or gets out of his parents' house to manifest his outburst against his parents attitude and behaviour.

If the child constantly receives negative stimulus from the parents or parent substitute, he forms an idea about himself as useless and good-for-nothing and starts losing self- confidence. His demand for love, affection, support, touch and intimacy from parents remains unfulfilled. He searches for a substitute who can provide positive stimulus to satiate his desired need. When the child succeeds in finding a substitute, he attaches less importance and weight to the negative stimulus received from his critical parents. It may occur that the substitute available for the child is not adequate to compensate the damage done by critical parents. In this eventuality the child re-researches the probable areas where he may get suppliers of positive input.

If the child receives positive stimuli from several substitutes, he feels secured and develops self-confidence and self-determination to face all sort of odds and hurdles to fulfil his aspirations, expectations and goals. When critical parents or parent substitutes play the role of punitive authority to ruin the child's development (generally when the person other than the father or mother of the child acts as a parent substitute or, in certain circumstances, when the father or mother or both are ill-motivated), the child forms reacts to his critical parents or parent substitute with hatred. Under such situations, the child keeps himself aloof from family ritual and activities, struggles for his maintenance and development, avoids participation in the game where cross transactions are likely to occur, stops keeping connections with the people who are closely related to the parents or parent substitute, and talks less or does not talk to parents or the parent substitute. The child becomes the victim of physical and mental torture and passes through uncertain, dark and intolerable phases. Sometimes, the extent of torture, harassment and oppression becomes so horrible that the child cannot sustain himself if he does not get a positive stimulus supplier (supportive relations) from his own family system.

In a situation where an elder brother of the child, or any person other than the parent, plays the role of the critical parent, and where the parent provides supportive stimulus to the child, the process of damaging the child's development projected in the case of the critical parent may not take place, if the positive stimulus of the parent tends to be much stronger than the negative stimulus of the 'role playing critical parent'. If the parent himself depends upon such a 'role playing critical parent' for his sustenance and survival, the child's development gets affected, as the parent cannot supply the necessary input to the child for growth because of his incapacitation. The dependent parent may continue to provide positive stimulus to whatever extent it may be, to generate confidence in the child to attain self-dependence and self-establishment. Under such circumstances, the child experiences loneliness and solitude while achieving his desired goal, set by himself on the basis of parents' expectation, societal demands and self-aspiration. By dint of hard labour and with strong self-determination and parents' supportive stimuli, the child may establish his position, despite persistent negative stimuli supplied by the 'role- playing critical parent'.

In a family where parents do little to facilitate the child's development, due to incapacitation, except providing calculated supportive stimuli, and where the 'role-playing critical parent' dominates over the child's activities, the child may not be successful in fulfilling his expectations. If the negative stimuli of such a 'role-playing' actor hits the child's emotional area and stands in the way of development, whereupon child decides his goal with strong determination, the child may achieve the target depending upon the positive stimuli received from the parents. In formative childhood, there is every possibility of the child following the wrong path, if not warned by the parent through an appropriate mix of stimuli.

The negative stimuli of the 'role playing critical parent' may not adversely affect to child's development process if the activities of the family system are controlled by different actors in the family who don't provide negative input to the child and the child strives hard with predetermined projections to achieve his desired goal. In such a family system, which is invariably bigger in size than microscope family unit, the parent may not be a participant in family activities but may manifest activities to communicate positive stimulus to the child. If the child can overcome some blocking hurdles standing in the way of his advancement, his driving force may derive extra energy to be put into action for achievement of goals. Thus the process of self- establishment of the child starts step by step, through struggle, with the desire to win. Some significant attitudinal changes may be noticed in such a child during this period. For example, the child may avoid the company of playmates, may spend less time playing, may not waste time, may structure time for useful allocation, may perform for positive stimulus, may make a sincere effort to come in close contact with the parent substitute to receive positive input, may exhibit activities acceptable to most people in the society. Once the child achieves some result in phased manner, it may become a routine process for him to move to other areas for achievement of his targeted goal. The child may explore the potential areas which he may consider his matching areas for diversion when one goal set by him is achieved. He may continue to overcome obstacles one after another with his forceful will power to win the desired goal.

It may happen in some family systems that a natural child gets non-identical, opposite instructions, advice, admonition from parents or parent substitutes. In such situations, the child gets confused, and cannot decide to decide what is right, what is wrong, what he should do, or what he should not do. Initially he may follow the role of observer and subsequently he may accept the behavioural patterns of the parent who gives positive input to him as per his desire. This uneasy, cross and discordant transaction which takes place between parents and parent substitutes due to differences in thought processes, conceptions, ideas, and perceptions may deter the growth and development of the child. The child suffers from deprivation of affection, love, and sympathy from the parent who provides stimuli not desired by him. He forms an image of such a negative stimuli provider parent as non-cooperative, unfriendly and a problem-maker, and may manifest some behavioural activities and attitudinal changes which may disintegrate the parent-child relationship. The child receives a big jolt to his emotional plane and may decide to develop his own career path with positive stimulus given by the other parent. The success of the child largely depends on how the positive stimuli supplier (the parent) considers the situation and what he intends to do in the present state of turmoil of the family. The longer the period of continuance of such a family climate, the more the damage to the child in his growth and development. If later on, both parents reach some sort of adjustment and understanding between themselves for the running of a peaceful and undisturbed family system, the child may erase out completely the impression, image and perception about the negative stimulus provider (parent) from his ego pattern. When both parents sincerely put in an effort to mould the child's perceptible structure, the child may incorporate the positive stimuli supplied by the parent to compensate for the vacuum created in the process of the formation of impressions about the parent and may try to forget the uncomfortable incidents experienced by him. However, in reality, absolute removal from the ego structure, once formed, may not happen.

The Trained Child or the Adapted Child

The terminology 'trained' or 'adapted' indicates that the child has adapted to the system through different processes of training and has become a trained child. Each organization, be it a club, hospital, school, college, university, family, society or any institution which has a definite objective, has its own separate entity. It has, therefore, its own culture, ethos, traditions, customs and beliefs, which may not be the same as those of other organizations. Every organization desires that its members get acclimatized to the organizational milieu for self-growth vis-à-vis organizational growth. Likewise, a child, immediately after he is born in the family, feels an environment different to that of his earlier one. The process of making him accustomed to the family atmosphere, through a process of imparting training, starts with parents or parent substitutes. Different communication techniques–verbal and non-verbal—are used from the very day of his birth in the world as a training/adapting measure through physical contact, touch, love, affection, sympathy, co-operation, guidance, assistance and protection. With the passage of time, the child comes to know what parents, family and society demand from him, what his role is as a member of the family what sort of stimuli he needs, how he should respond to the stimuli to be offered to him, what family strengths and weaknesses are, what customs, beliefs, and rules are prevalent in the family and the society. During the formative childhood, he therefore learns ways and means of adapting himself to the family system, as the parents want him to be accommodating, supportive and loyal to the family.

The child becomes easily adaptable to the family milieu if his learning process is based on a supportive and participative approach, with appropriate authoritarian behaviour by the parents as and when warranted. The adaptation of child, in such cases, is spontaneous, wilful, natural and without any impositions. The child finds pleasure in becoming a member of such a family, a feeling that he manifests through his activities, attitudes and behaviour. He becomes obedient, loyal and acceptable to the family. The child remains in happiness and comfort under such an environment in the family as he persistently receives positive stimulus from parents or parent substitutes through love, affection and acceptance of his deeds. All round development and growth in a child's mental faculties will occur if not otherwise affected. On most occasions, the child establishes complementary transactions while the exchange of stimulus and response takes place between him and the parent. In such situations, the child expects positive strokes from parents for his good performance and also negative strokes from them for any wrong deeds, so as to release his fear, anxiety and tension caused due to his misdeeds. Non-receipt of the appropriate strokes at the time of need from the parents may create a sense of parents having no concern for the child in the family, which may result in breaking down the understanding levels of child and parents. The child may subsequently exhibit negative behaviour and activities and may perpetuate cross transactions. The possibility of the occurrence of negative behaviour by the parents may be remote under such a family system.

Negative behavioural manifestations by both parents and child may be apparent in a family where the child is not adaptive and the training process does not suit the child's requirements. The child observes that parents are mostly critical by nature and impose restrictions on his activities arbitrarily and keep close watch and supervision on him without any positive and sympathetic outlook. Such parents believe only in the authoritarian principle to nurture the child and frequently provide negative stimuli to the child, with expectation of receiving the appropriate responses to form complementary transactions. The child may initially adapt to the family system unwillingly, may study the exact behavioural patterns of parents and may send the proper responses to the stimuli to establish congenial transactions.

Subsequently, when the child finds no improvement in the behavioural activities of the parents and they continue to provide negative stimuli to him, he may try to find ways and means to abstain from giving a response immediately and if he succeeds in his effort, he may stop giving responses in exchange of stimulus. But, if the child notices an uncongenial environment prevalent in the family and he is required to carry out instructions to complete a transaction, he may delay the process by being aloof for sometime. In such situations, a climate of distrust, disloyalty, lack of confidence, lack of a sense of belonging, lack of the feeling of oneness, wellness and togetherness prevails in the family. The child may search for a place to hide, he may not want to expose himself to the parent figure and he may restrict his activities, which may enhance the anger of the parents. When continuously negative stimuli are supplied to the child by the parents, the child may not be able to sustain the jolt of the negative input and consequently he may become the victim of oppression, torture and harassment by the parents. The child may form the impression that the parents are hateful, unsocial and biased personalities. He may manifest a rebellious attitude and non-compliance activities when he loses his tolerance. The manifestation of such activities occurs only when the child finds a substitute personality to protect him or determines to leave home to take shelter elsewhere. The problem of adaptation also arises if the child is not acceptable to the family. In such a cases, the authority figures impose restrictions on the activities of the child, which makes the situation much more painful for the child to bear. The child cannot adjust with the family environment and he feels dejected. He manifests behavioural activities which do not conform to family rules and norms.

During the formative childhood, the adapted child may manifest behavioural activities through the formation of complementary transactions, to the extent possible for him. He may, therefore, comply with the instructions and advice of the authority figures. If some activities, behaviours, restrictions, boundaries and limitations of the authority figures appear to be non-acceptable to the child, he may not directly go into confrontation. In such situations, he may prefer to diverting his activities to some other area where a comfortable milieu exists. He may take this course of action very silently, without exposing himself to any sort of activity. He may keep himself apparently normal and may participate in all sorts of family rituals. Since he is well aware, because of his adaptability, of the type of response to be given in exchange of stimulus provided by the parents, he may continue to respond appropriately though unwillingly, in order to transact in a complementary manner. In such situations, considering the potential force of resisting the disagreeable area and other limiting factors, the child finds no way other than to comply with the set rules of the family for the time being, till he gets alternative shelter. The period of such 'adaptation by compulsion' is very crucial to the child for his sustenance and self-growth. Any exposure to non-compliance or compliance under compulsion may damage the process of development of the child by curtailing or stopping the basic support and stimuli to the child

With the passage of time, the child passes through different phases of development. Such phases are:

Immature Phase → Mature Phase → Moderately Mature Phase → Highly Mature Phase

Each phase is vital for the growth and development of the child. The child's ego pattern is formed and set during the period he passes through such phases of development. There can be a desired level of growth in the child's personality if the situations mentioned below are prevalent during the formative childhood (that is, the intervening period from the immature phase to the highly mature phase).

1. The child adapts to family customs, traditions and beliefs.
2. The child is acceptable to parents, parent substitutes and other members of the family.
3. Parents/parent substitutes provide proper stimulus-negative, positive or both to the child at the appropriate time.
4. The child feels a sense of belonging, happiness and comfort, in the family.
5. More emphasis is given by the parents or parent substitutes on task behaviour (negative stimulus) during the initial phase/s of development. The relationship behaviour (positive stimulus) of the parents assumes importance whenever a child advances from one phase to other.
6. A conducive and congenial milieu exists in the family as well as the society, for peaceful existence.
7. Parents or parent substitutes are concerned for the all-round development of the child.
8. Parents are in no way under pressure from external people to create hindrances in the matter of the child's development.
9. The ego states and personality patterns of the parents are facilitative in providing the necessary input to the child.
10. Parents or parent substitutes provide clear-cut instructions, advice, admonitions, restrictions and boundaries of activities to the child in terms of his needs, requirements and necessities for growth and development.
11. Parents watch, observe and study the behavioural manifestations of the child in each and every activity and take immediate appropriate steps to lead him in the correct way if some activity appears to be un-warranted.
12. Parents make themselves available to the child to supply need based stimulus and respond to the stimulus to make smooth and complementary transactions.

It is, therefore, apparent that the adapted or trained child can have all-round growth and development in his childhood, provided all the factors exist that are mentioned above. The development of the child in different phases depends on the adaptation of the child, the ego patterns of the parents or parent substitutes and situational variables like the family environment, the social milieu, the opportunities available and infrastructural provisions. It thus follows that the development of the child is the function of the child, the parents and other situational variables: D=f (c, p, s). The D stands for development and C, P, and S stand for child (adaptation of child), parents (ego pattern of parents) and situations respectively. The extent of the development and growth of the child may be enumerated as follows:

> "The more the balanced ego patterns the parents or parent substitutes possess to meet the particular situation and needs of the child and the more the adaptability to the family and social system the child holds, the more the development and growth of the child in different phases will be noticed".

Witty Child

This child manifests his activities through intuition, imagination, creative performance and unusual and unexpected responses. This sort of child shows his reactive expressions in such a manner that the adult having no con-taminated influence of any ego state may not excel in the revelation of his reaction. Sometimes the child sounds con-fident in regard to his suggestions, opinions, actions and expressions and sticks to all his views until he is convinced otherwise.

Some behavioural:
Manifestations of the witty child:

The witty child makes some assumptions and thereafter forms perceptions on the matter to arrive at the conclusion stage. He expresses almost all his views with conviction. Some behavioural manifestations of the witty child are mentioned below:

1. The witty child ascertains the weak and soft areas of the parents and parent substitutes towards him and manipulates them for his own purposes.
2. Since the child remains in close contact with and under the supervision of the parents he experiences the quality

of stimuli given to him by them. He develops a sense of intuition and acquires the skill to predict the requirements of the parents in a particular situation. He activates his driving force to exercise intuitive power for the manifestation of activities.

However, the actions of the witty child may not always be in conformity with the requirements of the parents. Sometimes he fails to respond in a proper way.

3. Whenever the witty child does something on a thought provoking matter, he uses his analytical mind which he develops through an in depth study of the surrounding objects and an inquisitive approach towards knowing more about the things around him.
4. Sometime it appears that the witty child behaves and acts like a person having practical exposure and maturity on the aspect.
5. He is imaginative and chalks out an action plan for performance in the short-term period.
6. He watches and observes the situation and when the environment appears to be conducive he takes the full benefits to get his work done through his parents.
7. The witty child deeply studies the desires, expectations and aspirations of the parents and convinces them with corroborative facts about non-fulfilment.
8. The witty child expresses his behavioural indications in a serious manner if his views are not given due weight.
9. He is stubborn in imposing his thoughts, ideas and views on others.

Thus the witty child manifests his behavioural activities through his inherent skill and qualities, such as intuitive, creative and manipulative skills. He may have an uninterrupted and smooth expression of activities in a situation where he receives continuous positive and encouraging stimuli from parents and parent substitutes and communicates complementary transactions.

Under such circumstances, an environment of 'ok feelings' exists amongst the child, parents and parent substitutes. The inherent qualitative aspects may increase, new thoughts, ideas and projections may develop and the child may go for more and more manifestation of behavioural demonstration, if the parents or parent substitutes persistently supply positive stimuli.

The witty child may not be a successful actor in the manipulation of activities if the witty child ego of the parents or parent substitutes is stronger than his own ego-state. Success in intuitive work depends upon the perceptible quality the witty child possesses to analyse and ascertain the situation and to react accordingly. On some occasions it may happen that the attempt of the witty child at manipulative activities fails to win due to non-availability of proper information or data to study the situation, or the non-existence of a strong and sound ego pattern as compared to the ego pattern of the parents or parent substitutes. The witty child's innate skill to intuit may not always be effective to bring the desired result. There are instances that, due to wrong perceptions and misconceptions about the people around him, the witty child fails to demonstrate activities in the right direction.

The creative aspect of the witty child becomes prominently apparent when he demonstrates thought-provoking activities. With imaginative skill the witty child enhances his creativity to expose to new phenomena. The witty child may experience an uncomfortable, inconducive and uncongenial atmosphere in the family and society towards the demonstration of his creative activities. Under such situations, there may not be a qualitative development in the creative faculty of the witty child. The witty child may feel dejected when he persistently receives negative strokes and discouraging stimuli from authority figures, resulting in the creation of a halting position in the process of development. If such a situation prolongs, he may lose his efficacy in activating imaginative traits. But in a situation when the witty child is encouraged for his creative activities by authority figures by providing the appropriate stimuli in a conducive and congenial atmosphere, his driving force may lead him to explore potential creative areas. The witty child subsequently develops a strong base for his imaginative faculties, which supplies input for the manifestation of activities at the time of need. During formative childhood, the circumstances the witty child exposes, the stimuli he receives from his authority figures, and the situation he faces, may influence him to form some idea about all these, which may affect his judgement during adulthood.

CHAPTER 2

Role Dominance vis-à-vis Perceptible Demonstration of Behavioural Activities

In the foregoing discussion, it was evinced that an individual cannot manifest his activities rationally and judiciously if his adult ego is contaminated or dominated by any other ego. The proper response and judgement on any matter can be given only when adult ego is free from the clutches of any other ego. The adult ego may be contaminated in the following ways:

1. Contamination of adult ego by child ego.
2. Contamination of adult ego by parent ego.
3. Contamination of adult ego both by child ego and parent ego.
4. Contamination of adult ego by child ego and dominance of parent ego.
5. Contamination of adult ego by parent ego and dominance of child ego.
6. Contamination of adult ego by child ego and dominance of child ego
7. Contamination of adult ego by parent ego and dominance of parent ego.

Adult Ego Contaminated/Dominated by Child Ego

In a situation where a person's adult ego is contaminated or dominated by the child ego, the person concerned cannot function effectively. He becomes choosy towards a particular person, object, situation or issue. Some of the qualitative traits and behavioural patterns of such an individual, contaminated in (1), (3), (5) and (6) and dominated the by child ego as mentioned above are briefly discussed below:

1. He demonstrates a casual approach to each and every issue. He takes all issues lightly, even serious matters which require immediate intervention and solution on a war footing.
2. He expresses his emotional feelings whenever any occasion crops up and attaches prime importance to them, without considering its impact, outcome and pros and cons.
3. He is very self-centred and does not look to the situation where people need help, support and cooperation. He avoids involvement in any sort of arrangement or understanding which may require his presence and participation on a regular basis.
4. He cannot be patience about particular things, objects, matters or issues for a long period, becomes uncomfortable easily, and switches over to the other way when he feels restless.
5. He is non-committal. He cannot keep his commitment through his actions and deeds.
6. He is unreliable. He cannot keep any matter confidential.
7. He lacks the quality of objective evaluation of any situation or issue.
8. He is poor in the decision-making process. He cannot stick to the decisions taken by him. He changes his decisions under duress, intimidation and stress. He is a person who succumbs to pressure.
9. He lacks leadership qualities, which are a pre-requisite for the achievement of goals.
10. He cannot develop a sense of well being, togetherness and oneness amongst the people around him, since he does not have the necessary traits to create a team.
11. He is rights-conscious. He shirks responsibilities and holds others accountable.
12. He hesitates to take decisions on vital issues and keeps such issues unresolved until he is reminded.
13. He does not initiate changes in the existing system. He allows prevalent practices and systems to continue.
14. He is neither authoritative, nor democratic in his style of functioning. He follows the method which suits him at the particular point of time.

15. Since he does not have a clear mindset because of the influence of his child ego on adult functions, he is incapable of analysing problems objectively, finding out the genesis of issues and awarding solutions.
16. He cannot earn the confidence of people because of his incapacity at the people-orientated approach. He therefore cannot develop mutual trust, mutual understanding and mutual faith amongst the people around him.
17. He is not a task-oriented person. He fails to achieve the targeted goal due to his shortsighted vision, unrealistic thought processes, non-pragmatic projections and organizing ineffectiveness.
18. He lacks zeal, spirit, and the enthusiasm to complete the assignment in a time frame situation.
19. Since the adult ego of the person is non-performing, he can be manipulated and can be made agreeable to any matter, situation.
20. He can be made a tool of others, who may mis-utilise his services for some vested interests.
21. Because of the dominating influence of the child ego over the adult ego, the person demonstrates immature, child-like, irrational and unreasonable behavioural activities, resulting in uncomfortable, cross-transactions between him and others.
22. He remains pre-occupied by trifling issues and gives little or no attention to matters which require immediate disposal.
23. He is a fun-loving, merry making, 'don't know' type personality who does not keep himself aware of incidents happenings around him.

The above type of personality remains involved in wasteful and unproductive activities. This is remarkable and noticeable when a person's adult ego is substantially contaminated or dominated by his child ego. Such a person loses his individuality and the indispensable quality of role playing. He evinces his ineffectiveness through his actions and behavioural manifestations. He sometimes expresses his helplessness when something goes beyond his control.

The contamination of the adult ego by the child ego or the dominance of the child ego over the adult ego does not occur overnight. It is the result of interactions and interpersonal reactions between the individual and authority figures over a period of time, mostly during the formative childhood years of the individual under different situations and circumstances. The cardinal factors which push the driving force of the child to offer stimuli or respond to stimuli to form ego pattern through persistent transactions are mentioned below:

1. When the child feels the deprivation of fatherly affection, and when motherly affection is not sufficient to fill such vacuum, he searches out for authority figures to substitute his parent and get affection. The child may form an 'incomplete parent impression' in his brain computer if he fails to find such a personality to satiate his need for parental love. This sort of situation may not occur to a child if his mother compensates the deficiency of fatherly love through her nurturing process. In such a case, the mother, through her affection and love, does not make the child feel the absence of a father or fatherly love.

   The 'incomplete parent impression' that the child holds may drive the child to resort to the sort of activities which may not have a relation to propriety, reasonableness and rationality.

   The child may feel deprivation of fatherly affection (1)when he has lost his father in childhood, which he may or may not recollect, or (2) when his father has abandoned him and has been staying separately, or (3) when his father has remarried and pays no heed to his problems, or (4) when his father remains absent physically for a long period and is not concerned for his well- being, or (5) when his father does not accept him as member of the family.
2. When the child is deprived of motherly affection and his father cannot fill the gap created. Due to a deprivation of love from the mother, the child becomes restless and does whatever he wants to do. The child may have a deprivation of motherly affection when

   i. he has lost his mother in the formative period and no other 'parent substitute' compensates for the vacuum, or
   ii. his mother has remarried and stays at some other place, or
   iii. his mother gives him company after long intervals, or
   iv. his mother does not accept him as a member of the family.
3. When the child loses his parents in the beginning of his nurturing period and he is reared in a family where no-

body gives parental affection to him to compensate for his hunger for love, he cannot develop a distinct parent ego. He gets instructions, advice, suggestions and commands from different persons in a haphazard manner but he does not know what to choose as the appropriate stimulus for the manifestation of his activities. At that point of time, perhaps, the emotive stimuli, which are not at all facilitators for growth, may influence the child to respond. The receipt of inappropriate stimuli and the response to such stimuli make the child's ego pattern imperfect, unsound and unbalanced. Under such circumstances, the child feels that he is not accepted as a member of the family. He either keeps himself aloof from, or gets less involved in, family rituals and ceremonies. He passes his time under the family environment of threat, fear and suspicion. He feels dejected and curses himself for his birth in the family. It may happen that sometimes the child takes the extreme decision of leaving his house in search of peace and love elsewhere, or tries to end his life. He becomes completely perplexed and at a loss to decide what to do. He finds himself an unwanted person in the family. He obtains his education in an usual way in the family system. Nobody in the family asks him to talk about any difficulty, problem, need or any matter that he is supposed to face daily. He may get some help, guidance and advice from teachers of the school, or from near or distant relations in the family, which he may perceive as a paradigm in his life script. With the positive stimuli available from such personalities, the child may find some ray of hope in his life and continue his struggle for survival.

But unlike in the above case, in a situation where the child gets partial support either from his mother or from any authority figure in the family, he does not feel himself to be a completely rejected person. It is certain that the child does not get satisfaction on the overall activities of the family and the impressions perceived by them towards him bring an adverse affect in his mental state. The child may find a casual approach in his parent towards his career path and growth. The stimuli and responses of his parent are of a usual nature, which attach no specific mandate for the attainment of a stipulated goal. The child may notice a lack of spontaneity in his parent, and a failure to encourage him for achievements. Even for a successful event of the child, the parent may not come forward to greet him. Under such situations, the child may perceive his parent as an 'ineffective and non-playing actor'. He may go ahead with the idea formed by him. But it is not that the parent remains a simple spectator in all cases. The parent gives advice, directs and supervises the child, shows him the ways to follow and makes him understand that he is with him to help. Maybe this type of parental attitude is not abundantly prevalent, but the fact remains that under such situations the parent is not absolutely ineffective. The child may not get the support, impetus, encouragement and positive strokes from his parent to the extent that he needs for his development. Hence there may not always be congruent and appropriate transactions. The ego pattern of the child may not be in a sound state, as the child ego sometimes acts arbitrarily to influence the adult ego.

Adult Ego Contaminated/Dominated by Parent Ego

There are people whose adult ego is contaminated or dominated by the parent ego. Because of such contamination or dominance the adult ego cannot discharge its role performance neutrally and rationally. The information is supplied to the person by the adult ego after analysing and processing; the evaluation of the data may not be perfect, genuine and reliable. Thus the decision, instruction, judgement and advice given by the person on the basis of the information received by the contaminated adult ego is likely to be biased. The behavioural manifestations of the person whose adult ego is contaminated or dominated by the parent ego are very different to that of the person who has a balanced ego pattern. Some of the salient traits and behavioural expressions of such a person having an infected or a dominated adult ego by the parent ego are discussed below:

1. He considers himself a knowledgeable and enormously wise person.
2. He treats most of his competitors as inferior persons having no quality to compete with him. The persons who work with him in the same cadre and grade are not given due respect. He considers most of his colleagues as useless, non-performing and ineffective persons.

3. He always keeps his distance from most of the people in his locality, work place, club or in a get-together place, probably with pretensions of possessing superior qualities of merit, skill and expertise.
4. He is self-centred and has no concern for others.
5. He is very particular about his rights, privileges and benefits. He cannot sacrifice even a trifling share of benefit for the well being of people.
6. He keeps himself reserved and rarely exposes himself to the vagaries of the situation.
7. He is very vindictive and does not hesitate to retaliate even in a petty matter.
8. He is showy and projects himself before the people as a people-oriented person taking care of the needs of people.
9. He does not have the quality of an effective leader and he is not acceptable to the team members,
10. He creates a small coterie who supplies the required information to take appropriate measures.
11. He cannot have trust or faith in the people with whom he is working. Likewise, his colleagues, subordinates and superiors cannot trust him.
12. Ethics have no place for him. He can be purchased in exchange for anything.
13. He is greedy and miserly and desires many things in an unusual way.
14. He believes in the authoritarian approach and feels that he can gain anything through pressure and intimidation.
15. He has an inherent desire to grab power, authority, promotions and any sort of advantage, superseding his peers and legitimate incumbents in an irrational, unreasonable and improper way.
16. In reality he is alone. He may have some persons who may be considered to be his followers.
17. He is basically coward, timid. He does not have courage to expose truth or facts.
18. He does not like to mingle with people at work.
19. He is unsteady and unfirm in his decisions. He cannot keep promises.
20. He pretends to be disciplined, reasonable and rational.
21. He does not have the ability of stress tolerance. He may lose control and sometime he may succumb to pressure.

22. He never appreciates the people for good performance.
23. He exaggerates his performance to create a good image before people.
24. When an excellent job done by his subordinates, he takes the entire credit for such performance. But when anything goes wrong, he passes on accountability to others.
25. He is in the habit of criticizing the people and finding fault with their activities.
26. He cannot keep a balance between thought processes, words and deeds. What he says is not reflected in his actions.
27. He cannot tolerate his peers when they achieve something superseding him.

Salient Traits and Behavioural Manifestations in a Situation When the Adult Ego is Contaminated/Dominated by the Nurturing Parent Ego

1. The person whose adult ego is dominated or contaminated by nurturing parent ego is supportive, liberal and people-oriented.
2. He takes every matter, however important it is, casually and lightly. Even a matter which requires immediate disposal because of its gravity and importance is not given due weight.
3. He works as a facilitator and helper to solve the problems of the people around him. If somebody approaches him for assistance, he comes forward and extends his helping hand.
4. He never thinks of what he is going to get in exchange for his services given to people, but simply serves and helps them.
5. He has his paradigm to work as rescuer and protector of the people who are in extreme need of help and ask for it.
6. He is an unselfish, service-loving and image-building personality. He gives service at no cost and sometimes at his own cost.
7. He has a bossy tendency and expects respect from the assistance seeker.
8. He has an authoritarian approach based on the philosophy of helping people in a manner designed by him within his own framework.
9. He is weak in decision-making, and sluggish in action.

10. He cannot remain firm in action. He succumbs to pressure and surrenders. He has no stress tolerance capability and avoids situations which may cause worries and anxiety.
11. He is afraid of facing confrontation and settles issues and grievances through mutual process.
12. He cannot enforce discipline as he is liberal in administration.
13. He teaches rules and regulations and the necessity of its compliance. He also makes the people aware of consequences of non-compliance.
14. He is afraid of taking disciplinary action against erring people.
15. He is open-minded. He discusses problems with his subordinates and asks for suggestions.
16. He believes in settling issues over the table. He emphasises the need for a participative approach for threadbare discussion and to sort out the problem.
17. For any wrong doing he pleads innocence and establishes that it has been caused due to some situational factors.
18. He loves people, listens to their problem, assures them of consideration without commitment.
19. He is acceptable to people, and earns a reputation for his good behaviour and disposition.
20. He lacks the leadership traits required for the achievement of goals.
21. He makes a surface study of the issue. He does not go into the genesis of the problem, and does not make objective assessments and evaluations. The decisions taken by him are therefore devoid of natural justice, rationality and reasonableness.
22. He is soft spoken and timid. He usually does not show anger.
23. He is accessible to all. He does not impose any restrictions on people to visit him.
24. He develops an ethos where there is a climate of lawlessness, indiscipline and inaction.
25. He likes people who are free and frank, and does not like people who are complicated and harmful.
26. He believes people and, in the process, develops a soft corner for some people.
27. He strives for the well being of people in his own style of functioning.
28. He is not vindictive and tries to maintain congenial relations amongst people.

The individual's child witnesses the parent as command from critical or nurturing point of view. The child may observe either the critical parent or nurturing parent to play role in building perception about parents. The following are the circumstances under which a person's adult ego may get infected or dominated by the parent ego.

1. When the birth of a child is not welcomed by its parents, the child's entry in the family may bring unhappiness and anxieties for the parents. They may not accept the child wholeheartedly as a member of the family. In some cases, the child may witness total rejection by his family. In such a situation, the child finds that he is kept isolated from family activities. His desire, needs and aspirations are not given due weight and importance. He lacks appropriate parental love and affection. He may experience humiliation, differential treatment, or deprivation of basic amenities by the parent. He obtains negative stimuli from his parents. He may get harsh punishment for trivial offences. Parents express their behavioural manifestations as critical parents.
2. When the child's parent is already in possession of an adult ego contaminated or dominated by parent ego, he reacts, on most occasions, in a biased manner. The child's parent inherits some unverified qualities of child rearing and nurturing processes from his own parents, which he imposes on his child. Since the parent ego is of two types- critical and nurturing- the adult ego of the child may have contamination or a dominance of either the critical parent ego, or the nurturing parent ego, or both. The parent of the child may, therefore, supply stimuli to the child or may respond to the stimuli of the child, keeping in view the type of parent ego it possesses.
3. When the birth of the child in a family happens to be a blessing or a long-awaited event, the parents express an unusually warm welcome to the child. Parents provide positive stimuli to the child all the time. They nurture the child in such a manner that they forget to give negative stimuli at the time it is warranted for growth and development. Parents keep the child under their protective shadow, so that he may not be exposed to the vagaries of the elements. With such treatment and nourishing process of the parents, the child develops some image about his parents in his

perceptible region. He starts feeling that his presence in the family is indispensable and subsequently retains the feeling of 'I-ness'. He demands different types of articles one after another and, when he gets them immediately after expressing his desires, he thinks everything is receivable if a demand is placed. In such a situation, parents act irrationally and they fulfil the child's demands without ascertaining the necessity or the capability to supply, or the utility of the object or article demanded.

The child witnesses his parents as persons with open and liberal Personalities, believing in the philosophy of appeasement, patch-up solutions and adjustment. The child's adult ego cannot perform properly and judiciously, since the nurturing parent ego influences it too much. The person with such a contaminated or dominated adult ego is weak in Decision-making. He cannot shoulder responsibility and always tries to pass on responsibilities to others.

He lacks courage. He is afraid of undertaking risky projects. He wants not to lead but to be led. He avoids situations which are likely to create confrontation and complications. He does not analyse problems in the proper perspective. Whenever he faces a problem, he loses his will power to combat the situation. He always pays a defensive role in giving support to his own men. He blindly takes the side of his people to protect them from possible injury without giving proper thought to the issue. Since he has not experienced much in the matter of taking risks and responsibilities during the process of his nourishment in his childhood, he refrains from entrusting responsibility to his people.

Behavioural manifestations of the person whose adult ego is dominated or contaminated by critical parent are not same to that of a person whose adult is ego contaminated or dominated by a nurturing or nourishing parent ego. When a person's adult ego is contaminated or dominated by a critical parent ego, the person interferes in each and every matter of the people around him. He considers himself superior to others in all respects. He strives to exercise authority over his people through the autocratic process. He instructs his men to complete the job within a time frame without looking at any other aspect, like possibility, feasibility, capability, availability of infrastructure arrangement, etc. He makes the people accountable and responsible for non-performance and wrong doing. He criticises and abuses the people for no genuine cause. Most of his instructions are command-oriented. He wants everything immediately, right now.

Now let us examine the situation and overall milieu created due to the dominant role played by the person whose adult ego is remarkably influenced either by the child ego or the parent ego. The effect of the dominance of the child ego or parent ego is observable in the family, in the society, in the club or in the organization through the activities of the person.

Perceptible Effects in Functional Areas of the Person Whose Adult Ego is Dominated by the Child Ego

In a situation when a person's adult ego is dominated by the child ego, he demonstrates some behavioural activities which facilitate in developing ethos in the family, in society and in the organization to which he is directly associated. His behaviour, attitudes, beliefs and activities create an impression, in the minds of the people with whom he is related, about his personality, efficacy, competency, leadership qualities and expectations. The people around him, therefore, hold some assumption about the qualitative aspect of his style of functioning. During the course of his actions and interactions, the following situations are likely to occur in his functional area:

i. The person cannot maintain discipline, cannot take rational decisions, cannot do justice to others, cannot keep his commitments. The morale of his subordinates is eroded.
ii. The people working with or under the person cannot trust him. A climate prevails of lack of trust, and lack of faith and understanding on a mutual footing.
iii. Everything is taken very lightly. No seriousness is shown about issues which need seriousness. Hence the need requirements, aspirations and the desire of the members of the team to which he is leader do not receive due weight.
iv. People do not get appreciation and recognition for work well done by them. It is not that the person having the contaminated adult ego does not want to appreciate the best performers. It may be that he either forgets to recognize his people's excellence or is ignorant of judging

the necessity of giving positive strokes. His not giving recognition through positive stimuli is unintentional. The non-receipt of positive impulse in terms of appreciation makes the employees sluggish and indifferent towards achieving the desired goal. People may develop a feeling of unconcern and isolation which may worsen the relations between the two hierarchies.

v. The person lacks the requisite skills to convince people, to lead them and to achieve desired goals. He cannot run through a particular system for a period not necessarily long. He changes his decisions and switches over to other area of function in a different way. In the process, he invites unpredictable complications and cannot make effective attempts at successful venture. His frequent fluctuations in the task-performing approach creates a lot of ambiguity amongst his followers towards having a proper assessment of his mindset. Sometimes they may not get the proper message as to what to do, or they may feel that a shift in the task- performing approach is meaningless and uncalled for.

vi. The person may emphasize on unproductive work rather than productive work. He expresses his desire and gives emotional support to complete such a job in a time frame schedule. Such an unrealistic, untimely and unpragmatic approach may create a big jolt in the existing structure, which may eventually ruin the system.

vii. He does not make any plans for achieving goals. He gives less or no stress on the necessity of passing through the different processes of task accomplishment to achieve targets. He mostly puts in an effort for short term achievements in any matter, without giving consideration to quality, cost-benefit perspectives or possible effects in different areas.

viii. He cannot establish himself as a successful and effective person in the area of his activities. He lacks the qualitative traits essential for achieving perfection, accuracy and transparency.

ix. Before initiating any step or taking any action on any crucial issue, he does not make any analytical assessment of the case, the consequences likely to crop up and the remedial measures to be needed to face the situation. He acts as a defensive or reactive agent and not as a proactive agent. The actions taken by him may not be in proportion to the misdeeds. In some cases it even happens that the basis on which action is taken does not have solid footing or genuine ground. Hence, the whole process of an action-oriented exercise becomes a mockery or a farce. The people around him consider him a person with a fickle, casual and irrational character, having no sound conceptual base and determination.

x. Such a person, wherever he works, makes a mess inconducive to proper functioning. This sort of situation creates a security phobia amongst the members and an unhealthy environment in the entire system, which may collapse at any time if a rectification process is not undertaken.

The person may manifest an altogether different type of behavioural activity if his adult ego is contaminated by the parent ego. The parent ego has either the critical parent programming or the nurturing parent programming. The person whose adult ego is influenced by the critical parent demonstrates behavioural activities which are different from those activities manifested by a person whose adult ego is dominated by the nurturing parent ego.

Perceptible Effects in the Functional Area of the Person Whose Adult Ego is Contaminated by the Critical Parent Ego are as Follows

A person dominated by the critical parent develops an environment in his work situation, and at places with which he is associated, through demonstration of his behavioural activities. The overall work ethos and culture undergo a change in the process of the active participation/involvement in the crucial area of activities by the person who takes over the control of the whole system. The following conditions are noticed in the family, club or any organization where a persistently critical parent role is performed by the person as an executive:

1. Barring very few persons, nobody is happy with the person or with the environment created through his behavioural activities. Some people may show loyalty under compulsion, some people may evince, out of fear, that they are obedient

and blind followers. A state of unhappiness prevails so long as the person remains active in his role playing activities.

2. Most people are afraid of him. They sincerely try to keep themselves aloof from him and they maintain a distance between him and themselves. People cannot be free and frank, they cannot express their difficulties, disadvantages, troubles, shortcomings or limitations to him, as they are not given opportunities to come close and to discuss problems. The climate of fear psychosis is established during his regime.
3. The people do not get recognition for excellent work done. No appreciation, no sort of stroking to boost up emotional value is given by the person to the people for their achievements. The person does not give due weight to the people for outstanding performance. He thinks he is superman and he is the only person who is knowledgeable. He does not consider others as performers or achievers. An uncomfortable situation develops through the interaction process.
4. The person does not trust the people who are at his command. He always keeps a suspicious watch on them. He has an preconceived impression about the people. He believes that they are basically bad, betrayers, problem creators and people who cannot be relied upon. He has no confidence in people who are associated with him. The climate of mutual trust, mutual understanding and mutual cooperation does not exist.
5. The person is basically task-oriented. He is not concerned about the need and difficulties of the people. He wants the people to do what he wants them to do. He always exercises authoritarian tact to make the people work. He makes a thorough reshuffling of the people's assignments on a need based approach and places people according to his choice. A vested coterie is formed with some people, to supply necessary information to the person to strengthen the steps taken by him to achieve the objectives. Sometimes, people in the coterie become very powerful and they play vital role in the decision making process of the person. The environment of an autocratic system and the presence of a coterie regime is noticed.

6. The person remains in a critical mood. He never shows a sympathetic attitude. He criticises people for their actions, blames them for no genuine cause and reprimands them for no obvious reason. He gets his purpose served through exercising pressure on people. He creates havoc in the entire system. 'Hire and fire' is his weapon which he uses at the appropriate time. The human relations scenario depicts a bleak environment.
7. He is not liked by people in general. Nobody spontaneously pays respect to him, except his own men. He is, therefore, not acceptable to people. He does not have the requisite qualities of a team leader. He lacks the skill and ingredients to influence people. In fact, he becomes an ineffective and unsuccessful executive if he continues with the same assignment for a long period. A state of uncertainty and an unviable situation exists.

It also happens that the person's adult ego is dominated by the nurturing/nourishing parent ego. In such cases, the organization, club or family may witness a different situation to that of the previous one. In every field of activities, the appeasement technique works. Nobody hesitates to purchase peace and to remain in a trouble-free situation. Now, let us examine the perceptible effect in the functional area of person whose adult ego is contaminated by the nurturing/nourishing parent.

Perceptible Effect in the Functional Area of the Person Whose Adult Ego is Contaminated by the Nurturing Parent

1. The person is very liberal and soft towards his people. He rarely becomes harsh or adamant towards them. He takes lenient views even of gross irregularities or misdeeds. He cannot be strong and firm at the time of necessity. A climate of slack administration is noticed.
2. The person is not very particular about maintaining discipline. If he sees that his men have to face a lot of trouble, difficulties and painful exercises because of his imposition of discipline, he may discard the idea and may allow the running of the institution with a culture of indiscipline. A complete state of lawlessness and indiscipline hovers around.

3. He treats people as innocent and young, and considers them as having no experience or exposure to the situation arising out of cutthroat competition. He gives a lot of relaxation, benefits and facilities to his men, pays much more attention than needed, and keeps them under his shade of protection. In the process, he makes them ineffective and crippled. They become dependent upon him and lose their own identity; they need advice and guidance for each and every matter; their growth and development is halted, and the quality of tasks deteriorates. A static, or rather, a waning state of affairs exists.
4. As a person, he is good to one and all. He is loved by the people for his attitudes and behaviour but he is known as a person with no principles, norms or stipulated rules, boundaries or jurisdiction. He acts in a manner that suits him. The only thing he sees is that his action is for the benefit of the people who ask for it. An environment of following double standards may not, therefore, be ruled out. This sort of situation is unhealthy for any organization to grow. This not only vitiates the climate of mutual understanding and trust but also dampens the spirit of cohesiveness, the feeling of 'we-ness' and the sense of belonging. The ultimate result is a bleak situation in the prevalent system.
5. He is basically a group-oriented person. He does a lot for the amelioration of his own group. Here the 'own group' does not mean the coterie of the person or the very limited number of people who remain at his beck and call. In a broader sense, 'group' includes those people who are under his control or under his supervisory jurisdiction. Even at the cost of his own benefit or interest, he sacrifices some areas of his privileges and prerogatives for the benefit of his people. Looking to the attitude of the person as also the soft corner he has towards his men, who place their issues and grievances to him, including those that the 'group leader' may not be able to settle to the satisfaction of the people in their own forum. A climate of unrest, dissatisfaction and unhappiness in noticed amongst the people is noticed.
6. Since the person shows unwillingness and apathy in taking disciplinary measures against erring persons, people

become careless, negligent, disobedient and disloyal. They begin to feel a situation of laissez-faire in the entire system over which the concerned person has jurisdiction. They cannot deliver the goods in terms of need. Even the service rendered is rarely up to the mark. Both the productivity as well as the quantum of qualitative product get adversely affected in the organization. The overall growth of the organization reaches a standstill.

7. Sometimes, the person creates a 'situation for nobody' when he says 'yes' to everybody who approaches to him for help. In the process of giving commitment to all, very few people's aspirations and desires are fulfilled. A state of despair, frustration and helplessness is witnessed amongst the members.

CHAPTER 3

Influence of Need Factors in the Process of Activating the Driving Force towards Task Accomplishment

From the earlier discussion, we have seen that a human being receives stimuli—positive or negative—which push him to engage in activities for the achievement of his goals. Stimulus is essentially required for performance of a task and a quality task depends upon the type of stimulus received. It passes through different phases in a situation where positive stimulus is given.

Activity → Performance → Achievement → Growth and Development

In a situation where negative stimulus is offered, passing phases may depict an altogether different picture in the area of performance, achievement, growth and development. Stimulus is, therefore, connected with the passage of phases for the manifestation of activities.

There are different ways and means which stimulate the driving force to be activated to display behavioural activities. Physical contact, touch and recognition act as stimuli to move along a desired pathway. These are the basic needs of a human being while advancing from one stage to another. As soon as the child comes out of his mother's womb he urgently needs the physical touch of a person. Let us examine the necessity of physical touch as a part of the biological need of the person, especially for the child during the formative years of childhood.

PHYSICAL TOUCH AS A PART OF BIOLOGICAL NEED

It is the inherent desire of a person to have the love, care and affection of parents, family members, and other societal members. At the beginning of childhood, the infant is unaware about love, care and affection, since he has never tasted it earlier and has had no scope to experience it. What the infant wants immediately after he is born is to get somebody who ensures that he is available all the time to take care of him and shows his presence through physical touch or contact. The parent or parent substitute may initially appear to be a stranger to the child but after a period of time, when the child gets close to the parent or parent substitute at the time of diapering, fondling, caressing and bottle-feeding, he watches the parent substitute very minutely and considers him as his own man. The child becomes so acquainted with the parent or parent substitute that he can recognize the parent or the parent substitute easily. He develops a symbolic bond with them. He feels the absence of his parent greatly when the latter remains out of sight for some period. He expresses his desire to make his parent present through persistent shouting and crying and stops crying only after getting the physical touch of his parent or after becoming exhausted from shouting. The child responds to the expressions of love and affection of his parent through body language and movement. He wants to be embraced, for his body to be fondled, to be held in the lap by the parent. Physical touch or contact is as essential as food, water or air. It is a biological need for sustenance, growth and development. The child cannot sustain normally nor grow if he lacks touch or physical contact from his parent or parent substitute. His physical and mental health gets affected if he remains starved from touch or contact.

There can be all round development in the mental faculty and physical structure of the child if he gets proper and adequate touch and physical contact from the parent in a normal situation. Under such circumstances, the child feels comfortable in what he considers a pleasant, congenial environment. The child observes the surrounding milieu to be positive and facilitating for his advancement and experiences the spontaneity of the love and affection bestowed by the parent on him. The child realizes that his entry to the family is highly accepted. All these feeling, observation and realizations bring about a change in the mental state of health of the child, which keeps him contented and happy all the time. The happiness of the child tends to develop the physique if no congenital abnormality exists. In a situation whére child receives continuous physical contact from his parent, he manifests his happiness and contentment to be a part of the family through the process of the response to parental stimuli. He demonstrates his behavioural activities in the direction as expected by his parent. As long as he cannot express verbally his requirements, desires and expectations, he indicates through gestures and body language that he wishes to continue to receive physical affection. The child shows smooth and easy going characteristics in his behavioural pattern through the demonstration of performance of normal and routine activities. The above activities and expressions of posture and gestures of the child are noticeable in the very formative stages when the child cannot communicate verbally to his parent or anybody. But, with the passage of time, when the child advances from one stage to another, his mental state gets developed and the child starts placing his demands and queries through oral communication to the extent possible. At this stage the child gets stimuli from his parents, parent substitutes and other members of society, to respond appropriately at the time of necessity. The child tends to learn the skill to make responses for the completion of the transaction process, but at this age, he cannot respond properly as he cannot understand the exact meaning of each and every stimulus offered to him.

Company, Closeness, Intimacy

What the child needs during such a formative period (this period starts from the day he gives oral communication to the day prior to his entry to the primary school level) is the constant company, closeness and intimacy of the parent or parent substitute. He wants his parent to remain with him as a companion most of the day, if not throughout the day. He expects his parent to respond to the stimuli he offers: to play with him as a playmate, to reply to the queries as a guardian, to tell him stories of fantasy, ghosts, giants, wild animals etc., to give him anything he sees or intends to eat or drink, and to take him to the places he wants to go. He wants to be close to his parent to satisfy his needs and desires. He feels an inherent urge to know the heart and mind of his parent who gives him company and so he puts forward a lot of questions to his parent. He watches, observes and feels the behavioural activities of his parent and determines whether there is any transparent deviation from the earlier treatment/behaviour given to him through physical touch/contact during his early stages. If he notices a remarkable change in the behavioural pattern of his parent, he verifies and reverifies it by asking different questions, placing various demands and finally abandoning the issue.

The child wants to become intimate with his parent by getting close to him. He shows his smiling face to his parent whenever he comes to him, indicating his desire to make his presence available to him. He rushes to his parent, makes him sit before him, creates an environment to chit chat and continues to carry on non-stop talking, questioning and playing games. He does not allow his parent to go without getting his concurrence. If the parent leaves the place without consent, he creates a commotion to attract his parent and becomes quiet only when his parent attends, or if he otherwise gets exhausted. The child forgets his food and rest while playing with the parent. He gets annoyed if somebody disturbs or hinders him at the time of carrying on such activities. The child is very fond of playing, identifying the objects he sees, enjoying each and every incident he observes in day to day activities without knowing its significant aspects. The child wants to satiate his ego need of knowing things arising out of his emotional plane and he gets such knowledge from his parent by being intimate with him. If the child gets a reply to his each and every query immediately and comfortably from his parent he gets contented and develops a feeling of okayness. His mental faculty and other bodily organs start progressing under such a situation. But the reverse is the case when the parent communicates with the child about his unwillingness to reply to the queries, as also not to raise such questions any more in future. In this case, the child feels neglected, thinks he is not acceptable to his parent vis-à-vis the family, gets a sudden shock in his mental area leading to fear psychosis and a state of bewilderment. He cannot increase his area of conception and finds it difficult to cope with present day dynamic activities, as his all round development gets hindered. When the child does not get requisite treatment from his parent and rather obtains negative treatment from his parent he searches for other parent or substitute parents with whom he can play, gossip and spend most of his time and who can give him company as and when he needs. But, if the other parent (the father or mother, who comes to the rescue of the child) or parent substitute (the grand father/grand mother/aunt/elder sister or any body in the family or in the society) does not come forward to help the child or gives the same treatment to the child as was given by his parent earlier, he feels dejected and his need for company, closeness and intimacy remains unfulfilled. He starts thinking that he is alone and he has nobody in the universe as his own. He thus develops a state of solitude. He receives a big jolt in the formation of proper mental faculty for growth and development. At this age the child does not find anybody to give him company to satisfy his inherent desires but he may notice the occasional appearance of parents/parent substitutes to give him company during part of the day to satiate only a fraction of his requirement. In this case the child records the timing of his parent's visit in his memory and keeps waiting up to the scheduled timing to receive the company of his parent. Occasional participation of the parent in the child's game schedule facilitates development of the child's mental faculty only when the rest of the period the child is given company by the parent substitute to play with either at home or at somebody's house or in a crèche. Under such circumstances, the child's development depends upon different factors like the educational background, the time spent, and the level of intelligent quotient and behavioural attitude of the companion.

In the process of child rearing and satiating of the child's needs for coming close to parent, keeping the child regular company and developing intimacy, it may so happen that the child all of a sudden feels the deprivation of the parental presence due to the separation of the parent from the family to which the child belongs. In such cases, even if the absence of the parent is compensated by the other parent, the child cannot forget the parent, and the loving experience prior to the disappearance of the parent. In a consequential effect, the child may manifest behavioural activities to expose the mutual bond already established between them through role playing behaviour (viz. wearing the parent's dress, imitating the parent's specific activities, postures, gestures etc.) The child's development process confronts a severe traumatic effect due to the non-availability of the parent's positive stimuli, which were abundantly supplied by the parent at the time of his stay with the child.

During the period of infancy, as aforenoted, (i.e., the period prior to the attainment of the primary level class) the child forms a paradigmal concept of his parent through being in his company, and while being close and intimate with his parent. Now the child advances one stage further with regard to his period of entry to the universe, experiences gained, knowledge about objects, things, people in the family and society, and enters into a new era for the satisfaction of his needs, desires and exploration of potential areas to strengthen the ego pattern. Hence the immediate need of the child at this stage may be acceptance, involvement and recognition.

ACCEPTANCE, INVOLVMENT AND RECOGNITION

The child may by this time be aware of many things about his family (Such as: Who are the family members who like or love him? Who are on his side, who are his well wishers? How does the family run? What are his parents' professions? What are his parents' instructions to him? What are his parent's expectations from him? How do his parents behave? How do his parents regard him in the family?) An analysis of the child's queries indicates whether the child is accepted by his parents and other family members. The child wants to be accepted by his parents and parent substitutes spontaneously, from the core of their hearts, and he expects to be a desired member of the family. He needs a warm introduction to close relatives and other persons related to the family. From the activities and behavioural manifestation of any member of the family, especially parents, the child should not get the impression that his entry into the family is not welcome by both the parents or either of them. When the child goes to visit his parents' relatives or any person acquainted with his parents, he expects treatment at par with the treatment given to his parents. While introducing the child to another person or vice versa, the child minutely notices the postures, gestures or words used by his parents or parent substitutes, and draws inferences about the perception of his parents or parent substitutes about him. He tends to study the mind of his parents or parent substitutes. He keeps his mind open to analyse the stimuli given or responses made (to the stimuli) by his parents or parent substitutes to determine the impression they have of him. He also watches the activities and the behavioural expression of his parents or parent substitute when he makes some gross mistake. He observes and analyses the reaction/interaction of his parents to each and every activity in matters of eating food, resting, sleeping, playing games, attending school, doing hometasks, performing in examinations, going to the market, wearing dresses, visiting the doctor, and so on and so forth.

Hence one of direst needs of the child is acceptance by the parents in a manner indicating that his membership in the family comes after waiting for a long period. When the child earns acceptability, he may have free access to parents or parents substitutes to discuss most matters pertaining to his growth and development. If the child is loved by his parents or parents substitutes, he may be given undue importance and weightage even for matters not directly connected to him. The highly accepted child finds the freedom to play his role in the day-to-day activities of the family. It does not matter whether the issues over which the child exercises influence relate to his well being or not. The highly accepted child, if not appropriately supervised or controlled in a timely manner, sometimes become the victim of ruining his career path. He turns out to be undisci plined, stubborn and self-centred. He does not want to part with anything, and may have a feeling of 'I-ness'.

If the highly accepted child is nourished or reared through proper training and in congenial environment, where timely and proper stimuli are offered and appropriate responses are made, he may excel in performance. The all round development of his mental faculties may be positive. He remains happy and makes others happy. He now tends to involve himself in the family system.

The child wants to be involved in each and every ritualistic activity of the family to show his worth, value and importance. In some cases, the child wants to be prominent in role activities, indicating his willingness to participate as an effective team member. It is the initial desire of the human being to remain associated with the club, organisation or group to satisfy his need for belonging, and being involved in organisational activities, he desires to occupy the key position to show his importance and indispensability to other members. The child is therefore no exception to the rule of human needs. An in-depth study of needs indicates the following causative factors for the involvement of the child:

1. The child feels lonely and insecure. He observes the outside world being new and uncongenial for existence and he needs association in group activities.
2. The child wants more love and more affection from his parents or parent substitutes and feels that it is possible through involvement.
3. The qualitative traits become transparent when a person is exposed to the situation.
4. The child can get the courage and confidence to discharge the assigned job if he is involved in the proper spirit.
5. Effectiveness, efficacy and capability arise out of direct involvement in the team job.
6. The child feels ignored if he is not involved in family functions and activities.
7. Involvement clears accumulated queries and helps the child get acquainted with subjects with he was not familiar earlier.
8. The child is smooth and easygoing in his activities and does everything in a cheerful mood when he stays involved.
9. Involvement facilitates the child in enriching his knowledge and to exercise the skill for innovative work.
10. Mutual trust, understanding and faith are established if team members are knit together through the process of involvement.
11. The involved child becomes disciplined, loyal and obedient to the family, and manifests behavioural activities which are conducive and congenial to the growth and development of the child and other members of the family.
12. The child may get positive stimuli from parents or parent substitutes to form complimentary transactions in a situation where he is fully involved.
13. The deprivation of the child from involvement by parents or parent substitutes worsens the relationship between them and the child.

14. Involvement being a participative system, it makes the child feel that he is accepted as a desired member of the family. The child thus forms a perceptive idea about his parents' behavioural patterns, which helps him to grow.

The child, on having been accepted by the parents and on being involved in family activities and rituals, deserves to be recognised. The child needs recognition, as the development of his mental faculty largely depends upon how he is recognised by the members of his family and the society. Recognition does not mean only the recognition the child is given as member of the family; the recognition of the parents with regard to the activities and performance of the child is also seen. This recognition can be given through a range of signals: physical touch, contact, and gesture, verbal and written communication and sanction of pecuniary measures to boost up the driving force to activate it further for growth and development. Recognition symptoms may be prevalent in the following situations:

1. When the parents or parent substitutes provide constant positive stimuli to the child, the child enjoys a feeling of coming close to the parents.
2. Whenever the need for being embraced or held in the lap comes up, the parents caress with spontaneity. The child feels happy to be a member of the family. In such a family system, he never feels the deprivation of physical touch.
3. When the child's legitimate, proper and reasonable demands are met, he feels that he is not ignored.
4. If the child is given due appreciation, in presence of others, by his parents for his excellence in performances, be it in the area of his studies or any other areas, his morale gets heightened, which tends to develop a higher image about the parents in his perception.
5. When the child makes any mistake or resorts to any misdeed, he is not reprimanded or punished inappropriately. In such a situation, the child feels that biased or disproportionate punishment is not given.
6. When parents introduce the child to relatives or other persons known to them, the child feels his entity in the family.

7. When the child is allowed to participate actively in family rituals and functions as a customary measure, which he earnestly wants to do, his sense of belongingness to the family is enhanced. The child comes very close to the members of the family and develops a sense of we-feeling.
8. If the child is addressed in a sweet tone, calling his initial name and in a pleasing and sympathetic manner, he feels proud of being in the family. The child notices a congenial, comfortable environment in the family, which facilitates his growth and development.
9. If the child is afforded special care, treatment and attention at the time when he needs it physically, he develops his self concept as being part and parcel of the family.
10. The child gets a great jolt in his mental state and becomes upset if he does not get a response to the stimuli given repeatedly to the parents or receives a response contrary to the desired one.

    The child feels ignored, neglected and dejected and he may either suspend manifestation of his behavioural activities or display inimical activities. The child expects a proper response to the stimuli so as to make complementary transactions.

From the foregoing discussions, it is revealed that the child needs physical touch, company, closeness, intimacy, acceptance, involvement and recognition from parents or parent substitutes for his all round development and growth, so as to make him a perfect, complete and effective citizen of the country. It is presumed that the child's sustenance need (i.e. physiological need according to Maslow's hierarchy of needs) viz. food, shelter, clothing, medical facilities etc. and the need for ensuring continuance of the facilities (i.e., 'security need' in terms of Maslow's hierarchy of need framework) are taken care of by the parents and parent substitutes. The small baby can survive if he is given proper food etc. immediately after his birth in the new world. The discussion on such needs as a tool to make any attitudinal change of the child is, therefore, not required. But such needs (physiological and security-related) play a vital role in changing the attitudes and behavioural activities of the person. Discussion on this topic as a 'change-agent' of behaviour attitudes of the person appears to be essential.

Sustenance Need

This is the need which every human being has for his existence and survival. This is primarily a basic need which a child immediately coming to the earth requires for his existence in the new environment suiting his demands, intake capacity, physique etc. These needs are food, water, air, shelter, clothing, medicine etc. The renowned behavioural scientist, Abrahm H. Maslow, has described such needs as 'physiological' needs. This is the first order need out of five order needs in the hierarchy of need framework (the five order needs are physiological, security-related, social, esteem-related and self actualisation).

Every human being gives his best endeavour and puts in an all-out effort to satisfy his basic needs for his existence and survival. The person does not switch over to the next order of needs, if his basic needs remain unfulfilled. The person exhibits a lot of change in his behaviour and attitude if he fails to satiate his physiological need. Some of the salient behavioural manifestations of the person who fails to satisfy the basic needs are mentioned hereunder:

1. The person will resort to all possible measures to obtain the required quantum of food and other necessities for sustenance and growth. If, despite his sincerest attempts and hardest work, the person cannot earn to maintain a livelihood, he feels a 'sense of impossibility'.
2. The person may give-up altogether his optimistic approach to fulfil his needs.
3. The person may chalk out action plan and may objectively analyse the situation and the reason for not achieving the desired target.
4. The person may proceed further in a systematic and strategic manner with a view to reaching the optimum level of aspiration.
5. If the person, through objective assessment, comes to know that such a situation will not last long, the person may give renewed thought to starting afresh for need satisfaction.
6. If non-fulfilment of primary needs is due to some other factors which have nothing to do with the person

concerned, he enhances his zeal, vigour and spirit and takes an oath to win the situation.

7. If the person comes to learn that he has to suffer due to the malafide attempt of somebody, the person may strengthen his power and activity in a bid to achieve.
8. If the person is not an optimist with regard to the satisfaction of basic needs in the near future, he may change his approach, strategy and the ways and means to achieve.
9. In a situation of non-fulfilment of physiological needs, the person becomes unhappy and manifests signs and symptoms of anxiety, worries, tension, despair and a state of uncertainty.
10. If the person does not succeed, after repeated attempts, to satisfy his needs, he may exhibit behavioural activities in the form of lower productivity, worse customer service and deterioration of quality goods or products. On many occasions the person may not provide positive stimuli or may not respond to stimuli properly to form complementary transactions. In the whole system to which he is attached, he may experience an environment which is not at all conducive to his growth and development.
11. The non-achiever considers the people related to his profession or organizational activities as self-centred, opportunist, unconcerned. He keeps a close watch on the activities of such people, as their actions may cause danger or some other situation unbearable to him.
12. He may keep himself detached from social activities, rituals, ceremonial functions etc. and may avoid keeping connections with relatives and own people.
13. He may develop an inferiority complex and may have a feeling like 'I'm not OK, you are OK'.
14. If the person lacks self-confidence, determination and firmness, he may try to satisfy his physiological needs by other means. He may not think of whether such a method or way of satiation of needs suits him considering his stature, temperament, personality and other qualitative aspects.
15. If the non-achiever has strong will power, he sees the bright side of his life and he continues his struggle for survival and betterment of the situation.

The situation becomes altogether different when the person satiates his physiological need. The person passes through a series of interactive processes resulting in changes in attitudes and behavioural activities. Some such changes are discussed below:

1. The person becomes tension free and exhibits consolatory symptoms in behavioural activities.
2. As other vital needs of the person remain unfulfilled at this stage, he tries hard to meet his requirements as per the need hierarchy. All his activities are likely to be reflected in production, service and quality. The more a person feels happiness and satisfaction of their minimum needs, the greater his drive and urge to satisfy his subsequent order of needs.
3. The person manifests a complementary form of transaction in almost all interaction situations.
4. The achiever may receive positive stimuli from different quarters and may reciprocate while responding to stimuli.
5. If there is no apparent external intervention in personal activities or there is no remarkable social family obligation, the person may show his contentment at the basic order of needs. He may not exert his vigour and driving force to move towards the satisfaction of subsequent order of needs. However, the percentage of this category of persons is negligible.
6. The achiever may show his seriousness and sincere effort to grow and develop. He may activate his driving force to use the expertise, skill and knowledge to ensure perfection and accuracy in service and output.
7. The person may remain in a confused state of mind, as he does not know whether the same uninterrupted support will be provided to satisfy his sustenance needs.
8. The person becomes committed and delivers the goods to the satisfaction of higher ups in terms of the goals and objectives set by the organization.

When the lowest order needs (i.e., physiological needs) are fulfilled, the person ascertains whether primary sources or acting agents satisfying such needs are temporary in nature or have a solid base to continue on a permanent footing. The achiever wants to ensure that there is no danger involved in the process of continuation of satisfying basic needs in the prevalent situation. Such urges or insistence arise out of some inherent need which Abraham H. Maslow has described as the 'safety' or 'security' need. The person desires to continue to get at least the same, if not more, of what he is getting now. He therefore puts in all-out effort to secure a reliable indication for the smooth continuation of providing support to meet physiological needs. If the person is convinced of getting the requisite input to satisfy primary needs in an on-going process, or if his safety/security needs is satiated, he may manifest some behavioural changes which are more or less the same as in a situation when a person satisfies his physiological needs. However, some salient changes in behavioural activities are discussed below:

1. He shows his happiness and concern towards his job or organization. He exhibits his contentment which may reflect in his behaviour, attitude and communication process.
2. He can draw up action plans to move towards targeted sets of goals.
3. He remains free from anxiety and uncertainties and may undertake new assignments with vigour, perseverance and seriousness for growth and development. Such a state of mind may bring about a change in the work milieu.
4. He becomes committed to the organization, gives hard labour, and makes sacrifices for the growth and development of the organization.
5. His ultimate objective is to develop mindset for fulfilling higher order needs. He therefore ensures a constraint-free environment so that he does not face any difficulty achieving his goal.
6. He may keep on increasing his will power to combat any odd force that stands in the way of his functioning.
7. He may experience the environment as a source of strengthening self-determination which is a pre-requisite for the completion of any task. A qualitative change in his attitude towards his job and performance capacity may be noticed.
8. He may remain in preparedness to confront any untoward event for the achievement of his goal. He may, therefore, manifest his behavioural activities in terms of his level of perception and thought processes.
9. He may frame his mental set up to offer positive stimuli or to respond to stimuli and to form complimentary transactions.

It is noteworthy to mention that the needs of a person, whether he is attached to a hospital, school, college, university, club or any organization are more or less equal to the needs of a child. There may be variation in the degree in some areas of needs. Such kinds of needs are explored and analysed by Abraham H Maslow in his hierarchy of needs framework which are termed as the social (affiliation) need and the esteem (recognition) need.

Every human being, regardless of his profession or vocation, desires to satisfy social and recognition needs after the ..tiation of physiological and safety (security) needs and activates his driving force towards that direction. These needs emerge out of various behavioural activities manifested by different human beings at different points of time and in different situations, especially when they work with any club, hospital, educational institutions, organisations, etc. The significant and most remarkable situations causing to manifest behavioural expressions of human beings, which demand a fulfilment of concerned needs, are given below:

1. The person wants that he should be called by his boss a number of times a day, which can create an impact on the minds of his colleagues and subordinates about his importance to his boss; but the calling of the person several times a day to reprimand or abuse results in an adverse image about him in their minds.
2. The person wants reciprocity while giving the hello effect to his boss. Non-responding to the stimulus offered by the person to his boss while wishing him a good day may deter the development of mutual understanding between the person and his boss.
3. The person feels dejected and neglected if he is dressed down by the boss before his subordinates. It is the feeling of the person that in case of any mistake or misdeed committed by him, the boss should call him personally and not in the presence of any junior colleagues or subordinates, where he may point out the mistake, instruct him to rectify it and even go to the extent of abusing, reprimanding and punishing him. No human being wants his weaknesses be exposed to subordinates, as he knows that they become aware of his qualitative area and he will not be able to get their full potential.

4. The person wants the boss to be perfect, unbiased, honest and free from the influence of any caste, creed or religion. If he observes that the boss is hobnobbing with people who are identified as black sheep in society or the organisation, he feels that a proper decision of any issue requiring rational and natural justice may not be available.
5. The person becomes shaky, demotivated, ineffective, noncommittal, non-performing and unproductive if he receives constant negative stimuli from his boss in the form of intimidation, threats, abuse and curses for no fault of his own. The person develops a fear psychosis when he starts getting such stimuli from the boss day after day and does not notice any attitudinal change of his boss in day-to-day activities. In such a situation, whenever the person is called by his boss, he feels that he is going to face the test of his ability, competency and effectiveness and he is very much aware that boss can never be satisfied with his performance, sincerity, seriousness and capability. On the contrary, the boss calls him off and on to reprimand and so weaken his morale and delivering capacity.
6. If the boss does not like the person for any reason whatsoever, and if the person is retained to work under him by a higher boss, he wants to get the person out from him and to be successful in his attempt he prepares congenial grounds to prove the ineffectiveness, uselessness and inefficacy of the person. The boss harasses and humiliates the person for no genuine cause, keeps him under constant worries and anxieties, puts him under unbearable mental torture so that the person leaves the organization on his own.
7. The person wants his boss to consult him before he takes any decisions in the area of his activities.
8. When the boss acknowledges the importance and indispensability of the person and expresses his feeling before subordinates or a higher boss, the person's interest towards job and job role is enhanced. The person puts his all out effort to give his best to the satisfaction of his boss to the highest order.
9. When the boss involves the person in team work for the accomplishment of the specific job, the person realizes his importance and the respect given to him, and tries hard to achieve the team goal.

10. The person wants any matter which is within his jurisdiction not to be dealt with by the boss without his knowledge.
11. The person feels that the boss should be considerate in his approach.
12. If the boss develops some informal group to establish a mutual bond and understanding in the greater interest of the instruction, the human aspect is given due weightage.
13. If the person feels that the boss plays tricks with him and adopts a double standard policy, he remains alert and watches carefully the activities of the boss. Mutual trust between the boss and the person is not established in such cases.
14. If the boss acts as fault finder instead of fault rectifier and takes repressive measures against the fault doers without looking at the circumstances, situations and extenuating factors, the person finds it difficult to build up an understanding and rapport between them.
15. If the boss gets the work done through somebody else who is in no way related to the concerned department or through the junior person of the department superseding the person, the person feels humiliated and ignored. The person thinks that he is insignificant and unimportant and that he has no role to play.
16. When the boss speaks ill about the person to his subordinate or colleagues and the person gets such information, the possibility for development of mutual understanding and trust becomes remote.
17. When the person comes to know that, under the performance review system, he is rated by his boss as an excellent performer, his commitment to the organization is enhanced. He feels proud of being one of the members of the institution. The reverse is the situation when the person, after putting in a sincere effort, giving hard labour and rendering excellent service is given to learn that the performance rating made by his boss is average or below average, he considers the action of his boss as unjustified, highly motivated and biased. The person feels that the evaluation of the boss is done with malafide intentions to suppress his calibre, skill and other qualitative areas. The person becomes upset and gets a big jolt, resulting in a manifestation of lower-productivity and service or no transparency in achievement and growth.

18. In some cases the person observes that the boss wants only work and nothing else. The boss does not feel it worthwhile to attend rituals/ceremonies, he does not consider it important to establish human relations with his subordinates. The boss intentionally keeps himself away from participation in informal social festivities and does not feel a desire to see any of his team members in the hospital/nursing home, as and when such a member might be recovering from illness. In such a situation the person develops a sense of aloofness and separation from the organization and his need for belongingness to the institution is thwarted.
19. The person wants the dealings of the boss to be uniform. No particular person should be given undue importance or benefits. If the boss is inconsistent in his dealings and he is exposed to the people for his biased activities, the person's esteem need remains unfulfilled.
20. When the person earns the confidence of his boss by putting in hard labour and sincere effort, he intends to have some power and authority to satisfy his need for recognition in the organization and society as well. If the boss, even after having been satisfied with the performance of the person and having established confidence, does not feel the need to confer any authority and power to the person for discharging smooth function, the person gets frustrated and his hunger for power, authority and status remains unsatisfied.
21. When the boss is suspicious minded and he suspects each and every person in his team, and when he engages some persons of his coterie to collect information about the activities, linkages, connections and hidden ideas of the members of the team, the process of team- building is affected. In such a situation a climate of distrust and misunderstanding prevails. Nobody in the team dares to disclose any information to the boss, apprehending that the discloser may be dragged unnecessarily to substantiate the information. It may also happen that the discloser may have to face a series of humiliating processes.

From the foregoing discussion it is apparent that, like a child, a mature adult person has the need for acceptance, belonging, involvement, appreciation and recognition, to become an effective and successful member of the team to which he belongs.

But when the child advances from one stage to another, he feels an altogether different urge tending him to do such things that he is capable of doing. The child thinks that he is grown up and he has the necessary knowledge, skill and competence to do the right thing. He therefore sets, resets, tries, retries, opens, closes, and does anything that his inquisitive mind drives him to do. For such explorative work the child puts his sincere effort, expertise, persistent attempt and he gets satisfaction after accomplishment. In this case the child enjoys the feeling of getting something which brings an unusual thrill, emotion, enthusiasm, confidence and a sense of achievement.

The above need, which is mentioned by Maslow in his hierarchy of needs framework as the 'self actualisation' need, can be satisfied when a congenial environment exists in the family system. The parental attitude of support and encouragement help the child a lot in taking up a new and adventurous experiment. The child may not find it an easy task to satiate his need for self actualisation, when the family environment, parents' attitude, behaviour and activities do not provide support to him to carry out such work through which he intends to satisfy his needs.

Despite the best effort given by the child, if he cannot succeed in his attempt to satisfy the concerned need, he searches for the reason for his lack of success; if it is due to unfavourable/inimical family environment and parents' attitudinal exposure, he feels disgusted at the family milieu, begins to keep himself aloof from family activities, stays away from family involvement, develops an attitude of indifference towards his parents, and sometimes has outbursts of anger that he expresses through violent activities. If the cause of failure is due to personal reasons, such as the lack of adequate knowledge, skill, experience, ability, non-availability of latest information or incapacitation due to physical and mental immaturity, the child thinks himself unworthy and ineffective, and he becomes morose and frustrated. But if he gets persistent support and positive stimuli from his parents, he regains his will power and tries and retries for achieving his goal and subsequently he may get it.

Self Actualization Need

Thus, the self-actualisation need is something which is not easily satiable. This need comes last when more or less other types of needs are satisfied. Every human being, irrespective of age, sex, culture, creed and profession wishes to satisfy such needs. But the intensity of the need and the process of the satisfaction of the need may be same; it may vary from person to person considering the person's depth of knowledge, skill, expectancy, competency, desire and willingness. The self-actualisation need comes out of different situations, conditions and environment that a person has to pass through. The following diagrammatic representation gives an idea regarding the genesis of the need and the vital processes to be passed through for the satiation of such needs.

The self-actualisation need appears to a person as an important phenomenon which he deserves to satisfy through the application of his skill, expertise and tact. The person observes different phases of a situation for the achievement of the target (that is the satiation of the self-actualisation need). The phases are briefly mentioned below:

First Phase of Situation

i. Lower order needs are almost satisfied (viz., physiological Security, social and esteemed needs),
ii. Higher order need is prominent

Second Phase of Situation

i. Existence of positive milieu culture
ii. Prevalence of supportive and encouraging atmosphere
iii. Possession of traumatic, oppressive and humiliating influences that have occurred on earlier occasions.

Third Phase of Situation

i. Inherent desire and willingness
ii. Driving force is in action to push forward

Fourth Phase of Situation

i. Level of expectancy (i.e., what exactly the person wants to do)
ii. Level of competency
iii. Analysis of strength and weaknesses

Diagrammatical Representation of Self-actualisation need

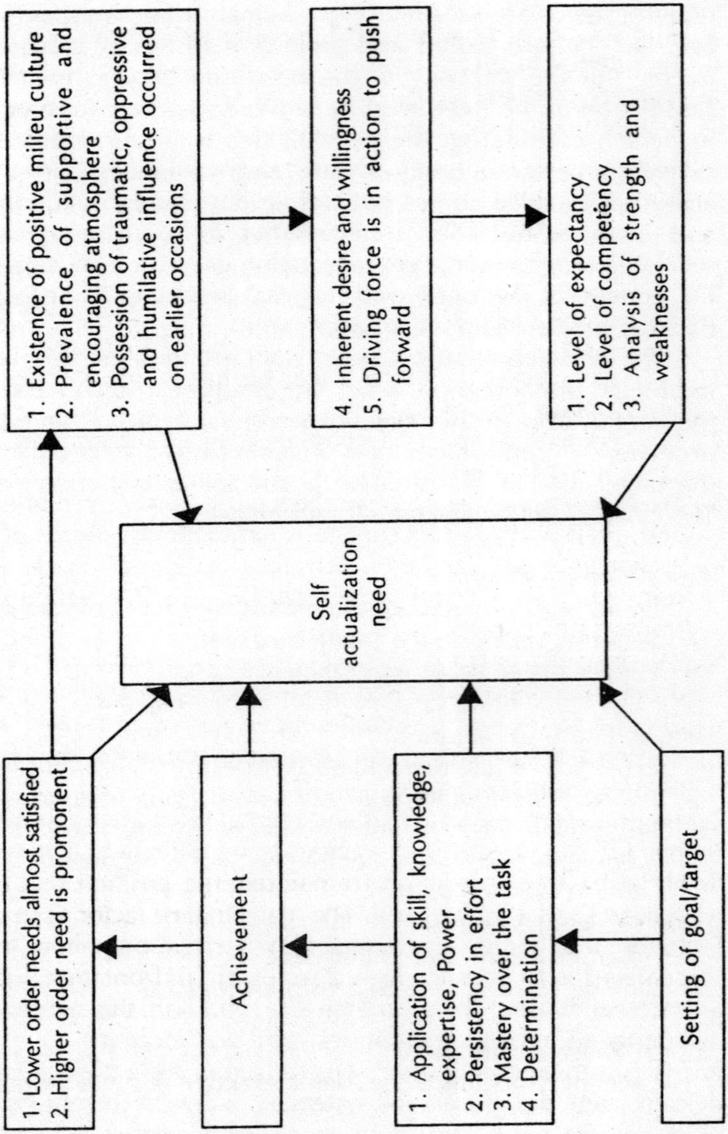

Fifth Phase of Situation

i. Setting of goal/target

Sixth Phase of Situation

i. Application of skill, knowledge, expertise, power
ii. Persistency in effort
iii. Mastery over the task
iv. Determination to achieve

When a person is successful at doing something that he is capable of doing, it means that he satisfies his need for self-actualisation. However, the self-actualisation need is such that each and every person may not be able to satiate this need.

The following situations may be observed when a person satisfies his self-actualisation need:

1. He feels worthy and thinks that he has a role to play, a contribution to make.
2. He becomes happy and contented and is committed to serve the community.
3. Productivity is increased, excellence in service is rendered, and quality in product/service is substantially improved.
4. A change in attitude and behavioural activities is markedly noticed. The person manifests his positive reaction/response to stimuli.
5. It increases the achiever's will power and will force. The achiever accepts more and more challenging assignments.
6. The person earns self-confidence, self-reliance and he develops a mindset to win over any situation. He feels nothing is unachievable.
7. He gets eternal satisfaction and mental relief after achievement of the target which appears to be difficult to achieve.
8. He gives an all out effort to maintain the position that he achieves to satisfy his need. The maintenance factor appears to be much more prominent in a situation when the achiever is to pass through a series of confrontation with external forces. To overcome the situation the achiever adopts all necessary measures on a war footing.
9. He resorts to all possible steps to further his activities in a calculated, disciplined and systematic way with the objective of gaining more and more recognition, power, authority from the society, the community and the organization.

10. The achiever maintains a cordial and congenial environment in the system through the manifestation of an optimum behavioural attitude, approach and activities.

Now, if the person cannot satisfy the need for self-actualisation despite putting in his best effort, it is likely that he may manifest a lot of changes in his behaviour, attitude and activities. Some of such attitudinal changes are mentioned below:

1. He may consider himself as being useless, ineffective and worthless.
2. He may question his capability and form an impression of 'nothing to do' if he fails to succeed even after making repeated attempts.
3. He objectively analyses the factors responsible for not achieving the desired target/goal.
4. The person may curse the situation and the entire system for not satiating his need.
5. The person becomes unhappy, morose and dejected about his unsuccessful endeavour.
6. The non-achiever may manifest his activities in the area of production, quality, distribution and services. Lower productivity, deterioration in quality product/service, fall in efficiency etc. is likely to appear, if the person becomes the victim of consecutive failures. But failure may not bring about substantial effects in production, service, quality, etc. under following circumstances:
   i. When the person identifies the sources/geneses of failure and the reason of such reactive measures as being based on bias, vindictiveness and personal gratification.
   ii. When the person is confident of his capability, skill and efficiency and he comes to know that the failure occurs due to the malafide motives or pre-planned actions of somebody who occupies a controlling position of the people around him.
   iii. When the person notices a congenial and supportive atmosphere in the office/place to which he is attached.
   iv. When the person continuously receives positive stimuli from the boss and a complementary transaction prevail.

CHAPTER 4

Changes in Behavioural Activities Due to Dispositional Variations

In the preceding discussions, it is clear that the needs at different points of time, the supply of stimuli and the spread of the ego state greatly influence the behavioural manifestations of a person. Different types of behavioural activities are noticed depending upon the mindset and mental constitution/disposition formed. People can, therefore, be placed in the following categories:

i. Person with volcanic disposition
ii. Person with cool disposition
iii. Person with moderate disposition
iv. Person with hot disposition Detailed discussion of the aforementioned people with different mindsets is needed to ascertain the nature, behavioural patterns, effectiveness, efficacy, leadership traits and qualitative aspects of the people in order to achieve the set-goal.

Person with Volcanic Disposition

This type of person is very harmful to the organization. He is always concerned about 'self'. For meeting his own needs and interests, he can go to any extent. The most salient nature, behavioural activities and temperament of this category of person are mentioned herein below:

1. He is vindictive and resorts to retaliatory measures for acts of omission or commission made by any person. He keeps in his mind the remarkable/upsetting incidents in his life

and chalks out plans to give a befitting jolt to the person responsible for the earlier misdeed.

2. He perceives others as dishonest, useless, unworthy, ineffective personalities.
3. He keeps himself watchful and vigilant to overall situation. He makes a hue and cry even over trifling issues just to show his concern and seriousness about the matter.
4. He gets pleasures at the plight of somebody. Whenever any person in a miserable state approaches him for any assistance and guidance, he keeps on showing his concern as sympathizer and gives false hopes/promises, saying that he will do something better for him.
5. He does not believe anybody and thinks everybody has his own vested interest in each dealing/transaction.
6. He appears to be loyal and obedient to boss. He is rough and harsh to his subordinates.
7. He rates everybody as inferior to him in respect of all parameters.
8. During the course of his work he is much more interested in detecting faults with others than in any other sphere of activities and he feels contented when someone is blacklisted.
9. He is self-centred. He does not have any concern for others.
10. He believes in the 'dictatorship' philosophy, which envisages that people are normally indolent and do not want to work unless compelled. This approach calls for authoritarian rules for the maintenance and enhancement of productivity/services.
11. He is normally rigid in his principles but succumbs to pressure, intimidation and threats.
12. He has no faith on the behavioural theory of motivation.
13. He keeps himself busy with small affairs, which is unproductive in nature.
14. He does not like to delegate authority to his subordinates. Even if, on rare occasions, he delegates, he retains the controlling power to route all matters through him.
15. He does not treat people as human beings. His mode of talking and behavioural activities appear to be something other than usual.

16. He is biased. He blindly encourages the activities that he feels proper without looking to their pros and cons, propriety and genuineness.
17. He conveys each and every issue of whatever nature to his boss in order to get close to him and to build up a good rapport with him.
18. Because of his anti-people approach, he is not acceptable to the people. He is perceived by the people around him as a selfish, vindictive and fickle minded personality.
19. He is poor in decision-making. Sometimes, he makes some patch-up decision to overcome the situation, leaving the scope to crop up the issue afterwards.
20. He may play the role of a 'dubious character' if the opportunity is available to him. In such cases, he may pass on information of secret nature which is exclusively internal and confidential, to outsiders or persons not directly related to such matters. This he does without the knowledge or permission of his superior. He may open up another channel within the existing system with the people who are either members of the opposite lobby of his immediate boss or persons with substantial influence in the organization. His main objective is to show his link or connection to his boss/superior in order to make him understand that he is an important personality and that he can influence the lobby to which he belongs to get his work done.

Such a person underestimates and undermines his superior and continues to be under the suspicion that something unusual may occur to him. He may show artificial loyalty, obedience and trustworthiness to his superior/boss. But in reality and from the core of his heart he dislikes and distrusts his boss.

He suffers from a superiority complex and considers himself to be a superman with extraordinary qualities. He thinks the people around him do not have any qualities to match his. He is a man who likes to obtain each and every desired thing through the back door by passing over people with genuine, legitimate and reasonable claims.

He thinks of his 'self' and not for others. He does not like people in general, and likewise he is not acceptable to people.

The person with 'dubious character' is not normally happy in his profession and environment, his place of his work, the people around him like his peers, his boss or his sub-ordinates. The main reason is probably his overestimation of his merit, capabilities, level of maturity, thought-process, creativity, imagination and other qualitative areas.

He is very materialistic. Money is the only thing to him. He may do anything and everything for money or for any material substance within the purview of his jurisdiction even at the cost of his ideology. He may surrender his qualitative traits to anybody in exchange for money.

But in some cases, the person with dubious character plays the opposite role to the one aforementioned with regard to material needs. He spends money to get his purpose served. He develops a rapport with the big guys in and outside organizations through his money power. He has a strong feeling that he can manage any problematic situation by getting himself involved in the 'powerful group' as an active member or through somebody in the group at the cost of money and he does so whenever he faces such hard situation. He strives his best to appease the people standing in the way by giving economic support. He takes advantage of weak mental areas through the display of artificial loyalty and obedience and by being an activist of the coterie. This type of man remains active in his role-playing task so long as his vested purpose/interest exists. He does not mind changing colours and switching over to the opposite lobby, if the existing group turns to be a weak one. He only goes by his own interest and he does not mind getting his purpose served at the cost of moral and ethical values, reputation, status and recognition.

21. He is a person with unpredictable character. It is very difficult to study his thought processes as, in most cases, his deeds and actions do not conform to what he preaches and says. He immediately changes his decision if it does not suit the people in whose favour he makes it.
22. He lacks the courage to admit his fault. He always shifts the responsibilities to others and does not keep anything with him for which he may be held accountable.
23. Since he suspects the integrity and honesty of people, he intentionally involves them in matters with which they are in no way connected.

24. He prepares his mindset with an illusive impression and ideas about the people around him. He starts thinking on any issue pertaining to the people from a negative perspective. The decisions that he makes are likely to be biased and imperfect, based on false perceptions.
25. He is most dishonest but pretends to be the one who has no other concern other than to serve the organization selflessly and in dedicated manner.
26. To protect his interests, benefits and privileges and to obtain feedback and information about the goings-on among people, he informally forms a very small group with people of same beliefs, ethical values, and ego patterns within the organization.

Person with Cool Disposition

This type of person remains cool and calm. He oversees the situation, studies the matter discreetly, examines and evaluates analytically and thoroughly, keeps on watching for some period till he arrives at conclusion. He generally does not pass any remark/comment on the matter under examination/investigation. Some of the qualitative aspects, behavioural manifestation and mental dispositions of such person are discussed herein below:

1. He is a person with excessive tolerance skills and a high degree of power to sustain situational hazards.
2. He continues to carry on his assigned task without fear or favour and keeps a strong vigil on the overall situation. He does not let others know about activities which are secret in nature.
3. Normally, he does not get irritated, angry. He is not over-enthusiastic or emotional about any issue. He never allows any issue to flare up. He strives to settle issues in a systematic manner.
4. As soon as any issue crops up or he comes to know about any issue which may stand in the way of inter-personnel relations, he takes up the matter, looks at it with seriousness in his own way, listens to the persons who are related to the issue, tries to understand the genesis of the issue and takes necessary measures.
5. He is generally non-vindictive, sympathetic and co-operative and stretches hand to support/help in case of need.

6. He is more or less acceptable to the people around him. In the normal course, he does not get into confrontations.
7. He believes in openness, mutuality of understanding, trust and confidence, building up of informal relations rather than formal relations.
8. Normally, he does not take hasty decisions, but rather only after protracted and threadbare observation, examination and analysis. His decisions may not necessarily be perfectly judicious, but to arrive at some judgement he makes qualitative and objective assessment.
9. In some cases this category of person may be shrewd, cunning and clever; it is likely that he may wait for the opportune time to utilize the situation for his own purpose. The possibility of manipulating the situation cannot be ruled out.
10. In very rare cases, this person plays a role of a dubious nature. He thinks minutely about each and every matter, studies the pros and cons and resultant effects of a situation. If such a person plays a dubious role, he is not exposed to the people like the person having a volcanic disposition. He maintains top secrecy in the matter.
11. The person with a cool temperament, who may also have manipulative and shrewd ingredients, may have the following qualitative traits.

    i. He talks nicely to people, irrespective of the position they hold.
    ii. He expresses his seriousness and desire to help when any matter requiring his attention is referred to him, but in reality he does not help.
    iii. He shows his empathetic feelings outwardly, when any aggrieved person approaches him to interfere.
    iv. He pays extraordinary heed to any issue and listens to the problem, in order to make the affected person know that he is very sympathetic and has a serious concern.
    v. He forms an imaginary impression in his mind about the people around him and searches for the ways and means to put them into trouble.
    vi. He does not hesitate to play double standards on any issue to suit his requirement.
    vii. He never admits his fault or misdeeds. He blames others

when his wrong action comes out and claims credit when his team yields results.

viii. He pleads forgetfulness whenever he is exposed to others for his inaction or misdeed.

ix. He is self-centred and remains busy to meet his own needs. He does not sacrifice even a tiny thing for the greater general interest.

x. He prepares plans and projections to trap people in his fold in order to fulfil his malafide intentions.

xi. He delays matters pertaining to the well being of people and pretends to not know about them.

xii. He does not treat people as human beings. He always keeps a distance from them but, publicly and during interface discussion, he appears to be much more people oriented than anything else. His acceptability to the people is not transparent.

xiii. Each and every part of his activity aims at satisfying his ulterior motives. He therefore suppresses facts, lingers on matters for long, keeps on watching behavioural manifestations and takes immediate measures to bring it in his favour.

xiv. He is harmful and vindictive. He chalks out plans secretly to resort to retaliatory measures.

xv. He is not reliable. He cannot be trusted. He can do any work for his own sake.

xvi. He remains very silent and does his job silently in a planned manner.

xvii. He is a man with 'cobra vision' and does not allow the targeted man to pass by unnoticed.

xviii. Most people in such categories are believers in the philosophy of 'sweet words and bitter actions'. His actions and speech are not the same. There is no relation between his words and deeds.

xix. He is fully informed and keeps his records up-to-date.

xx. He may have analytical ability and conceptual skill which, in most cases, he uses for strengthening his case.

xxi. Outwardly he is disciplined, loyal to superiors and obedient to the boss. He wants to remain in the good books of the boss in order to form a good impression in the mind of the boss.

xxii. He critically evaluates the performance of people and seldom remains happy with the output/service of his sub ordinates. He suspects the integrity and honesty of people.

xxiii. He keeps people under close supervision. He makes people accountable for their assigned work.

Person with Moderate Disposition

The mindset of this type of person is such that he does not have an extreme degree either of the cool or the hot temperament. He neither gets angry immediately on sensing the issue like the volcanic person, nor does he remain cool for long without looking to the pros and cons of the situation. His mental faculty may have more or less equal proportions of the dispositional factors—cool and hot. The following salient behavioural manifestation and activities of the above category of person are discussed below:

1. He is considerate, listens to the problem and does not take hurried decisions.
2. He keeps patient for some time just to watch the situation, to study it properly and to find out the factual position of the issue.
3. He does not succumb to pressure. He has the skill to convince the people.
4. He is open minded, unbiased, free and frank and has the ability to foresee any issue.
5. He does not get irritated and angry all of a sudden. He remains calm, quiet and seems to others to be a silent spectator/observer.
6. He appears to be a person with the life position 'I am OK, you are OK' or 'I am OK, you are not OK'.
7. He is believer in the philosophy of amicable settlement of any issue through mutual discussion.
8. He has the adequate ability of stress tolerance. He can face any situation requiring capability to sustain it.
9. He can predict the situation and the probable prognostic effect.
10. After a thorough examination and discreet inspection he can take remedial measures if something goes wrong.
11. He does not leave a serious issue unattended. He takes drastic action so that it does not recur.

12. He can make appropriate equations to overcome a crisis period.
13. He shows his inclination to carry on complimentary transactions in order to develop understanding, faith and confidence.
14. He cannot tolerate injustice or hate-filled activities.
15. He is accepted by people. Very few remain unhappy with his behaviour. He is sober in nature. In most cases, he shows his empathetic approach.
16. His decision-making processes may take little bit more time, as he has to pass through some phases to achieve accuracy and perfection and to make an unbiased decision.
17. He is co-operative and gives a lot of emphasis to human factors. He is positive in his attitude and approach.
18. He believes in the philosophy that 'no motivation is better than demotivation'. Demotivation does much more harm than no motivation.
19. He has the qualitative skill to develop understanding and mutual ties with people around him.
20. His style of functioning is based on the approach 'wait, observe, study and then work'.
21. A negligible percentage of such type of people may be having a dubious characteristic quality with manipulative skills. In this case, such a category of persons may have the traits mentioned in the foregoing discussions.

Person with Hot Disposition

The mindset of such a type of person is such that he immediately responds/reacts to any stimulus activity in an authoritative manner without going into the depth of the issue. He does not think of the probable consequences to his reaction. Some of his behavioural activities, traits, mental and dispositional reflections are discussed below:

1. He thinks he is a super person and whatever he says or does is correct.
2. He is not afraid of anything. He remains bold and discharges his entrusted assignment in a courageous way.
3. His mode of talking and style of functioning has the tint of supremacy.

4. He forms his own life position like, I am OK, you are not OK.
5. From the manifestation of his behavioural activities it appears that most of the time he sends stimuli or responds to stimuli from his critical parent ego.
6. When he says or does something he forgets his role position. He does not even pay respect to his superiors when he carries out transactions.
7. He is straightforward in his action and deeds.
8. He tries his best to establish his opinion, stand and decisions through pressure, intimidation and compulsion.
9. He is the person who generally does not bend and makes others bend.
10. It is his nature to dress down subordinates in presence of peers and others.
11. He takes the matter exceptionally if he is questioned/ blamed for his deeds and actions.
12. He is a person who is not easily amenable. He suffers from a superiority complex and treats others as his subordinates. He forms perceptions about other people around him as much inferior to him. He thinks they do not match him in any parameter.
13. Since, his ego pattern is highly contaminated (the adult ego is contaminated by the critical parent) he does not want to take any advice from his friends, colleagues and others on any issue. He feels it is beyond his dignity to consult anybody other than his boss/superiors on any matter which requires his decision.
14. He is incorrigible as he is already biased. If anybody with bonafide intentions makes him aware of his weaknesses, shortcomings and mistakes, he takes it otherwise and develops bitter relations with him.
15. He wants his subordinates and people around him to be sober, loyal and obedient. They must always remain ready at his disposal. They must comply with his instructions. They must not be argumentative or complicated in nature.
16. He makes a hue and cry and creates a rowdy scene if things do not move according to his desire.
17. He takes a serious view if any subordinate delays compliance with his orders or his advice. He does not hesitate to reprimand and rebuke such a person.

18. He is nagging in nature. He constantly hammers the person for wrongdoing, whether it is intentional or unintentional and whether it is on trifling or major issues. He does not easily erase from his mind somebody's misdeeds until he takes up and discusses the matter with some authority figures, who may or may not be concerned with the matter.
19. He does not remain happy with any situation, any person or anything. He aspires to things which may not always be available.
20. He fixes the performance targets of his subordinates much higher than their strength. He does not listen to subordinates speak about their difficulties, suggestions and requirements. He remains adamant and sticks to his own point. In case of non-achievement of goals/targets set by him, he crushes person through appropriate measures.
21. He is revengeful and remains always alert to retaliate. He does not leave anybody who has once been targeted for retaliation.
22. He is harmful and unacceptable to people.
23. He cannot remain in a peaceful and congenial environment. He creates problems, pollutes the situation and makes the entire climate filthy, sullen and unhealthy.
24. He believes in the 'dictatorship' philosophy and develops the approach that others are non-performers and non-willing to work. He feels that he may not be successful in achieving his goals if this lot of people remains with him.
25. He suffers much from mental anxieties, worries and agony. He is a frustrated person. To cover up his areas of limitation and self created mental sufferings, he keeps himself busy with unpleasant activities.
26. He has a bossing tendency. He wants his subordinates to be 'yes men'. He has a cabinitis ego, (i.e., the ego for separating him from peers to show his special super power and authority to others). He is crazy for special treatment and favour from his boss.
27. He has very few people of his own. He can never be good to anybody except a few.
28. He is faultfinding person. He searches and examines each and every aspect discreetly to detect misdeeds or faults. Whenever he finds any mistake, he feels it is a sort of achievement.

29. He gets pleasure when any person around him is punished. He is a strong believer in the punishment concept which envisages the imposition of punishment to the wrong-doer irrespective of the nature and gravity of the misdeed.
30. He does not believe in the 'human relations' approach for better performance. He feels productivity can be increased through close and constant supervision with no relaxation of the time frame schedule. He emphasizes the concept of 'work by compulsion'.
31. He appears to be a person who goes by rules, regulations and norms. But for his own case or for the benefit of the person who is closely connected to him, he pleads for relaxation and deviation from the set rules.
32. He is very self-centred and does not care for others.
33. He wants respect from others but does not pay respect to them.
34. He wants to have complimentary transactions in each and every 'stimulus-response' exchange made between him and his subordinates. In most cases, such transactions occur from a parent-child relationship (such a person acts or reacts from a critical parent ego while the subordinate acts or reacts from a child ego)
35. During interactions between him and his subordinate, he observes the mode and way of talking of the subordinate, the words used by him and his posture and gestures, and then critically analyses the overall transaction process to indicate the act subversion of discipline. He tries to establish that the subordinate uses the words while talking to him that are unparliamentary and highly derogatory.
36. He may play the role of a dubious person. He forms a small coterie comprising his own people. He transmits information which is very much secret in nature to higher authorities, superseding his immediate boss. At the opportune time, he speaks ill of his boss to the higher authority. More or less the same qualitative traits and behavioural activities are manifested as discussed in the foregoing deliberation when the person acts as a dubious personality.
37. He is a person with an arrogant mindset, false vanity and some disproportionate ego components. He thinks he knows everything, has excelled in every area, has got

everything to overpower others and nobody on earth can contest him over any issue.

38. He is self-exalted and highly critical. He chalks out plans and programmes to do harm to others.

People have different mindsets, perceptions and thought patterns and they interact with each other according to the level of their dispositional state. Two such cases of interactions, which make cross transactions in their deliberations are discussed below:

Case Illustration 1

Mrs. Sulochana is intelligent and particular about her assigned task. She completes the allotted job much earlier than the usual time. Her output is more than average. She is smart, sophisticated and polished. She excels in communication. Normally, she commits no mistake in her work. She enjoys positive strokes from her immediate boss, Mr. Naresh for perfection and accuracy in her work. She can grasp her assigned job in no time and delivers the goods to the utmost satisfaction of her boss. She never says no to her superior whenever any additional task is given.

Mrs. Sulochana has some shortcomings. She likes leisure periods. She cannot work for long at a stretch. After doing some work, she feels bored, uneasy and fatigued. She cannot remain in her seat and moves to her other colleagues who remain engaged at their job. She starts gossiping and disturbs their work.

She has the habit of remaining absent frequently without taking prior permission. She sends messages to her boss about her not coming to office. On resumption to duties she submits an application for sanction of leave. She frequently leaves office before the scheduled time of departure on flimsy pretexts.

She keeps her immediate boss happy. He appreciates her and gives her recognition for quality work. Since she does not keep allotted jobs pending, her boss gives her some relaxation in attending/departing office. She develops a good understanding with the boss and earns his confidence in her work.

Though she is responsible and accountable to her immediate boss, Mr. Naresh, for her work performance and assignments, her attendance, punctuality, salary and leave administration are controlled by Mr. Chanakya in Senior Office Management. Mrs. Salochana comes under the direct supervision of Mr. Chanakya who keeps a close watch on her mobility and attendance activities at the office.

Mr. Chanakya is a non-acceptable person. He is a negative personality. He never helps people. He does not believe in the motivational approach. He does not treat people as human beings. He perceives people as non-performers and leisure seekers. He is an autocrat in his behaviour and activities.

In one case scenario, Mrs. Sulochana resumed her duties after three days of absence. All these three days, she informed office about her absence. Mr. Chanakya was away from headquarters during those days. The day Mrs. Sulochana came to report for duties, Mr. Chanakya was present. On seeing Mrs. Sulochana, Mr. Chanakya started firing her. The following transactions/exchange of stimuli and responses occurred between them.

Mr. Chanakya: Why you have not submitted your leave application?
Mrs. Sulochana: Sir, it is now 5 minutes to 10 a.m. I have just come to attenu office after my illness.
Mr. Chanakya: On earlier occasions also you have delayed submission of your application for sanction of leave of absence.
Mrs. Sulochana: Sir, it has not happened in my case. Every time either I get my leave sanctioned before I proceed for leave, if it is privileged leave, or I send a communication to office about my inability to attend office when it is casual or sick leave.
Mr. Chanakya: No, no, you are not correct. You are in the habit of not submitting leave applications on time. This time also you have repeated the same thing. You did not bother to inform us about your not coming to office.
Mrs. Sulochana: Sir, I telephoned at the office. I wanted to talk to you but you were out of headquarter three days ago. I gave the information to Mr. Naresh, my boss, about my indisposition. I also told him that I would not be able to join duty for three or four days.
I never delayed submitting my application for sanction of leave of absence. I know the rules as I have put 20 years of service with the organization.
Mr. Chanakya: Don't talk about 20 years' service. I know how to set the thing right. Yo· have no casual leave to your credit. You will have to be put on loss of pay for the period of your absence. As for sanctioning privileged leave, one has to apply 30 days ahead of the date of availing of privileged leave.

Mrs. Sulochana: Since, I have no casual leave credit balance, you have to sanction privileged leave.

Mr. Chanakya: You have become over smart. You do not know how to talk. Are you commanding me to sanction privileged leave? I will teach you a lesson.

Mrs. Sulochana: Sir, I did not mean that. I simply wanted to say that if my casual leave was exhausted, it is up to you, my superior boss, to see how my absence period would be adjusted, maybe by debiting privileged leave. (Then she started crying).

Case Illustration 2

Mr. Madan Lal is a person who always thinks of himself as superperson with all the powers in the universe to dominate people. He treats people around him as weak personalities and keeps on getting their services through intimidation, pressure and humiliation. He displays his authority and power so that people remain afraid of him and surrender to him.

He is very proud of his position, which he considers to be in a higher order of achievement. He keeps rapport with like-minded people and takes their help to serve his vested interests.

He is always obedient and loyal to his boss. He cannot tolerate the activities of any person against his boss. He is biased and stubborn and wants to get things done according to his desires and whims.

He cannot see any person in a good spirit if he argues with him on any issue. He gets irritated and takes the matter exceptionally, if a complementary transaction fails to form. Mr. Mohan Chand is more or less a balanced person. His adult ego functions in a rational and systematic manner. He is sober and gentle and does not normally hurt anybody. He is very adaptable to any situation. He likes people, whom he treats as human beings. He has acceptability and recognition amongst members of society. He is open minded, straightforward, calm and quiet. He cannot tolerate injustice but takes decisions after a thorough review of the situation. Mr. Mohan Chand had the occasion to interact with Mr. Madan Lal while travelling by train. They had short span of conversation on some issue pertaining to socio-ethical values.

Mr. Mohan Chand: They have no common sense. How did they keep the water jug over there? It was sure to fall down from the insecure place.

Mr. Madan Lal: It was not their fault that they kept the jug over there.

Mr. Mohan Chand: But it is true that they had no foresight about its fall. See, how it has injured my finger and has made my dress wet! If they could give some little thought to safekeeping, such a situation would not have occurred.

Mr. Madan Lal: Don't talk rubbish. Stop talking, otherwise, I will throw you outside.

Mr. Mohan Chand: What are you saying? Don't I have any right to discuss this?

Mr. Madan Lal: No, you cannot talk anymore. I have already warned you. If you open up your mouth, I will throw you through the door of the train compartment. This is my area. There is none to question my actions.

Such were the transactions exchanged, the prolongation of which would have resulted in unprecedented and unexpected activity. Mr. Madan Lal had a contaminated adult ego (an adult ego contaminated by the critical parent) which manifested autocratic, dictatorial and arrogant activities. His behavioural indication was that of a fierce commander who believes in the compliance of his commands without question. Mr. Madan Lal considered Mr. Mohan Chand as a trifling and negligible guy.

CHAPTER 5

A Bird's Eye View of the Behavioural Manifestation of the Boss and Subordinates with Different Ego Patterns

In the earlier deliberations we have seen that people have different ego states, causing varied behavioural patterns, senses of perception and formations of mindsets, which influences dominate the entire gamut of the interactive process. People with a contaminated ego pattern may not have proper adjustment with their peers, subordinates, bosses and members of the team. In each and every step of activity people experience an unhealthy and uncomfortable situation, emanating from a basic difference in mental set up. On most occasions they may have to search for alternative ways to get rid of unpleasant interaction. Be it in the organization, club, society, family, hospital or educational institution, people have to pass through such sorts of situation.

Effect of Contamination

Contamination blocks the adult ego from exercising its rational and judicious thought process. Hence the person becomes biased, forms perception about people and surrounding objects suiting his own taste, vision, habits, desires and values. Such a person subsequently develops the appropriate mindset with his dispositional state or temperament. The following tabular representation reveals the probable effects of contamination of the adult ego on person's dispositional/temperamental states:

Probable Effect of Contamination

Type of disposition/ temperament	Degree and ego state of contamination
1. Person with volcanic disposition	1. To a great extent contamination of adult ego by (critical) parent ego. 2. To minimal extent: Contamination of adult ego by child ego.
2. Person with cool disposition	1. Largely it is due to contamination of adult ego by parent (nurturing) ego.
3. Person with a moderate disposition	1. All the three ego states exist in more or less equal proportions. 2. Tendency to influence / contaminate slightly the adult ego by parent ego may be prevalent. Adult may not find uncomfortable climate to use his analytical and evaluative power to reach to a concluding decision. 3. Healthy and balanced state of ego pattern (with coherent existence) with little or no influence of any particular ego state.
4. Person with hot disposition	1. Adult cannot function freely and independently. 2. Adult ego is predominantly influenced by parent ego (critical parent). 3. Adult ego is exclusively and largely contaminated by critical parent ego.

People with a Moderate State of Disposition

If people have a moderate state of disposition (that is, having a more or less proportionate state of ego pattern) they may not face any difficulty in developing a congruent understanding amongst themselves for the effective and smooth functioning of the system. The on going transactional processes may have an uninterrupted situation to achieve the desired goal. Complementary forms of transactions occur under such an environment. Where any system of activity, whether a club, hospital, family, educational institution or organization, has a large size of people with a moderate state of disposition/temperament, the following manifesting circumstances is likely to be transparent:

1. A healthy and comfortable environment exists all over the system.

2. Since people have faith, belief and understanding in each other, a harmonious relation amongst them is established.
3. Each and every member of the team makes an all out effort for the growth and development of the team. Everybody is busy fulfilling their own targets.
4. A 'win-win' culture prevails. Nobody is born to lose, but to win.
5. A state of okayness amongst most people may be prevalent. The individual may feel, about himself and others surrounding him, as 'I am OK, you are OK'.
6. Differences of opinion on any matter, inter-personal conflicts and confrontations may not be experienced a lot under such a system. Instead, a coherent existence prevails.
7. People demonstrate a sense of contentment, happiness and belonging to the system of activity.
8. A culture of justice, rationality, logical interpretation and reasoning based on moral, ethical and social values plays a vital role in influencing decisions on any major issue.
9. The interaction process may demonstrate itself to be more or less congruent as most of the followers/reactors mould their pattern of behaviour, if any divergent area is noticed. In very rare cases people come out with opposition in conflicting states of a situation. The whole system sees a milieu based on mutuality amongst the people themselves.

Boss with a Moderate State of Disposition

In reality, it is rarely noticed that such a state of mental disposition exists amongst people with a homogeneous mindset, perception quality and balanced ego patterns in any system of activity. In any system, some may have a moderate disposition but others may have one contrary to this. Hence the reaction to each other may have an adverse effect to the smooth running of activities. But this may not affect the proper functioning of any system, if the boss/superior possesses a balanced/moderate temperament. It is the boss who holds the reins of the system under his jurisdiction to run it in ways suiting his own ego patterns and conforming to the needs of the system. A balanced/moderate boss acts as a moulder to the ego pattern of the subordinates to the extent feasible. Under such circumstances the boss, to become an effective and competent leader of the team, may relax/compromise some area to reach some sort of understanding with subordinates, but obviously not at the cost of the organization. As a measure to help the subordinates who do not have a considerate disposition the boss may adopt the observation tactic, i.e., 'watch and see the reaction of the subordinates', giving them some time to rectify/ compensate their thought process. This is done when the boss finds that positive indications to change behavioural activities of subordinates exists and the situation does not warrant the need to take hasty steps. Under this 'moulding therapy measure', appropriate stimuli are provided by the boss to remove contamination and to accept substitution so as to respond in a manner to form a complementary transaction.

It is easier for the boss to convince the subordinates to move in a particular way as per his direction in view of his being acceptable to them. Even the most hot-tempered subordinates accept his leadership and appreciate his mode of talking, directing and functioning. Very few subordinates are incorrigible as they are exceptionally biased or contaminated and may not have the capability to study the mindset and behavioural manifestations of their boss initially but subsequently they may have a pragmatic realization about their boss's quality, approach and desire.

The observation technique as discussed above is a 'positive moulding therapy' used by the boss through the interactive processes with the objective of changing the behavioural pattern of the subordinates. This therapy motivates the subordinates and brings changes in their activities in the following ways:

1. The boss's activities create a sensational impression in the mental faculty of the subordinates, which subsequently helps to form perceptive ideas about the boss.
2. Subordinates may come across commendable incidents which may be the outcome of proper and rational handling of the issues by the boss.
3. A change in the working environment based on the principle of justice, equity and rationality is noticed.
4. Subordinates experience a system basically free of oppression, deprivation and malafide intentions of the boss.
5. In most cases the activities of the boss may appear to be pro-people which may give a fillip to the subordinates to rethink issues.

6. Subordinates may receive a message that the boss is a person for the people, of the people and on behalf of the people.
7. Subordinates may have the impression that their boss is honest, free from corruption, helpful, co-operative and open minded. Such perception may help to bring closeness amongst them and to develop some sort of hidden understanding for mutual existence and growth. A clean image of the individuality of the boss also makes a safe room in the mental arena of the subordinates to manifest respect, concern, agreement and support.
8. Subordinates may witness a change in the system in its entirety, through spontaneous and active participation concerning the well being of each and every member of the organization, the introduction of involvement model, philanthropic and benevolent schemes and welfare measures.
9. The sincere and honest effort of the boss to implement his message to 'stay together, think together, and work together' brings an attitudinal change in the subordinates and prompts them to respond and react appropriately to the stimuli.
10. After a critical analysis of the behavioural aspect and the role performance of the boss, if the subordinates come to the conclusion that their boss possesses the qualities of dynamic personality and effective leadership with a people oriented cum task oriented approach, they develop a feeling of 'we-ness', of 'doing something for the boss', 'belonging to the same family'.

In some situations 'positive moulding therapy' under the observation technique may not work to bring a change in the behavioural activities of the subordinates due to excessive contamination of their adult egos either by the child ego or by the parent ego. In such cases, 'negative moulding therapy' may become useful. After giving ample opportunities to the subordinates to rectify the probable areas of disagreement for the coherent existence and for the smooth running of the activities of the system, if the subordinates fail or refuse to make available the services for their accommodation/adjustment, the boss may resort to punitive measures to mould their behavioural pattern. This measure of rectification may be called 'negative moulding therapy'.

Negative moulding therapy is an effective tool to set the house in order. Delinquent/highly contaminated subordinates in some cases accept the necessity of using such device. This therapy holds to make changes in the behavioural activities of the subordinates in the following manner:

1. The therapy gives a signal to the subordinates not to proceed further and to put a check on the behavioural activities.
2. The subordinates may escape from exposure to a bigger jolt as they take precautionary measures immediately on having been alerted by the boss.
3. Subordinates feel that punitive action is taken as a welfare measure in giving them the chance to rectify their behaviour.
4. Punitive measures bring a feeling of relief from misdeeds amongst subordinates and indicates the areas where they require appropriate upliftment and accommodation.
5. When subordinates feel that punitive actions are adequate, timely and warranted and that no malafide intention exists, they get motivated to change their attitude. Their value systems and morale pass through a phase of change.
6. Subordinates find that their behavioural activities are always closely watched by the boss and at the time of going beyond a certain level they are cautioned to maintain the line of decorum. They also notice that initially, through persuasive measures, an effort is made by the boss to check excessive activities, and after giving sufficient time to them and indicating on several occasions as to the consequences of such activities, punitive action is taken. The process through which negative therapy is used may not, therefore, afford any scope for subordinates to consider the action as an imposition. Rather, they find a new way of life for better living and meaningful survival.
7. Subordinates feel that 'negative therapy' is a necessity to correct the excesses in their behaviour and attitudes and the absence of such therapy may result in grave and unpardonable activities tending towards a ruinous state of conditions. They may, therefore, feel that they get saved by the use of this approach.
8. After being exposed to such therapy, every subordinate of this category takes much more caution than earlier at the time of giving any stimulus or responding to stimulus, so that there is not any repetition of his previous excesses in his attitude and behavioural activities. When such a subordinate develops a better image and perception about

boss as a reasonable and rational personality, he tries to remove his 'excesses' to the extent possible and comes close to the boss as a refined person.

9. Some subordinates may feel that 'negative therapy' is better than no therapy. This situation arises when such subordinates are not given due importance, their activities and behaviour are ignored and the boss takes vital decisions keeping them in dark. To draw the attention of the boss and to make him aware of their existence they may resort to such activities that may warrant punitive action.
10. The boss may use negative therapy in extreme situations when there is no other alternative than to invoke punitive measures. It may happen that boss expresses the compelling circumstances under which he has to take negative measures to set the concerned subordinates on right track. The boss may also convey his feeling, sentiment and emotion for the suffering/hardship they are likely to face because of non-compliance of the repeated caution.

Subordinates watch the situation, study the boss's mind/intentions, analyse the causative factors for using negative therapy and the role of the boss and critically ascertain whether the boss's actions have a hint of vindictiveness. When the subordinates come to conclusion that boss is a clean and unbiased personality and that he has no desire to play double standards, they may perceive their boss as a 'super person'.

From the foregoing discussion, it becomes transparent that the boss with a moderate disposition uses the moulding therapy—positive or negative, after making an analytical assessment of the magnitude of the contamination of the subordinates in order to bring appropriate changes in behavioural activities. The mental state of the subordinates is not open or free from contamination. They may have hot, a cool or a volcanic disposition. The adult ego of the subordinates may, therefore, have contamination either from the parent or child, or from both.

Developing Inter-Personal Relations between the Moderate Boss and the Contaminated Subordinate: Rational Dealing of Some Probable Problems

Subordinates, whether attached to a hospital, club, educational institution, family or organization, as members of the team under the leadership of the boss who has a more or less balanced pattern of ego structures, should follow some norms of interaction for responding to the stimuli of the boss. In order to create a healthy and conducive environment for the growth and prosperity of the organization, some of the probable problematic cases arising out of transactional processes between the moderate boss and subordinates with contaminated adult egos, together with suggested steps for rational handling, are discussed herein below:

Case No. 1

Whenever any problem is placed before any subordinate by the boss for discussion and subsequent disposal, he should not immediately react without making an in-depth and wide-ranged analysis of the issue. But if an immediate decision is required to be taken, the subordinate should give topmost priority to the problem. He should take the following measures:

i. He should collect the information with regard to past history and the background of the issue, the persons involved, the prevalence of the practice, if any, the undercurrent history, if any, the acceptability of the problem from different corners and general opinions on the issue.
ii. He should make an analytical study on the basis of the above information as also of rules/norms framed thereon and find out the genesis of problem.
iii. He should assess the probable effects if the problem were settled in some direction.
iv. He should ascertain whether a settlement would bring any demotivating effect on a large number of people.
v. He should see whether the settlement of the problem would invite complication in future.

After going through the different phases of activities as aforementioned, the subordinate may now have a conference with his boss and, if he is asked to comment or give suggestions on the issue, only then should he give his observations. The presentation of the subordinate should be such that under no circumstance should he impose his suggestions on the boss. It happens sometimes that the boss gives the indication of a specific solution and wants to know the reaction from his subordinate in the matter. In such cases, the subordinate should not oppose the proposition or should not give any hint of disagreement. If the subordinate thinks that the decision may have a far-reaching affect on the smooth functioning and running of the system, he may apprise the boss of that, indicating the probable consequences, and then submit his opinions/ suggestions. Now, it is left to the boss whether he should take the advice of the subordinate or ignore it. The subordinate should not feel offended or should not keep it in his mind if his suggestion is not honoured. When the boss does not accept the suggestions of the subordinate and takes a decision ignoring the advice given by the subordinate, the subordinate may earn the confidence of the boss after the latter realizes the accurate and perfect indication given by him.

For maintaining a good rapport and developing better understanding between the boss and subordinate, complementary transactions are normally desirable and this is possible if the subordinate follows the guidelines given above in the context of the situation as narrated.

Case No. 2

If the boss gives any assignment to any subordinate and indicates its importance for disposal on top priority basis, the subordinate should take the following steps:

i. He should prioritise his job activities and should attend to the new job assigned, leaving aside the other jobs. However, if any job which is lying at hand seems to be more important than the job now assigned, the subordinate should bring it to the knowledge of the boss.
ii. He should show his interest, willingness and sincerity and give his best effort to complete the job on a war footing.
iii. He should chalk out an action plan and make it a time bound programme.
iv. He should not argue with the boss on matters related to the urgency of the job assigned.
v. He should not feel annoyed or irritated and should not consider it as an imposition when any job is given on a priority basis.
vi. He should utilize the available resources and show enthusiasm for the completion of the job prior to the scheduled period.
vii. While making expeditious/early disposal of the assignment, he should see that quality of the work does not suffer.

viii. If, in the process of performance of the job, or at any stage right from the initiation of the planning process to the controlling/directing stage, the subordinate comes across any sort of trouble or difficulty in the completion of the assigned task, he should immediately bring the matter to the notice of his boss. The boss then can understand the real cause of delay in accomplishment, if it has happened.

ix. The subordinate should not say 'no' to the boss for completion of the task. Even if the task is difficult to carry out, the subordinate should never show his incapacity or inability to perform. Rather he should come forward, take the lead, put in his energy and vigour and assure the boss that the assignment will be done.

Case No. 3

When the boss pins down the subordinate with regard to his weaknesses, limitations and deficiencies for performance and directs him to something in particular way for completion of the assigned task, the subordinate should take the following steps:

i. He should take the advice of the boss in good spirit.

ii. He should set his mind in such a way that he morally accepts his weaknesses.

iii. He should consider his boss as a well wisher, guide and friend.

iv. He should wash away from his mind any suspicions he has of the boss.

v. He should listen to the boss minutely and attentively without interrupting or showing any disregard.

vi. If he is hurt mentally when the boss indicates his blind spots, he should bear it for some time. But in any case, he should not keep it in his mind for retaliatory activities.

vii. 'Watch, study and initiate' should be the guiding principle of the subordinate. Initiating activities should have close and direct relation with the perceptible activities of the boss.

viii. He should take remedial measures to improve. He should even solicit suggestions from the boss to reset his mind.

ix. He should not be casual in his approach for the performance of his job. He should give due weightage and serious thought to matters expressed by the boss for ratification.

Case No. 4

When the boss questions him regarding delayed performance or non-performance of the assigned task, the subordinate, in order to form complementary transactions, should adopt the following steps:

i. He should listen to his boss attentively and should not get irritated or show his anger while his boss talks to him or directs him to do something.
ii. He should not interrupt while the boss talks.
iii. When boss finishes his talk and gives him a chance to talk, only only should he talk. He may also talk after studying the situation, in case he is not specifically asked to do so.
iv. When he talks to the boss, he should see that he does not go beyond the level of official decorum, decency and courtesy.
v. He should represent his case in a very sober and modest manner. There should not be any tint of a hostile attitude, gesture and posture. His submission should be based on the factual position and the data available on record.
vi. If the delayed performance or non-performance of any assigned or delegated task is due to some reason which is beyond his control, he should place the matter before his boss in a submissive tone.
vii. If the non-performance or delayed performance is his fault, he should narrate the circumstances giving cogent reasons for his delay/failure to perform.
   It is advisable that in both the situations mentioned in point (vi) & (vii) the subordinate should own responsibility and should ensure timely delivery of the goods/services. However, the subordinate may request infrastructure facility or any sort of help/assistance for the above purpose if he feels so.
viii. When, he submits his representation he should not question the authority of the boss who is asking for an explanation nor should he ask the boss the reason for not questioning the other subordinates about his/their non-performance or delayed performance of assigned tasks.

Case No. 5

When the boss makes a query on some issues or ascertains the development of some pending issues, the subordinate shou'd resort to the following activities to develop mutual understanding, mutual faith and confidence:

i. The subordinate should not be offended or misinterpret the situation when the boss wants to know the development of issues, including pending cases. On the other hand he should, on his own, come forward and make the boss acquainted with the issues, the development thereof, areas of disputes/disagreement, if any and the reasons for non-disposal.

ii. He should make an in-depth study of the issues, should analyse critically the issues and then submit them before the boss in a systematic and polite manner.

iii. When the boss asks for submission of further details, the subordinate should not feel that his boss does not have trust or confidence in him. The subordinate should immediately furnish details of issues.

iv. The subordinate should always respond to the stimuli provided by the boss in appropriate terms so that a complementary transaction is formed. Parent-Child, Adult-Adult transactions are the modest way of forming and developing understanding between the receiver and giver of the stimuli.

v. The subordinate should not keep any information suppressed. He should disclose the matter to the boss if anything which is secret in nature comes to his knowledge.

vi. The subordinate should not feel that the boss is a fault finding personality. He should think from a positive perspective. He should have a high regard for his boss and should remember that 'the boss is the boss' and that the boss does good for the people.

vii. The subordinate should take notice of the queries that the boss puts before him and should reply suitably after he himself is convinced about the right handling of the issues, the monitoring follow-up etc. The subordinate should present the matter before the boss when a congenial and conducive atmosphere prevails, but if the matter is such that requires immediate intervention, the subordinate should submit information on a war footing.

viii. The subordinate should control his emotions. He should not exhibit over-enthusiasm, extraordinary zeal or energy to submit the factual position of the issues. He should reply to the boss or should furnish information strictly to the point in the normal course if otherwise not required exigently.

The aforenoted illustrations indicate some procedural steps which the subordinates with a contaminated adult ego should follow for developing an understanding with boss and to make complementary transactions for the growth and prosperity of the organization. For subordinates who have a balanced mental disposition (moderate disposition) the above guidelines may help them additionally in reminding them of the situational aspects of the issues. Generally, moderate subordinates do not come across any problematic situation in the transactional process when they work with a moderate team leader.

Contaminated Boss vs. Moderate Subordinates

A problematic situation arises in the organization where boss does not have a moderate disposition or a balanced ego pattern. Such a boss cannot function freely and independently. His every decision has the effect of his ego-contamination. He cannot gain mass acceptability from his subordinates. Moderate team-members feel uneasy and uncomfortable accepting their boss as team leader. Hence, a spontaneous team environment may not prevail in a situation where moderate team members outnumber the other members. An adult-contaminated boss may initially find that an uncongenial environment exists in the system which hinders effective functioning, but subsequently he prepares his ground to rule his own territory. To be successful as boss, especially in the performance parameter, he takes the following steps immediately after he takes over the assignment:

i. Informally, he forms his own coterie with very few subordinates, hardly five or six who act as unofficial representatives. The basis of the selection of coterie members is mainly caste, creed, community, place and linkage to the boss through any channel. The coterie people tend to be the 'yes men' of the boss.
ii. The boss specifically directs them or, through posture and activities, tries to create positive image of himself in the minds of the subordinates and to pass on untrue information to the subordinates in order to establish himself as having a clean and unbiased position.

iii. The boss gets all information through this unofficial sub-system.
iv. The boss makes some reshuffles amongst the subordinates in order to form a smooth channel of communication between the people of his own group.
v. The boss compiles data and keeps records for subsequent use.

In most cases, it may happen that a boss whose adult ego is contaminated by the generally critical parent is a workaholic and creates an environment of work by staying late in the office and attending office early. He makes his subordinates sit late, calling them frequently to his chamber for supply of information or to answer any questions he may have while he is at the office.

The salient characteristics of the biased boss are discussed below in a nutshell:

1. He nakedly supports his pet subordinates. If any mistake or even misdeed is committed by such subordinates, initially he does not give cognisance to the genuineness of such information, but when the matter is placed before him with supporting evidence then he either tries to cover up the issue or takes the matter very casually in order to make others understand that the issue is neither grave nor one which requires serious thought.
2. He always looks to the interests of his coterie members. He gives special thought to extending any facility to them beyond the stipulated norms.
3. He is so biased that he cannot have faith or confidence in subordinates other than his 'own men'.
4. He lacks skill in motivating people and does not believe in the 'human resource development approach' as a tool to increase productivity and profitability.
5. He holds a crude assumption about people at work. He considers mostly all people, barring a few, to be selfish, ineffective and unworthy, who remain busy with own work.
6. He wants only work from subordinates but never thinks about the personal needs, demands and requirements of such subordinates.
7. He appreciates his 'own members' in the presence of others, irrespective of the quality work such people deliver. Even in extreme cases he appeases the people in his coterie through appreciation letters and commendable citations.

8. In key posts he puts people who are docile, sober, unaggressive, unargumentative and silent workers.
9. He succumbs to pressure, threat and intimidation. He is indecisive and has no clarity and transparency in his functioning.
10. He wants to do everything in haste without looking to its quality, perfection and accuracy.
11. He has no principles about tackling issues nor does he want to follow the principles governing the system.

When the boss is biased and unbalanced in his ego pattern, no fair and rational judgement can be expected. In such a situation, there is an altogether different type of atmosphere in work performance, a change in behavioural activities, interactive processes and in the perception people hold about their surroundings. Some transparent areas arising out of the situational environment are discussed below:

1. Nobody wants to stay with the organization from the core of their heart under the leadership of a contaminated boss. People remain with the team under compulsion and whosoever gets a chance to leave, leaves immediately.
2. There is a distinct state of mistrust and lack of confidence. Hence a mutual understanding based on the reciprocality is not developed.
3. Team members cannot work freely and independently. They feel helpless and uncomfortable working in the prevailing environment.
4. Subordinates do not get support, not even moral support, from their boss when they pass through difficult situations.
5. An informal group is formed very secretly by the boss with his own people to provide him information and feedback with regard to the activities and impressions of the team members towards him. The creation of such a group in the name of effective working within the organization hinders the growth and development of the institution as the boss is busy taking retaliatory measures against the team members who do not work as his yes men.
6. An unhealthy inter-personal situation becomes transparent in the organization, which adversely effects the achievement of goals.

7. People get demotivated and demoralized as they are not given impetus, appreciation or positive strokes by the boss at the proper time for their excellent performances. Rather they find that the people who are not supposed to get appreciation are presented to the higher boss as excellent performers.
8. A state of adhocism may be prevalent in the organization as the boss lacks foresight, decision making skills and the guts to take risks and responsibilities. Hence the organization development comes to a halt.
9. An uncongenial and unconducive working environment is created through the interaction processes. The man-management relationships developed through behavioural activities are not based on a comfortable climate. Such a relationship, if is in existence, gets worse after taking over the assignment by the contaminated boss.

Interpersonal Problems between a Contaminated Boss and Subordinates: Some Case Problems with Effective Measures

It is clear that the quality of the working environment depends on how the team leader tackles issues pertaining to the team members and how he interacts with them during the course of functioning. It is also revealed that the head of the institution or the leader of the team cannot expect a healthy and congenial atmosphere in the work place if, due to his biased ego pattern, he cannot give free and fair judgements. The situation becomes much more aggravated when team members working under such a biased leader are also biased and are not able to respond appropriately to the stimuli offered by the leader. The foregoing case illustrations may help team members sort out problems and form complementary transactions. Mutual understanding and confidence between team members and boss are established.

The activities of the boss or team leader may bring some changes in the process of forming impressions in the minds of the subordinates which subsequently influences the building up of a mindset and perception about the boss. The subordinates get a mental jolt and develop a fixed idea about the boss when they are convinced about the biased and motivated support of the boss to the subordinates of his 'own group'.

The mental set-up, disposition and bias of the boss or team leader makes the team members unhappy and creates a feeling of a leaderless team. This is expressed through some case interactions given below:

Case Illustration No. 1

Mr. Stubborn is a Chief Executive of a multi-national company. He is posted in a metropolitan city. He has a good number of executives, nearly 60 in number, working directly under him. He is critical by nature. He has a feeling that others are non-performers. They do not want to work. Nor do they have job knowledge. He suspects the integrity and honesty of mostly all executives, barring very few. He has formed a small group informally with people who are loyal, obedient and 'yes men' to him. Through them, he collects secret information about the people at work, their activities and their impressions about him. He uses their services to confidentially work as detectives of personnel. He also assigns them some unofficial and unconventional job to create a good impression before them about his behaviour, activities and thinking.

He is a person with a biased disposition. His adult ego does not work with accuracy due to its contamination. He gives undue benefits and facilities to his 'group men'. He exaggerates the performance achievement of his own men and openly appreciates them in the presence of other people, though he is quite aware of their low performance or average performance. Mr. Stubborn tells his mission or his plan of action to his own men only and keeps other executives in the dark.

Mr. Winner is an executive working directly under Mr. Stubborn. Mr. Winner is very considerate, rational, sacrificing and reasonable. He is sincere, loyal and disciplined. His ego pattern is more or less balanced. He is acceptable to the people at work. On some occasions, through his tact and skilful interaction with the 'yes men' of Mr. Stubborn, he snatches some top secret information from them.

Mr. Winner pays respect to his boss, Mr Stubborn, and honours the official decorum. He strongly believes in the dictum that 'the boss is boss'. Mr. Stubborn considers Mr. Winner to be a harmless, non-vindictive person.

Mr. Stubborn does not disclose or divulge some vital information to Mr. Winner. But in this instance, Mr. Winner has managed to collect the secret information anyhow and enters into a transaction with Mr. Stubborn.

Mr. Winner: Good Morning, Sir.
Mr. Stubborn: Good Morning Mr. Winner. What is the matter with you to be here?
Mr. Winner: I have just come this side. Sir, when are you coming back to the office?
Mr. Stubborn: I am not going anywhere.
Mr. Winner: Sir, I got to know that you are going to Mangolane on special mission-perhaps to investigate some matter.
Mr. Stubborn: How strange! How did you come to know? This is very much secret. Only a few persons, probably two or three, know it. How come this top secret got leaked! I have not told you as this is TOP SECRET.

The above interaction process exposes openly the thought process of Mr. Stubborn with regard to forming a small group of three or four persons with whom any secret or vital matter is discussed. It is not new in the organization to form an informal group to monitor activities. In the family system also, all matters are not discussed with all the family members. There are some matters which are discussed with one or two members only and others are kept in the dark. Be it in the family or any organization, if the intention of creating a small group is for the well-being of the members vis-à-vis the institution, there is nothing wrong in the formation of group. In this instance case, Mr. Winner holds a very important portfolio in no way lesser in importance than any other portfolio held by the person with whom Mr. Stubborn forms a group. Furthermore, the matter on which Mr. Stubborn conducts investigations relates to the Department of Mr. Winner and as per the norms and practices the Departmental Head is taken into confidence for disposal of the concerned issues. The intention of forming a group is, therefore, malafide and keeping Mr. Winner in dark may bring a lot of change in his mindset and perceptions about Mr. Stubborn which may adversely affect his work performance. The prolonging of such a situation arising out of frequent incidents may lead to the degeneration of the mental set up if there is no vigorous support, either through internal forces or external avenues, to sustain the stress.

When such a situation arises (as happened to Mr. Winner) creating a big turmoil in his mental faculty, resorting to 'disposition therapy' may soothe and increase the stress tolerance capability to overcome the situation. Details of such therapy are discussed below:

1. The affected person (that is, the subordinate) should take it easy and should not manifest any gesture, posture or any sort of activities against the secret mission undertaken by the boss with his group members.
2. On having confirmed the fact that an informal group has been formed, the subordinate should not express his displeasure to anybody.
3. The subordinate should not discuss with the boss, even casually, the outcome of the mission. However, if the boss raises the issue the subordinate must respond appropriately. But in no case should the subordinate show eagerness or over-enthusiasm to collect information from the boss on the above matter.
4. The subordinate should keep patient and should not burst out when the boss does something in matters pertaining to his department without his knowledge. The subordinate should remain in low profile and should adhere to the principle 'watch and see the consequences'.
5. The subordinate should, as far as possible, keep good rapport and understanding with the group members. He should not do anything unusual which makes the group members aware that he is well aware of the formation of the small group with the boss.
6. If the subordinate comes to know about the secret mission of the boss through some member of the group in a manipulative manner, he should not disclose it to anybody.
7. The subordinate should remain steady, keep his tolerance level high, prepare his mindset appropriately to face the challenges and accept the situational activities as part of the game of day-to-day life.
8. There should not be any fall or decrease in productivity and quality levels of products or services of the subordinate after the boss is exposed to the subordinate about his nexus with some persons and the secret job undertaken by them. Rather, the subordinate should make an all-out effort to increase his productivity and respond to all stimuli emerging from the boss or his associates, to make a complimentary transaction.

9. The subordinate should build up his mental set up with strong determination and self-confidence to overcome any situation, to achieve his goal through his hard labour, foresight, honesty and integrity.
10. The subordinate should always think of issues and assignments from a positive perspective. Whenever any hard task is undertaken he should keep in his mind that he is 'born to win' and he must succeed.
11. The subordinate should not keep anything in his mind which may affect his working when he comes to know that his boss gets the work done through somebody ignoring him. He should sincerely put his best effort to perform the job assigned to him and should set an example of an effective and workaholic worker.
12. He should never show his anger, aggression or hostility to his boss and should carry out instructions as a loyal worker. If any instruction, however, appears to be detrimental to the interest of the institution or violative of rules and norms, he should bring this to the notice of the boss in an amiable manner and should convince him, placing the rules, supporting documents and the relevant fact and figures before him.

Case Illustration No. 2

Mr. Critic is an executive of a big organization. He is Area Manager of the North Eastern States and posted at Guwahati. He is a biased personality. He does not like people nor does he accept them as human beings. He is not acceptable to the people at work. People do not pay him respect. He is afraid of Mr. Suspicion working under him. Mr. Suspicion is also a biased person. His acceptability by his colleagues is negligible. He is hard in his heart. He is vindictive like Mr. Critic. Both personalities are more or less the same in regard to their activities, their role character, ego patterns and behavioural manifestation.

Mr. Critic discusses problems with Mr. Suspicion pertaining to other department and seeks suggestions from him in the presence of the concerned Department Head. It also happens that Mr. Critic sometimes considers the issues of other departments raised by Mr. Suspicion with an intention to apparently strengthen his understanding with Mr. Suspicion.

Mr. Critic expresses his feeling to Mr. Normal, Head of one Department, in the matter of the interference of Mr. Suspicion on the issues and problems pertaining to his department. Mr. Critic emphasizes that Mr. Suspicion's entry to his department should be minimized and no information which is confidential in nature be supplied to Mr. Suspicion if requested.

Mr. Critic elaborates the dubious character of Mr. Suspicion and advises Mr. Normal to refrain from discussing or seeking suggestions on any matter relating to his Department.

Mr. Normal gets surprised and tries to find out the reality as he observes that his boss, Mr. Critic, gives much more importance on Mr. Suspicion and on vital aspects including those confidential in nature, which the boss discusses with him. The interaction between the subordinate, Mr. Normal, and the boss Mr. Critic which often takes place is given hereunder:

Mr. Critic: Mr. Normal, does Mr. Suspicion come to your department frequently?

Mr. Normal: Not frequently, Sir. Occasionally, and that too on urgent work.

Mr. Critic: How is the important and confidential information divulged? Mr. Suspicion gets all the information and supplies it to the right person before our official communication reaches.

Mr. Normal: Sir, I confirm that no information, whether confidential or unimportant in nature, is leaked through our Department Staff.

Mr. Critic: I have information that staff members of your department have a good rapport and understanding with Mr. Suspicion. Is it true?

Mr. Normal: Sir, it is quite usual that staff members build up good human relations and understanding amongst all the staff members of the office. But, in no way does this relation affect department secrecy and privacy.

Mr. Normal: Sir, I have a small appeal to you.

Mr. Critic: Yes, Mr. Normal, come on. Tell me.

Mr. Normal: Sir, you attach undue importance on Mr. Suspicion. In my presence you ask for suggestions on vital and confidential issues pertaining to our department and you act upon his suggestion.

Mr. Critic: Mr. Normal, it is not that. I do not want his intervention on matters not connected with his department.

Mr. Normal: It is fine. Sir, then why do you discuss with Mr. Suspicion issues pertaining to our department?

Mr. Critic: I discuss those with him just to study his mindset on the matter and sometimes I also consider his suggestions to appease his sentiment. You know, all these are outward shows. I make him understand that he is an important person which he is not and I take decision on vital issues after consultation with him.

Mr. Normal: That's right. I assure you Sir, no information pertaining to our department be given to Mr. Suspicion without your permission.

From the above case illustration, it transpires that the boss plays confusing role to his subordinate Mr. Normal. Mr. Normal is at a loss to decide what to do as he develops doubt about the activities of both his boss and Mr. Suspicion. He is not sure whether his boss really wants to keep Mr. Suspicion in the dark about the activities of his department or the boss is testing his feelings and perceptions about Mr. Suspicion. Since this is a very sensitive issue to be dealt with cautiously, it is advisable to follow the guidelines as under mentioned. It may be mentioned that whenever such a situation arises (as happened to Mr. Normal) the problem may be dealt with in same manner:

1. The subordinate (Mr. Normal) should ensure the compliance of instructions of his boss. He should categorically tell people of his department about the impression the boss carries in the matter of divulging information to some other people.
2. The subordinate should take his people into confidence and discuss at length the steps to be taken for maintenance of secrecy and privacy of information. He should make them feel that leakage of information from the department implies that team members of the department do not have understanding, confidence and trust in each other. The suggestion of the departmental people should be examined and be given due weightage.
3. He should keep in mind that the boss does not want involvement of the other person (Mr. Suspicion) on any issue pertaining to his department. So the visits of other person to his department should be minimized.
4. The subordinate should also keep a vigil about the movement and activities of other person. He should also study the mindset of the boss, his perceptions about the person who makes unwarranted interventions in other departments' job to ascertain whether the boss really wants what he advises or not.

5. The subordinate should not argue with the boss if he gives undue importance, relaxation or leverage to the person concerned. He should rather take it for granted as a special gesture shown to the person.
6. If the subordinate has self-confidence in the area of his job role, performance of assignment and the boss as well as a good impression about the work or responsibility assigned to him, he may express his feelings to his boss (when the boss is in a good mood) for making a room for other person in his department. The subordinate, this way, can understand what the boss actually thinks about the person.
7. As a member of the whole team the subordinate should remain aloof from group politics and should not share his views in informal discussions held by different groups or subgroups which invite his opinion with regard to the functioning, activities and behavioural phenomena of the boss.
8. If Mr. Suspicion wants any information even in an official capacity, the subordinate should furnish information to him after bringing the matter to the notice of the boss.
9. The subordinate should identify the person who gives wrong feedback and incorrect information to the boss on the basis of which the boss takes decisions and should remain away from him to the extent possible within the framework of official decorum. The subordinate should not express his ill feeling about any person in the hearing of the informer.
10. The subordinate should create an environment of staying together in the department which emerges out of the feeling of oneness through discussion, persuasion, exchange of views concerning each other's problem, openness in approach and treating each other as members of the same family. This human relations approach binds them in such a way that nobody can even think of divulging any information which goes against the interest of the group or department.

CHAPTER 6

Qualitative Traits of the Boss vis-à-vis Human Relations

From the preceding deliberation it transpires that different situations crop up in the organization in the process of interaction due to the existence of the heterogeneous nature of mindsets, perceptions, thought processes and ego patterns of people. It is quite possible that people do not respond to the stimuli in a manner as expected. The possibility of having a large number of cross transactions may not, therefore, be ruled out. An unhealthy and uncongenial environment may exist if the interacting people are not properly educated, trained and motivated to feel the necessity of mutual understanding, mutual faith and mutual confidence in each other for their growth and development vis-à-vis the growth of the organization to which they belong. Whenever there is a sense of belonging and togetherness, the team members start to feel a change in the entire gamut of environment, the mode of working, behavioural patterns, perceptions and thought processes may be noticed. The mental set-up, disposition, temperament and ego structure of people may undergo a transformational change on the receipt of moulding stimuli, which reflects.

QUALTATIVE TRAITS OF THE BOSS FOR THE DEVELOPMENT OF HUMAN RELATIONS

In order to bring a healthy, conducive and facilitating environment to develop better human relations for the smooth and effective interaction between boss (team leader) and subordinates (team members), it is suggested that the boss, regardless of his temperamental set-up, should have the following qualitative traits:

I. Patient Hearing

The boss should remain cool and calm when any subordinate comes to him with any problem or grievance. He should show his eagerness and earnest desire to hear from the subordinate. He should create an atmosphere of active concentration to hear him. The boss should give appropriate stimuli or make queries/question to the subordinate to clear his ambiguity. The boss should not argue with the subordinate on any point raised by him. He should not ignore his issue or should not consider the issue as trifling or unimportant. In the hearing session, the boss should hear the issue patiently and should excel in convincing the subordinate that his representation is well-heard. There should not be any interruption when the subordinate narrates his case. The boss, through posture and gesture and with brief and appropriate queries during pauses, should make the subordinate feel that he has listened to his problem with an open mind. During the time of listening the boss should remain exclusively engaged for such a purpose and should not attend to any other job. In the listening session there should not be any third person. If, However, any other person enters into the hearing-session cabin, the boss should tell him to come some time after the session is over.

While listening to the problem of the subordinate the boss should think of th. problem of the subordinate as his own and should feel the suffering and hardship of the subordinate by putting himself in his place. The empathetic feeling of the boss does not cost anything but pays in removing suspicion, ill-feeling and adverse impressions of the subordinate about his boss, so as to develop a better human relations and a mutual understanding and closeness.

The boss may note down the important aspects of the representation of the subordinate in brief while he listens to the problem. Since this is a listening session boss should not give any commitment. The boss may however give his assurance to look into the problem at the earliest. The boss should not create any situation during the hearing session which:

i. irritates the subordinate while placing his representation before him
ii. compels the subordinate to stop deliberations and to leave the session room
iii. brings a change in perception (negative perception) of the subordinate about boss
iv. keeps him away from the common understanding level already achieved
v. gives any indication to make the subordinate understand that the boss has a doubtful role to play
vi. creates confusion in the mind of the subordinate as to the continuance of mutual trust and confidence established earlier
vii. makes the subordinate believe that the boss plays double standards
viii. makes the subordinate feel that he is ignored and belittled by his boss
ix. gives the indication of his biased and partial activities to the subordinate.

2. Emphathetic Feelings Towards the Problems/Grievances

The boss should make a sincere and honest effort to sort out the problems, to settle the grievances, to dispose of the issues referred to or noticed by him. He should give due weightage and importance to the issues of the subordinate. The boss should consider the problems of his subordinate as his own problems and should convey his feeling for the hardship and suffering he has to pass through. The boss should initiate such steps which, in the opinion of the subordinate, are timely and appropriate for the settlement of the issues. The handling of the issues by the boss should bring confidence to the subordinate.

When the subordinate feels that the boss deals the with the matter effectively and unbiasedly and attaches due importance to his problems, a congenial and conducive environment becomes prevalent in the system. In such situations both the boss and the subordinate get satisfied with regard to tackling the issues.

3. Considering the Subordinate as Teammate

The boss as a team leader should treat his subordinate as a team mate. The suggestions, opinion and views of the subordinate should be solicited and discussed with the subordinate threadbare, in order to have a better understanding, conception and a different perspective on the matter. This gives a feeling to the subordinate that he has a role in the organization. The subordinate also starts thinking that he is not ignored and that he has a say in the decision making process.

The boss should consider the subordinate as a team member in the true sense. It should not be that, as a customary process, the boss treats the subordinate as team member without offering him any opportunity or scope to participate in the decision making forum; or even when participating, not attach any value to the suggestions and views of the subordinate.

The boss, through personal interactions, behavioural activities, circumstantial environment and organizational set-norms, may indicate his desire and intentions about inclusion of his subordinate as one of the members of his team. The boss may also create some situational incidents which may give some hint to the subordinate as to how he is treated. If the subordinate is convinced about his inclusion or if he develops the idea that he is part and parcel of the team, he sees the interest of the team first, and sees his own interest only afterwards. The subordinate also makes an all-out effort to achieve the team goal. He becomes team-biased, faithful and loval to the team leader.

4. Human Treatment

The boss should have a strong belief that the human touch and human treatment makes impossible phenomenon possible. He should treat his subordinate not as working tool but as a human being in possession of five sense of organs through which he can watch and evaluate each and every action. He can counteract, react and can make altogether different situation arising out of the kind of treatment he gets. The boss should have positive thinking about the people around him. He should, therefore, form a mindset about the people with a positive approach. Whenever any subordinate approaches him for any assistance or co-operation, he should start thinking in a positive manner (that is, how to help him) rather than in a negative manner (that is, how to get him out). Positive thinking about the performance, activities and behaviour of the subordinate facilitates a comfortable position of interactions between both boss and subordinate, which may tend to form complimentary transactions in their 'stimuli-responses' exercise. In dealing with people, here are the guidelines that the boss should follow as facilitator to human therapy:

i. If the subordinate has some apparent weaknesses which is in the knowledge of the boss, the boss should give him support (at least moral support) to restore and recover the lost ground and to set him right. The boss should never exploit the opportunity and the weaknesses of his subordinate to derive personal gain out of such a deal. Rather the boss should sacrifice some of his personal interest to the benefit of his subordinate. This approach on the part of the boss will bring some change in the mindset of the subordinate, which strategy will consequently develop a sense of gratification of the subordinate towards his boss. The subordinate may search out an opportune time and situation to express his spontaneous gratitude to his boss. With this a congenial and conducive interaction process starts. Transaction analysis shows a complementary diagram and formal relations substitute human relation.

ii. When the subordinate suffers a mental upset due to the sudden demise of a near relation or for some unusual happening, the boss should console him, should assure him that he will extend cooperation and assistance as and when needed, should provide him mental strength to cope with the situation through consolatory measures. If the subordinate is staying home, the boss should visit him at his house to express his concern at such a time. The visit of boss to the subordinate's house at such time counts a lot and it helps to develop informal relations between them.

iii. The boss should invariably accept social invitations made by the subordinate and he should express his spontaneous presence in the celebration. If, due to unavoidable reasons, the boss is unable to attend, the subordinate should be convinced about the urgency and the reason for his having remained absent. Proper and due intimation to this effect should be given by the boss. Attending rituals by the boss at the invitation of the subordinate makes them close and develops healthy human relations.

iv. The boss may invite the subordinate to his house off and on for a chitchat. The boss himself may visit the subordinate's house unnoticed occasionally. The intention of the informal meeting is to develop personal relations and rapport for better understanding. Through such informal chitchats the boss may get some information which may help him deal with some cases effectively. While calling the subordinate at his residence or while visiting the subordinate's residence the boss should minutely study the subordinate's feelings, behavioural activities and reactions to such an informal meeting, in order to ascertain whether the subordinate welcomes this process of developing interpersonal relations or whether he feels awkward and uneasy and wants to get rid of the situation. If the subordinate does not like such meetings, the boss should desist from visiting to subordinate's house unless invited and for the same reason the boss should call him at his residence only when the situation warrants his presence or some ritual celebration takes place.

v. The boss should not forget to express his compliments to the subordinate for the achievement of the assigned task or for excellent performance in some area. The boss should appreciate him immediately on being aware of his outstanding work, in the presence of other colleagues. The boss should also express his sentiments regarding the outstanding performance of the subordinate before an audience at the earliest available forum. It should be remembered that delay in conveying appreciation does not bring any additional message to boost up his morale nor does it help the conveyor establish a personal rapport with him. Appreciation to the subordinate by the boss for excellent performance on time before peers, superiors and other colleagues plays a dual role to act as a positive stroker for the maintenance and furthering of the spirit of achievement and, as a facilitator of human relations, to establish a better understanding and confidence between the boss and the subordinate.

The boss should also appreciate the subordinate when he completes a time-bound assignment prior to the scheduled time or when his suggestions and views on any issue requiring a decision are accepted or for his timely and qualitative performance, through posture, gesture, verbal communication and physical contact, depending upon the situation, the type of work performed, labour spent and the infrastructure provided.

Appreciation of performance in any form gives the recognition of the dignity of labour, perseverance and sincerity to the performer who feels a sense of belonging, oneness, togetherness and closeness. Such feelings of the subordinate help bring them close to each other and develops a good rapport and better personal relations.

vi. The boss should develop personal and informal relations with the subordinate through the interactive process. At a convenient time, he may discuss personal matters with the subordinate so as to obtain information about his family background and social linkage. The boss may also casually make him aware of his vital family matters like his children's education, service, pleasure trips abroad or other matter relevant for discussion. The discussion should be free and frank and it should take place in a congenial and healthy environment of understanding so that the subordinate cannot think that boss wants the information for some malafide intention.

If the boss comes to know that any of his family members has been conferred a distinction in the academic field, he should call the subordinate to his chamber and should convey his congratulations to the concerned family member for his excellent achievement. Such expression of feeling may appear to be a small matter, but in the reality it is important. It has a strong impact on the mental set up of the subordinate, who starts feeling a sense of family environment arising out of the human treatment from the boss.

vii. The boss may develop better human relations with his subordinate by offering some small gift to him on the occasion of some festival, on resumption of duties after a pleasure trip from abroad or after attending some training programme outside the headquarters. The material value of such gifts is negligible considering its effect in building up mutual ties and understanding. Likewise, the boss may develop human relations by offering good wishes to the subordinate on New Year's Day or on the anniversary day of his birth, marriage or joining of service.

viii. When the subordinate resumes his duties after availing of long leave for a pleasure trip to different places or after participating in sports, workshops or conferences, the boss may, on the very day if not immediately after his resumption, call the subordinate and enquire about the trip, his feelings, any difficulties he faced or any remarkable incident. The boss is like the 'karta' of the family (head of the family); and he may show his interest in such personal matters in order to make the subordinate feel that he is part of the 'family'. This caregiving approach bridges the gap of official relations between boss and the subordinate.

Likewise, when the subordinate resumes to his duties after recovery from ailment or after attending to an ailing relation, the boss may enquire about his health or the health of his relation, the nature of the problem, medical treatment, the advice of the doctor and the rest period. Through the personal query the boss may express his feeling and may volunteer his services, if needed. The boss may also assure all sorts of help and facilities available to the subordinate to overcome the situation. The boss should invariably provide moral support to the subordinate to reduce the mental trauma. This approach of the boss towards the subordinate creates a sensitive area for developing mutual understanding and ties for better human relations.

The foregoing deliberation under the heading 'human treatment' indicates the proper way of dealing with the issues under different situations for developing human/personal relations as also mutual understanding, faith and confidence in each other. Tackling the issues for establishing healthy human relations arises out of the 'human approach' which offers appropriate strokes (generally positive strokes are given, except in situations where negative strokes are applied to move in the right direction) after giving due weightage to human consideration. Human treatment is possible only if the individual is considered as a human being by the treatment giver (here, the boss). The mindset, disposition and mental set up of such a boss is formed to develop human relations through interactive processes, activities and behavioural manifestations.

SOME SITUATIONAL PROBLEMS VIS-À-VIS EFFECTIVE MEASURES FOR APPLICATION

If the boss forms a perception about the individuals around him as human beings, this is manifested in his every activity. The boss shows his concern for the people at work and the people in the team and deals with the issues—both personal and formal—from the perspective of people-orientation cum task-orientation. The boss should, therefore, take special care while tackling the situations. Some such situations with appropriate tackling measures are discussed below:

Situation no. 1

If the subordinate is in urgent need of financial assistance to meet expenses relating to hospitalisation, marriage, celebration of festivals, children's admission to higher classes, construction of a house, etc., the boss should express his positive outlook and make an all-out effort to help. If no such scheme is available to help him, the boss should offer financial help to the extent possible from personal sources. The boss should remember that he should not ask for any consideration from the subordinate in exchange for making arrangements of financial assistance to him. Through effort and activities the boss should make the subordinate feel that he is leaving no stone unturned to help him. If the boss, after making an honest and sincere attempt, cannot provide pecuniary help, the subordinate will not mind for this; rather, he will feel ashamed at giving him trouble and pain for such matters. The subordinate does not forget the hospitality, co-operation and assistance extended by the boss and keeps it in his mind to reciprocate at the appropriate time. The subordinate develops a sense of gratitude which facilitates the establishing of a personal rapport with the boss. He comes very close to the boss and gets the opportunity to show his loyalty, obedience and willingness to perform any job even beyond the job role assigned to him. This way he develops a congenial and conducive atmosphere of sharing views/exchanging opinions with the boss and makes complimentary transactions in most cases.

Situation No. 2

The subordinate may be required to remain on leave for some period immediately and may approach to the boss for sanction of leave. The boss should take the following measures to arrive at a decision:

a. The boss should call the subordinate in his chamber and ask him the reason for taking leave and the period of leave he desires. The boss may ascertain whether the leave asked for can be postponed for the time being and be sanctioned after that time schedule.
b. If the boss, after a long deliberation, comes to conclusion that the need for leave is urgent and is for some specific purpose, he should sanction the leave.

It may also happen that subordinate wants leave for going to his native place on receipt of a telegraphic message or a telephonic communication for some urgent work or for the serious ailment of a near relation. In such situations, the boss should sanction leave immediately and offer his help, if required, for arranging the journey ticket or any financial assistance. Generally it occurs that the subordinate does not need such assistance. But, when the boss volunteers services, there is an invariable impact on the attitude and the behavioural activities of the subordinate. The subordinate gets a sensitive impulse from the boss arising out of the human touch provided by him and forms a positive impression about the boss to establish healthy human relations between them.

Situation No. 3

Sometimes, in special circumstances, the subordinate may request a change of his duty hours. He may also request a transfer to the place of his choice as he has remained away from his native place for a long period and his presence is required to look after the family.

It may be that the boss cannot easily accede to the request of the subordinate as each and every activity of the organization is decided on merit within a prescribed framework of policy and norms. The boss may find that the request of the subordinate is genuine and need based, and a favourable consideration of the request may bring contentment and satisfaction with belonging to the institution. If the boss feels it is difficult to consider the representation of the subordinate, he should take the following measures:

a. The boss should call his subordinate in his chamber and inform him about his request application.

b. The boss should show his concern at the suffering and hardship the subordinate has to face.
c. The boss should express his earnest desire and willingness to help him. He should impress upon the subordinate the existing norms and practices followed to deal with such cases.
d. The boss may ask for suggestions from the subordinate to sort out the issues within the existing framework. The boss should always show his positive outlook to assist the subordinate. The boss may give some relaxation to the subordinate to the extent possible within his jurisdiction, as a token gesture to show his liberal and people-oriented activities.
e. The boss should create such an environment that the subordinate gets convinced as to the rightful direction taken to sort out the issues. The boss should remember that in the whole process, right from calling the subordinate to his chamber to the convincing stage, he should manifest his positive attitude and behaviour towards his subordinate.

Through inter-personal activities and the exchange of ideas and views the boss should create such an image to the subordinate that he considers his boss as the ideal personality who is never biased in his decision. Under such situations the subordinate gradually becomes the follower of his boss and develops a harmonious relation with the boss and he may not feel resentful if his request is not acceded to.

Situation No. 4

The subordinate may sometimes request a small favour to allow him to go early (say one hour before the scheduled time of departure) from his office due to his indisposition or for some exigent need at his home. The subordinate may also request the boss to give him a light job or some other job in view of his not being well to perform the assigned task as per the job role schedule. When the boss receives such requests as mentioned above from his subordinate, he may deal with the matter in the following ways:

i. *In case of seeking permission to leave office early due to indisposition*

The boss should call the subordinate to his chamber and enquire after his health and the period since when he is feeling unwell. He may ask him whether he needs medical treatment and assistance to give him relief. If the subordinate wants medical help, the boss should make an honest effort to arrange for that. The boss should allow the subordinate to leave office early. The boss should closely watch the suffering of the subordinate. If the ailment is severe and the subordinate may not like to travel alone, the boss should advise any colleague who knows the residence of the subordinate to accompany him. The boss may offer the subordinate his accompaniment for any service if required.

In such situations the boss should show his enlightened and human approach and should spontaneously assist the subordinate. If the subordinate approaches him frequently to leave office early on medical grounds, the boss, in a sympathetic manner, may ask him for a thorough and proper medical check-up and treatment. The boss may volunteer his services for any sort of help to this effect. In a positive and helping outlook the boss should express his deep concern about his frequent sickness and the magnitude of suffering he has to bear. The boss may draw the notice of the subordinate to the whole scenario if permission of early departure is accorded on a regular basis. The interface discussion on the impact on other colleagues and discipline management between the boss and the subordinate may be arranged in a cordial atmosphere so that there cannot be any room to breed misunderstanding between them. The boss may suggest complete rest at home and to remain under the treatment and advice of the physician.

In the above discussion the boss, instead of saying 'no' directly to the request for regular early departure, should invite suggestions and action from the subordinate under such circumstances.

He should make him feel the importance and necessity of discipline for the greater interest of the organization. However, if the time off is for a shorter period (say, for 10 - 15 days) the boss may consider this as a special case. The boss should also see the gravity of his request considering nature of the illness, the type of disease, the need for recuperation and the probable effect on other people at work. If the boss finds that the suffering of the subordinate is due to the attack of some incurable disease and more or less every person shows great concern for the subordinate and approaches to extend relaxation to leave office early (one hour before the scheduled hour), the boss may, without precedent in future, allow him to leave office early purely on humanitarian grounds for a temporary period. This is a sensitive issue and should be settled cautiously, looking to different perspectives and on merit. The boss should look upon such issue from a human angle.

ii. *In case of seeking permission to leave office early for some exigent need at home or outside*

It may also happen that the subordinate may need to go home early for some urgent domestic work. The boss may ask him the nature of the urgent work, the time at which he wants to leave office, whether any other person can be substituted in his place etc. If the purpose of going early is genuinely urgent and convincing and the subordinate normally does not request for early departure from office, the boss may allow the subordinate to go early. The boss should ascertain from his subordinate whether any urgent work is kept pending which requires immediate disposal. The boss may advise the subordinate to leave office after attending some job on top priority basis. The boss should deal with such cases on merit without any prejudice or bias, but on each and every case the boss should give the human touch to make the subordinate feel that the boss does not play double standards.

iii. *In case of a request for giving a light job or some alternative job*

The boss may come across some situation when the subordinate may request a light job or alternative job in view of his recent suffering from serious ailment. The subordinate may bring to the notice of the boss that he cannot take rest or recuperation at home as he has exhausted and all his leave balance is finished due to his sickness and he has to attend office on compulsion.

The boss may deal with the matter cautiously as the decision of the boss may have an all-round impact on the activities of other subordinates. The boss may take the following steps:

STEP 1: The boss should call the subordinate and ask about his health. The boss may enquire about the medical treatment he has had and what is the attending doctor's advice in regard to rest and recuperation. The boss should create such an environment during the interaction process that the subordinate, on his own, narrates his ailment, suffering and treatment.

STEP 2: The boss should initiate discussion in a very informal way and show his interest and willingness to cooperate and help the subordinate. The boss, in a sympathetic outlook and with a positive approach, should examine the matter and make the subordinate aware of the feeling of the boss.

STEP 3: The boss should explore the possibilities to help the subordinate by giving him an alternative job which may be lighter than the assigned one at least for some period (say 3/4 months) for restoration as prescribed by the doctor. The boss should honestly and sincerely try to accommodate the subordinate. If the boss does not find any alternative job available for the subordinate despite his best endeavours, he should call the subordinate and discuss the matter and inform him of the unsuccessful effort.

STEP 4: The boss may give a less burdensome job to the subordinate for some period. If any additional assignment is required to be performed, it may be distributed amongst others. The boss should develop an understanding with his subordinate and through his behavioural manifestation he may communicate the sentiment, thought process and perceptions about the subordinate.

The boss may find it difficult to have an enlightened and liberal view in the case of such a subordinate who wants relief from doing his scheduled work in normal times throughout his service career on the pretext of this or that. Such a subordinate demonstrates, off and on, his ailing state of health and seeks relaxation of his duty hours. The boss should tactfully ascertain the genuineness of his representation through medical documents and other informal sources. He should initiate his 'activity to help' only when he is satisfied about the factual aspects of the representation. But in a case where there is doubt as to the genuineness of the request of the subordinate the boss may wisely avoid the situation.

5. Confidence Building

The boss should possess the required qualities for building confidence between him and his subordinate. Through his behavioural activities, style of functioning and responses to different stimuli he should prepare the ground for open and frank discussion between him and the subordinate without fear in order to develop intimacy vis-à-vis human relations. With his supportive outlook he may show his keenness to help the subordinate and may ask him to indicate the problematic issues and inconveniences which stand in the way of his performing the assigned task. The boss may express his 'helping approach' through behavioural manifestations and the interaction process. Under such congenial environment the subordinate gives his immediate response to make complimentary transactions in order to establish mutual trust between them.

In an organizational set-up the following are the ways through which the boss may build up confidence among people:

i. When the boss leaves headquarters for official work on a secret mission he may give this information to the subordinate before leaving strictly on a confidential basis. The subordinate may be told to keep this information secret and not to divulge the same to anybody if otherwise not instructed.

   The boss, on reaching the destination, may enquire about the office-issues, problems, etc., through telephonic discussions with the subordinate.

   In the above instance, when the subordinate finds that he is the only person or one of the very few persons who knows the movements of the boss, he feels proud of being in the team as also of coming close to his boss. This feeling drives away misunderstandings or disputed areas if any, and binds both the boss and the subordinate in a single thread of harmony. The subordinate, under such a situation, finds his own room of supremacy over others who may feel jealous of him. The same state of feeling may appear to the subordinate when he gets a telephone call from his boss on tour. Talking to the subordinate by the boss over the phone creates an elating effect which brings contentment and happiness to the subordinate.

   When the boss talks to the subordinate on any issue he should keep in mind that either the subordinate is the next senior in rank of the office or he is the head of the concerned department the issues pertaining to which are discussed by him over phone. It happens in some cases that the boss, ignoring some of his subordinates who are either department heads or next senior persons in the office, communicates messages or collects information on some matter from the subordinates who are juniors to other subordinates and do not belong to the relevant departments. This style of functioning of the boss clearly indicates his biased feeling and attitude towards some subordinates, which not only demoralizes the affected subordinates but also creates a bottleneck in the confidence building process.

If the boss thinks that other subordinates are ineffective and non-performers, he should initiate measures through motivational and stroking devices so as to bring them to the desired level of performance.

It is desirable that the boss on tour should convey messages and information pertaining to any department either directly to the head of the concerned department or through the next senior most person in the cadre or rank of the office. It may not be over-emphasized to mention that subordinates keep their eyes open to watch the boss's activities, linkages, attitudes and informal ties and if anything beyond the accepted norms of behaviour is observed, it may give a tremendous jolt to the image building process.

ii. When the boss goes on an official visit and takes the subordinate with him, the subordinate gets ample opportunity to interact with the boss. The boss also, through the interactive process, comes to know the strengths and weaknesses of the subordinate and gets the chance to strengthen the deficit areas.

The subordinate feels a sense of belonging with the team vis-à-vis the institution and offers gratitude, loyalty and obedience to the team boss. Frequent visit of the subordinate with the boss may develop such a state of mind of the subordinate which prompts him to surrender to the boss to establish informal relations with him. It is noticed that confidence is built on a solid foundation when the boss takes the subordinate on informal visits, ritual tours and customary gatherings. In such situations both the subordinate and the boss forget official relations and develop a family tie. This informal relation facilitates the formation of a confidence building process.

iii. It is seen in some cases that the boss develops confidence in the subordinate within a very short period of time, if the subordinate has a connection and a good rapport with some person who is related to the boss. The linkage phenomenon brings both the boss and the subordinate close to each other and makes ample room for the establishment of an informal relationship between them. The basic fabric for building confidence is the development of mutual understanding and this is feasible only when the boss displays his frankness and invites the subordinate for free and open discussions on any matter without fear. In the organizational frame-work the boss may, therefore, call the subordinate for open discussion on the issues for giving suggestions and opinions without fear. The boss may create a conducive climate for the exchange of views and opinions between them. The boss should always consult with the subordinate and take his suggestion on matters pertaining to his department. There cannot be any situation allowed to crop up when, ignoring the subordinate, the boss takes the assistance and suggestions of other subordinates on the issue not connected with the latter's department. The activities of the boss and the treatment towards the subordinate should not be biased, vindictive and unjustified and the boss should be free from pre-conceived notions about the subordinate. Under such situations the subordinate feels a comfortable state of environment to build up mutual understanding and confidence. The greater the mutual understanding they develop, the more solid will be their mutual confidence.

iv. The boss should be broad-minded. He should see each and every issue from a positive perspective. His perception about the subordinate should be clear. He should have a cooperative approach based on equity, justice and reasonableness. He should not indulge in discriminatory activities. He should believe in a single standard policy and should never practice double standards. He should have transparency in activities. He should manifest his behavioural activities as a 'model actor' to influence the subordinate.

The aforementioned qualities of the boss may bring attitudinal changes in the subordinate who, in a bid to develop understanding, may come close to the boss through transactional activities. In such situations both the boss and subordinate make as much complementary transaction as possible in a short span period of time. In the process mutual understanding and confidence is built and each of them feels an integral part of the team and develops healthy human relations.

v. The following activities of the boss may facilitate the establishing of mutual ties between him and his subordinate so as to develop mutual understanding and confidence in each other:

A. *Proper Evaluation of Performance*

This is the most sensitive area to the subordinate. It is human nature to want to get the optimum or due share, if not more. If he is not given his proper share he feels dejected and forms an indifferent impression about the provider of his share. This is equally applicable in the case of evaluation of the performance of the subordinate by the boss. If the subordinate is an effective, sincere worker, delivers the goods in the desired manner and the track record of his performance is excellent, he obviously expects just, proper and unbiased assessment of his performance from his superior/boss. If the service and performance of the subordinate is rightly evaluated, this not only motivates the subordinate to tone up his spirit and zeal for higher production and services but also brings a chance for a good image in the subordinate's perception about the boss. The reverse is the case when the above kind of subordinate finds that his boss does not give him his due share in evaluation of performance.

Evaluation of performance is a useful device to bring the two 'partners' of the team close to each other if rightly reviewed by the reviewer. This closeness creates a sense of 'we-feeling' and togetherness which subsequently helps to establish mutual understanding and trustworthiness.

B. *Setting an Example of a Clean Personality*

Everybody is born to win. He wants respect, regard and recognition as an honest and clean person. He desires to be acceptable to people and to win their hearts through good work. He may, therefore, play the 'model' and 'ideal' role through the manifestation of commendable activities to earn a reputation as a clean personality. He may be able to come close to people and to influence them as a leader when his role behaviour is appreciated by the people around him.

The boss may set an example of a clean personality before his subordinate and others through his activities. Some of such activities are mentioned below:

a. Claiming reimbursement for travelling expenses for such amounts defrayed by him subject to his entitlement, ignoring some expenses which are negligible and trifling to claim.
b. Not giving extraordinary time to ascertain his receivable dues from the organization after implementation of any financial scheme.
c. Not expressing unwarranted and unethical enthusiasm for any pecuniary gain.
d. Not showing any interest in getting or taking anything out of the way.
e. Sacrificing his own interest for the benefit of others.
f. Not taking any undue benefit from the organization or from outsiders.
g. Obeying and complying with the norms of discipline, punctuality in attendance, rules and regulations without any deviation.
h. Maintaining official decorum and decency.

In an organizational set-up the 'role behaviour' of the team leader or boss has a great impact on the subordinate. If the boss projects his image to his subordinate as an honest and clean person through his actions the subordinate may accept him as a leader and may develop a feeling of deep respect towards him. This feeling of being proud of his association with the boss may drive him to come close to the boss and to develop ties with and confidence in his boss.

C. *Impartial Treatment/Action in Case of Special Assignment*

In each and every organization some special assignment may need to be made to subordinates and for effective functioning subordinates may have to undergo training which is attractive and rarely available. It is generally expected that selection of subordinates for such training and the special assignment thereafter be made on the basis of objective assessment and on merit. The boss should, therefore, remain neutral and take impartial decisions after proper and rational evaluation of performance and other perspectives. The boss's role, whatever capacity he holds, in the matter of selection of subordinate is crucial as it creates a definite image in the mental faculty of the subordinate.

If the subordinate finds that the action of the boss is in the right direction and there is no instance of bias, nepotism and favouritism, the subordinate will develop a positive perception about the boss. But in case of reverse situation a negative perception is formed.

It may happen that the decision making boss is the immediate boss of the subordinate and the concerned subordinate is nominated for the specialized training. In such a case, the subordinate develops a sense of respect for his boss and delivers his best to please his boss as a token of consideration. Both the boss and the subordinate reach some level of understanding and establish confidence in each other.

D. *Unbiased Accommodation*

It is quite natural that the boss receives requests and representations from his subordinates seeking favourable consideration in respect of the difficulties and problems faced by them at different times. The boss should come forward, show his sympathetic attitude and positive approach to sort out problems and give serious thought to solving them. To mitigate the hardship and problems of the subordinate as time to time represented, some sort of accommodation or adjustment is required to be made sometime within the frame of stipulated norms, sometimes as a special case without precedent in future.

Some of the accommodations may be in the nature of deputing subordinates to a nearby place, nominating them for the usual training and staggering duty hours for a temporary period. It is very important for the boss to keep in mind that such issues may create unhealthy industrial relations scenarios if a casual approach is taken in the process of settlement. If the boss makes such accommodation as a kind of gesture exclusively on merit, without bias and without any malafide intention, the concerned subordinate takes the boss's helping action as a special favour shown to him. The subordinate gets the opportunity to come close to the boss through the interaction process and develops confidence in the boss.

E. *Shouldering Responsibilities of Wrongdoing by the Subordinate*

The boss may delegate the authority to his subordinate for the effective and smooth functioning of the system. In the process of performance the subordinate may make inadvertent mistakes, causing loss to the organization, for which he may be held accountable. The subordinate accepts his wrong - doing, feels repentant, expresses regret and assures non-repetition of such incidents. In such situations the boss should stretch his helping hand and assume the responsibility of the wrongdoer as his own. When the subordinate observes that he is relinquished from his responsibilities by his boss and the whole blame of his misdeed is taken over by the boss, his faith on his boss increases manifold. After this, the subordinate starts thinking afresh about the behavioural activities of his boss and develops an altogether different perception about the boss, if no such incident has taken place earlier. The subordinate feels proud of his working with such a boss and makes as many complimentary transactions with the boss as possible in order to establish cordial human relations and thereby to develop confidence in each other. The reverse may be the case when the boss passes the responsibilities on the subordinate and holds him responsible for his wrong activities. This sort of activity of the boss distances the boss and his subordinate from each other and the possibility of developing mutual confidence may be a rare occurrence.

CHAPTER 7

An Overview of Subordinate Qualitative Traits as Also the Organizational Milieu from the Perspective of Human Relations

The preceding discussion depicts a detailed study of the qualitative traits an executive, boss or a team leader should possess in order to create a positive image in the minds of subordinates, to develop mutual understanding, trust and confidence in each other and to establish harmonious human relations between the boss and subordinates. The role of the boss and his characteristic abilities undoubtedly bring a changed environment in the work situation as also a conducive climate for inter-personal relations. But the role-performance of the subordinates and their qualitative traits cannot be ignored in the context of establishing cordial human relations. The subordinates should be equally enthusiastic, initiators and facilitators for developing a congenial human relations environment. The boss can succeed in his objectives to bring a healthy climate of human relations only when his subordinate interacts equally in the desired direction and possesses the requisite qualities for carrying out the interactive process.

Qualitative Traits of Subordinate

The subordinate should have the following qualitative traits in order to make complimentary transactions to the extent possible with the objective of establishing cordial interpersonal relations.

i. *Analytical Capability to Assess the thought Process of the Boss*

The subordinate should acquire an analytical ability through numerous interaction exercises to study the thought process of the boss. What the boss really needs, what he means, what he wants in a particular situation: subordinate should minutely analyse all these factors with relevant facts, events, timing and sequence and then arrive at a conclusion. Sometimes the boss only gives some hints to the subordinate to indicate his line of action for disposal. The subordinate should have the requisite ability to assess the latest development of the issue and the boss's strategy tc deal with it and to chalk out the tentative measures to be taken for providing assistance and support. This is possible only when the subordinate is well aware of the problem—its genesis, causative factors, development and probable effects and is acquainted with the style of functioning of the boss, specific observations made by the boss and the comments of the boss on the concerned issue.

ii. *Maintenance of Individual Entity*

The subordinate should remain an individual. He should not lose his entity in the process of his performance of duty. Though on some occasions the subordinate may gain by surrendering individuality, in long run it may not bring any result. The boss (team leader) in reality does not rely on the subordinate who lacks the quality of individual entity, but rather appreciates the subordinate who courageously maintains individual entity and may even encourage him to continue with the individual quality and to develop an inter-personal relationship. In some small organization of unorganised sectors the boss may, however, expect that the subordinate should perform his job out of the way even at the cost of individuality. The same situation may be observable in the offices of large organizations where bosses with contaminated adult egos run the show. Bosses with such qualitative traits come close easily to the subordinates and establish cordial human relations However, in general bosses do not like subordinates who lose their own individual entity. The subordinate having his own individual quality may, therefore, come close to the boss and may get the opportunity to interact for the building of mutual understanding.

iii. *Adaptable/Adjustable Disposition*

The subordinate should have the quality of adjustment/ adaptation to a situation that may emerge out of the functional processes of the boss. The subordinate should observe and study the boss regarding his strengths and weakness, his dispositional state, likes and dislikes and his perception about the subordinate. The subordinate should remain mentally prepared to face any sort of hindrance if one stands in the way for performing the assigned task in the changed environment. He should update his record of events, activities, achievements and special assignments made by his boss and ascertain the probable areas of deviation and difference for adjustment. If the difference in thought processes, perceptions and mindset between the boss and the subordinate is negligible, it is easy for the subordinate to adjust. Whatever the situation the subordinate may have, for establishment of cordial human relation between him and his boss, he should be adaptable/adjustable to any sort of environment. The greater the adjustability of the subordinate, the better will be the interpersonal relations to establish mutual understanding, trust and confidence.

iv. *Acceptability*

The subordinate should be acceptable to the people around him, particularly to the boss with whom he works. It is generally noticed that some bosses indicate the qualities the subordinate should possess and they cannot work with the subordinate who does not have the requisite qualities as per his specification. For a better understanding and for establishing cordial human relations, the subordinate should possess the following attributes:

a. *Simplicity and Soberness:* The subordinate should be sober in his behavioural manifestations. He should be a person of simple mentality and should not have any hidden intentions. He should be free and frank in his delivery of transactions with his boss.
b. *Loyalty and Obedience:* The subordinate should be loyal to the boss. He should be obedient in carrying out instructions and should not be a person who argues over job roles, assigned tasks or any matter to show unwillingness to perform functions or to disregard instruction.

c. *Positive thought Process:* The subordinate should have a positive approach for dealing with issues. He should be a personality who takes initiative to dispose of the issues, looking to the interest of the institution and has no disposition to say 'no' to any task assigned to him.

d. *Quality to 'Like the Job, Love the Job and Do the Job':* The subordinate should be happy with his profession. If he gets happiness out of his work, he will develop the quality 'to like the job, love the job and do the job'. Such a person cannot waste time simply by sitting idle or doing nothing. The inherent instinct of his liking his work will not permit him to engage in ritualistic games and will prompt him to remain busy with the task. The above personal qualities of the subordinate create a 'people-image' about him and he becomes acceptable to his boss for making complimentary transactions in order to establish better human relations between them.

v. *Work-Addiction, Consciousness of Duty and Involvement in Work Accomplishment*

The subordinate should be dutiful and very conscious about job performance in a time-frame schedule. He should lay stress on job perfection, accuracy and completeness. He should be a person who exclusively invests his time and efforts for task accomplishment. Such a subordinate gets involved in each and every activity of teamwork with the objective of the completion of the task/assignment in due time.

The subordinate does not keep his time of departure as followed by others. He leaves the office according to his work schedule, normally much after the stipulated time and obviously not before the scheduled time of departure. It may occur that work involvement makes such a subordinate a workaholic or a work addict. He gives maximum time of his active period towards work accomplishment and development of the system, work procedure and methods of his own territorial area of portfolio. Even on Sundays and holidays such a subordinate keeps busy in the performance of assigned task.

The boss likes subordinates of the above quality, as he finds the potential ingredients existing in such subordinates ideal for the achievement of the target set by him. The above type of subordinate may come close to his boss and may get a chance to interact frequently to form complimentary transactions essential for the establishment of healthy human relations.

vi. *Model Personality*

The subordinate should set an example of the ideal worker through his work performance, behavioural pattern, manifestation of activities, compliance of norms of attendance and punctuality and adherence to rules and regulations. He should be a disciplined worker right from obeying the instructions of the boss/superior to percolating messages of the higher authority for compliance amongst other peers and subordinates. He not only manifests disciplined activities but also creates a conducive environment to activate others to be disciplined in all spheres of activity. He ensures discipline among the people of his department or his office. He gives his all to inculcate in people the spirit and necessity of spontaneous discipline and adherence to the norms, rules and regulations of the organization for their personal growth and development vis-à-vis organizational development.

The subordinate may become a successful motivator to influence his own thoughts and perceptions to his people at work in respect of spontaneous discipline and compliance of organizational set- standard if he is acceptable to them as an 'ideal person' for his role performance, behaviour, activities and adherence to all set-norms in the area of attendance, punctuality and other administrative aspects.

The boss may like the subordinate who possesses the above quality, inter alia, to facilitate smooth and effective interactions in order to establish a congenial and understanding scenario. Healthy human relations are developed when both the partners—the boss and the subordinate—have more or less similar thought processes to arrive at some decision. It is presumed that the boss, being the formulator and facilitator of the norms and rules, is in possession of the quality and he may like the subordinate who owns the 'model personality' for the formation of a close association and complimentary transactions.

vi. *Honesty*

The subordinate should be honest and should not have any stigma in the area of financial transactions. He should not have any past history of misappropriation or embezzlement of funds, nor should he have resorted to any sort of fraudulent activities in the past. It is observed that the person who has had a past background of fraudulent activities and has rectified and corrected himself, cannot gain the trust and confidence of peers, subordinates or bosses. This is very sensitive issue. If once a subordinate loses confidence, it is very difficult to get back to the pre-fraudulent state. The subordinate with a past background of dishonest activities is never really liked by the boss. The boss wants a person as his subordinate who is clean from all corners so that he may rely on him and have confidence in him. The honest subordinate may have greater scope and opportunity to interact with the boss and may expect to make complementary transactions in the interactive process. The boss generally likes to build up team spirit with such types of subordinates who also possess qualities as aforenoted for establishing mutual ties, mutual bond and understanding.

vii. *Rational thought Process, Decision Making and Judgement*

The subordinate should be unbiased, rational, impartial and judicious in decision-making. He should not have any personal grudges against his peers or other people in the organization which may affect his judgement process. If the subordinate has any occasion to interact in an unpleasant way with any of his colleagues or any member of the team, he should not bear the grudge. He should forget such incidents otherwise they will create their own room in his mental faculty and subsequently develop a feeling of enmity which may depict a bad syndrome in the rational decision making process of the boss. The subordinate may be required to provide feedback, information, data, facts and figures, after making an objective analysis and evaluation at his end, for his boss to arrive at a conclusive decision. If the subordinate has a hostile impression against somebody, he may send the information to his boss, even though it should be necessarily filtered. The decision-making may thus be biased.

The boss may rely on the information supplied by the subordinate for analytical evaluation if he considers the subordinate unbiased, fair and reasonable. Such a subordinate may easily a develop team relationship with his boss.

viii. *Non-involvement in Group' Politics*

It may be observed that in the club, hospital, school, college or any organization two, three or even more groups are formed with people who have more or less homogenic thought patterns, mindsets and qualitative traits. These unofficial groups do not have a legal or administrative status but they may sometimes become active from the background to push forward someone's interest. The boss keeps a vigil on the underground activities of the group members as some groups may remain engaged in critical analysis of boss's activities and may develop an anti-boss impression amongst group members.

No boss likes it when the subordinates is involved in group politics with the objective of indulging in non-productive and unpleasant activities.

The subordinate should minutely study the activities of the groups and the role of the group members. He should keep himself aloof from the clutches of group members. He should not be involved in group politics but should have the unofficial machinery to collect information about the on-going developments of the group's activities. He should also provide feedback about the group activities to the boss and create the impression in the boss's mind that he is neutral and does not belong to any group.

When the boss gets confirmatory reports from his own sources that the subordinate has no involvement in group politics and he is a neutral person, he remains open for further interactions with the subordinate. In such situations the boss starts re-thinking his opinions about the subordinate, if he has already formed impressions about him, and develops his mindset afresh. The subordinate may have uninterrupted opportunities to interact with his boss and may exchange expected levels of views and deliberations with the boss to make complementary transactions. With this he will earn recognition from his boss and they can develop a better understanding between each other to establish a healthy state of human relations.

ix. *Sense of Propriety of Authority*

The subordinate should have a clear concept about the propriety of authority—the jurisdictional hierarchy of authorities, reporting authority and superior authority. In a multidimensional authoritative approach the subordinate should be very careful in his interactions with other line or staff authority as the comments and opinions of such an authority play a crucial role in the image-building processes of the boss. The boss collects information, incidents, reports and opinions about the subordinate from different sources including line/staff authority personnel before he develops a mindset about the subordinate.

The subordinate should pay proper respect to the persons in position. He should not bypass any information to the superior office unless it is called for. Even in such cases, the subordinate should bring it to the notice of his boss if he remains present in headquarters. Whatever information is furnished to the higher office it should be within the knowledge of the boss. It may happen that the subordinate may be well acquainted with the boss's boss, because of his working with him in the past, or through contact with him through some person they know in common. In such cases the boss should not get offended if information is communicated to higher office without his knowledge. Since the career path, promotion and elevation of the boss largely depends on the performance evaluation by his boss, the boss encourages the subordinate, albeit reluctantly, to strengthen links with his boss. The boss may superficially manifest his healthy human relations with the subordinate and may develop mutual ties and understanding. The boss may also keep such a subordinate happy and contented through various motivational and interactive measures. The boss may not hesitate to evaluate the performance of the subordinate extraordinarily without looking to the objectivity of the assessment. The boss does all this simply to be in the good books of his own boss through the subordinate who, in reciprocation, gives commendable feedback about the boss and his work-performance to his boss's boss. The subordinate should always remember the idiom 'boss is boss' and should not do anything to supersede his boss or to bypass him. He should develop a sense of propriety of authority in the process of discharging responsibilities.

x. *Dependability*

The subordinate should manifest his work activities and role performance in different forums so as to develop mutual trust and confidence between him and the boss. The subordinate should always bring to the notice of the boss any difficulties and obstacles faced by him while discharging the assigned task.

The boss may be very concerned about the transparency of performance as also of accountability and responsibility. The subordinate should, therefore, identify the areas of achievement, the areas of his failure and the reasons thereof, measures taken to eradicate constraints, the responsibilities shouldered, etc., and give his all out effort to achieve the target. The subordinate should be assertive in getting the work done and should display a clean record of transparency in his task performance. He should be confident in completion of the assigned job on time with perfection and accuracy. He should create an impression in the mind of his boss about his competency and effectiveness through his work performance, sincerity and seriousness towards job completion and unstinted effort for discharging delegated responsibilities. The boss may, subsequently, be dependant on the subordinate. It may happen that initially the boss may be reluctant to give higher responsibilities to the subordinate in discharging assigned tasks, but on subsequent occasions when the calibre, ability and skilful activities of the subordinate and his capability of shouldering higher responsibilities becomes transparent, the boss may repent his past activities for not giving the desired recognition to the subordinate.

A dependable subordinate can easily come close to the boss and become a trustworthy person after a series of interaction exercises. Such a subordinate may develop mutual understanding and confidence between him and his boss only when the latter gives a positive signal after a lot of complimentary transactions take place.

xii. *Link-finding Quality*

The subordinate should be capable of studying the overall environment of the office and organization particularly in the area of 'link-relations' related to formal and informal relationships and group dynamics. It happens in almost every organization that besides man-management and the boss-subordinate relationship, some other relationships (informal and individual) exists with the boss. The boss may have some persons as his 'own men' and may develop informal and individual relationships with them. These individuals may keep the boss informed about the day to day activities and incidents of the entire organizational system and may establish a solid rapport with the boss. Sometimes they may also exercise the boss's authority in vital decision making processes. They may, therefore, be very powerful in organizational activities.

The subordinate with the 'helicopter' quality is able to scan people and their attitudes towards the boss through interactions with the people on different occasions and in different situations. They will notice the boss's reactions and his interaction with different types of people, as well as the overall circumstantial factors for the sanction of special leverage to some person by the boss. The subordinate can, after consideration of the situational requirement and objective assessment with analytical evaluation, arrive at a concrete finding of the people who have informal nexus with the boss.

The subordinate should keep in mind that he should not divulge to anybody his identification of people having informal individual relations with the boss. He should be cautious and careful while dealing with any matter pertaining to any member of the informal group. He should not express ill feeling about the activities of such people or on any matter concerning any person of such a group.

The subordinate should develop a good rapport and better understanding with people who have informal links with the boss. It may occur that such people create a positive image about the subordinate in the mind of the boss in the usual process by providing better feedback about him. This may possibly change the attitude of the boss towards the subordinate and the boss may give a lot of scope to him to interact with the intention of building up congenial human relation between him and his subordinate.

From the preceding deliberations it is transparent that both the subordinate and the boss should be in possession of qualitative traits for establishing healthy human relations through the interaction process. Mutual understanding, faith and confidence are prerequisites for better human relations. This occurs when the interactions between the subordinate and the boss are comfortable, cordial and congruent so as to make complimentary transactions.

The qualitative traits, as discussed in the foregoing deliberations, are effective for developing better human relations. There could be some qualities existing with some subordinates or bosses other than those mentioned in earlier discussions. It is observed that these traits and qualities may not have strength to activate the driving force of the person concerned to move forward for any sort of transaction. However, lack of any of the vital traits as mentioned above may hamper the interaction process and the human relations as well. The whole process of human relations is shown below through graphical representation:

The Genesis of Human Relations

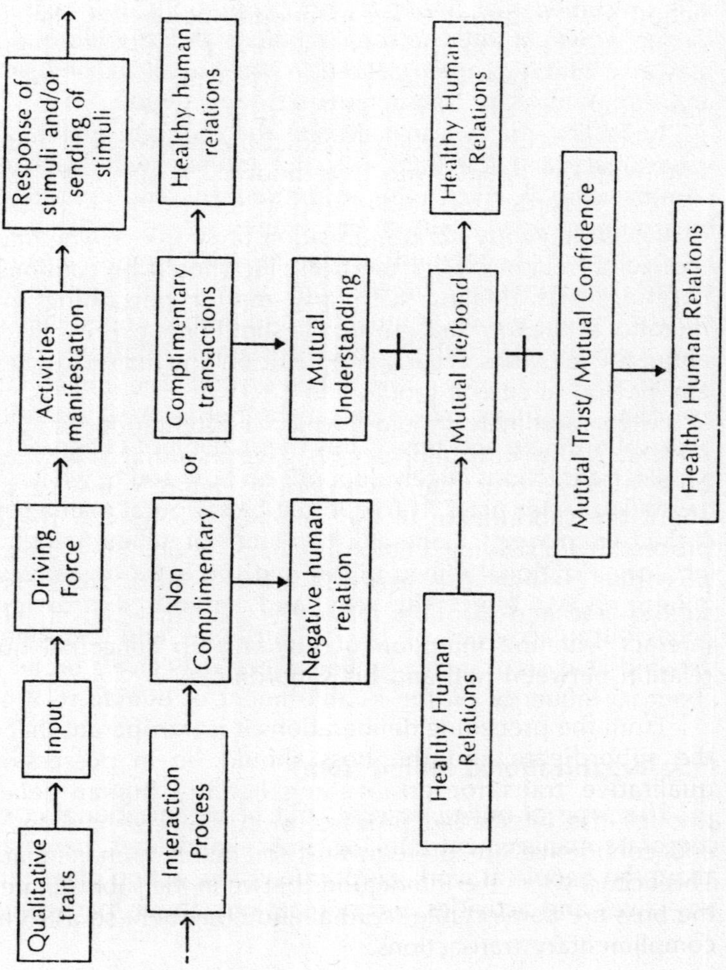

From the above discussion, it is transparent that both subordinate and boss should possess some qualitative traits to exchange free and frank opinions through the interaction process to establish personal relations in the organizational framework. This personal relation which is the same as human relation develops when both the partners own more or less identical or semi-identical thought pattern on specific objects and behave accordingly to make complimentary transactions. In the process of interactions both of them reach a certain level of understanding to build rapport which subsequently facilitates the development of mutual ties and confidence. In such cases it is presumed that 'other factors'/'conditions' are favourable for the growth of inter-personal relations and, therefore, do not play any inhibiting role to stand in the way of making smooth and complimentary transactions between them.

In reality it occurs that despite the requisite qualities, the subordinate and the boss may not interact with each other comfortably as they feel an unhealthy and uncongenial environment exists within the whole set-up to hinder the establishment of congruent human relation. Even in a situation when complimentary transactions take place, the chain of mutual understanding, mutual ties and mutual confidence does not form to strengthen inter-personal relations due to impediments inherent in the milieu system. The 'milieu factor' exercises significant influence on the behavioural activities of both subordinate and boss. Thus the making of congruent and parallel transactions largely depends on how and to what extent the milieu factor plays its role in the behavioural manifestation of the two 'players'. Generally, two kinds of milieu-namely, the intra-organizational milieu (IOM) and the extra-organizational milieu (EOM) affect the free and smooth expression of behavioural activities of the subordinate and the boss. A detailed analysis of such a 'milieu affect' may give a broad idea about its influence on the establishment of human relations.

Intra-organizational Milieu (Iom)

This type of milieu emerges out of organizational culture, corporate management thinking, policy guidelines, perceptions about the people at work, corporate vision, action plans, union objectives and activities and perceptions about management.

The corporate management style of functioning conveys the message to the lower rung of the management with regard to the methods to be adopted to deal with the issues. Corporate management may resort to a single or combined style of functioning as under mentioned:

i. authoritative style of functioning
ii. participative/motivating style of functioning
iii. open style of functioning
iv. Laissez-fair style of functioning

Sensing the higher management style of functioning, the boss may try to change his methods of functioning to suit the corporate climate. The authoritative style indicates strained relationships which restricts the boss to make free and open dialogue with the subordinate to establish mutual understanding. In such situations frequent complimentary transactions may not take place. Even if complimentary transactions occur the possibility of building up confidence and mutual ties and bonds may be remote as the condition emanates from the 'parent-child' relationship (boss gives stimuli or reacts or responds to stimuli from 'parent ego' and subordinate responds to or gives stimuli from 'child ego'), which is not an ideal state of ego pattern (Adult-Adult relationship). The subordinate may keep himself away from the boss, he may not like to come close to the boss, he may want to pass on time without performing the job, he may not like to perform the functions unless he is compelled. The subordinate shows an indolent, idle, good-for-nothing, disobedient, work-avoiding nature. It may be, therefore, possible that the boss may not take the subordinate into confidence and may not develop healthy human relations with him.

The participative or open management style is entirely reverse to the authoritative style. When the boss comes to know through various actions of the higher management and from different ameliorative measures introduced under welfare schemes that corporate management is liberal, enlightened, participative, employee-oriented and lays emphasis on open discussion forums for disposal of issues to build up mutual understanding, he may update his perceptible area with necessary feelings and prepare his mindset accordingly. In such situations the boss may start thinking on any issue from a positive perspective as and when referred to him. Even the issue which may require forthwith rejection may come up for thorough perusal to find out ways and means to sort it out within the existing norms and rules.

Under the participative/open management system, the boss opens up channels of communications for discussion with the subordinates to remove ambiguity of issues if any. The boss may hold structured or unstructured conferences and meet with the subordinate to study, ascertain and understand his perception about the subject matter through an interface discussion, exchange of ideas, views, opinions, and objective analysis and deliberations. Constructive suggestions are offered by the subordinate to remove the turmoil situation, if any, and to reach an amicable solution. The subordinate feels that he is part and parcel of the system when he is invited to offer suggestions. He develops a sense of recognition when his suggestions are taken for implementation. He develops a sense of belonging, we-feeling and togetherness. He expresses his willingness to shoulder responsibilities to fulfil team expectation and objectives.

In such cases there may not be any scope for breeding any misunderstanding or mistrust; as an 'on-going process', the boss holds free and frank discussions with the subordinate mostly on all the issues. Since the subordinate has free access to the boss, he may also discuss with the boss on any issue which he thinks confusing, ambiguous. He may thus clear his misconception and may develop a complete perception on the matter.

Under this style of functioning the boss offers ample opportunities to his subordinate to come close through interaction process. The subordinate provides appropriate stimuli and responds to stimuli in order to make complimentary transactions. He finds pleasure in forming parallel transactions and so he creates a lot of complimentary transactions. Formation of parallel transactions is a prerequisite for developing mutual understanding, confidence and trust. This may subsequently lead to the establishment of healthy human relations.

In a participative system the subordinate may have a communication forum to interact with the higher authority (i.e., the boss's boss or upper hierarchy) on different issues of the organizations. He may also make the higher authority aware of vital incidents as and when they occur. If the subordinate is not happy with his boss or if he notices some shortcomings of his boss or finds off-the-track games being played by him, he immediately brings it to the notice of the higher authority. It happens that higher authority knows the subordinate's boss better than the subordinate knows his boss. This may be possible when the subordinate is an active member of a team, committee or association. In some cases, the higher authority may not have any occasion to interact with the boss of the subordinate.

When the boss comes to know that his subordinate has a good rapport, link with his own boss; he gives special attention to solve the problems of the subordinate. The boss may offer some relaxation to the subordinate to extend any benefit or assistance in his favour and may indicate through behavioural manifestations and activities that the subordinate may ask for any kind of help, cooperation and service as and when need arises. The boss exchanges a series of complementary transactions with the subordinate and then keeps open the doors for the subordinate to make intimacy, participate in partnership of the team, develop mutual understanding and establish personal relations. The subordinate also finds a congenial and conducive environment existing for building up mutual ties and confidence between him and the boss.

The policy guidelines of the corporate management, corporate vision in the forthcoming years, corporate management thinking, action plans, perception about the people at work and the introduction of welfare measures bring a lot of changes in the attitude of both the boss and the subordinate. The policy guidelines linked to employee growth and development under the human resource management strategy, corporate vision for making happy and contented work force community and the introduction of various welfare measures for well-being and amelioration of work- people creates an impact on the working of the subordinate. The subordinate may start thinking about the positive steps being taken by the higher management to improve living and working conditions of the workforce and to satiate their psychological needs. He may, therefore, discharge his assigned task with great zeal and enthusiasm and deliver the goods to the highest satisfaction of the boss. He will make an effort to increase productivity and to enhance the image of the organization through rendering excellent service.

The boss may experience the existence of an easygoing environment due to introduction of several welfare measures and employee growth and development oriented schemes as envisaged from corporate policy guidelines and vision for ensuing years. In such situations the boss changes his method of tackling the issues considering the above perspectives and takes a liberal and lenient view even in harsh circumstances. The boss may lay emphasis on individual growth and development as a strategy to create a contented working force who on their own may convert themselves to committed soldiers to serve the institution at the desired direction. The boss implements all instructions of the higher management in the spirit and action of the policy guidelines, vision and welfare schemes and manifests his positive attitude and behavioural activities as a people oriented person. He may earn a reputation as a dynamic and successful team leader. He develops a cordial relation with his subordinate through frequent interaction, exchange of views and deliberations.

Corporate management objectives vis-à-vis union/ association objectives plays a significant role in changing the attitudes of boss and subordinate. If the objective of the association/union is more or less the same to that of the objective of the management, some changes in behavioural patterns, activities, modes of treatment, lines of actions and attitudes of both subordinate and boss may be noticed. Some such vital changes are discussed below:

i. The boss may not find any major difference in perception between him and the subordinate on matters relating to service conditions of people, productivity, profitability, customer service, and the growth and development of the people and the organization. Both the boss and subordinate show eagerness, sincerity and seriousness in implementing and complying with the instructions mentioned in the respective framed objective.
ii. The boss may draw up an action plan to take necessary steps to achieve their goals. For this, he involves the subordinate as a team member, assigns him tasks and analyses task accomplishment through feedback discussions.
iii. The boss treats the subordinate as a human being who needs motivation, praise, recognition, appreciation and

identification as an 'important partner' and initiates necessary steps to meet the psychological needs of the subordinate.

iv. The boss may give emphasis on settling issues through discussions, dialogue, exchange of views and suggestion. He believes that an amicable disposal of issues is the way to remove differences and doubt and to establish mutual understanding and confidence.

v. The subordinate may not dispute the settlement of any matter by the boss as he knows that the boss follows guidelines given in the objective framework.

vi. The subordinate extends cooperation to complete the task undertaken by the boss.

vii. The boss earns acceptability from the subordinate through the process of interactions, exposure to different situational states, manifestation of behavioural activities and application of judicious and reasonable approach for settlement of issues.

viii. The subordinate considers the boss as the 'head' of the family who thinks for the good of his family members

ix. The subordinate shows disciplined activities, loyalty, obedience and stress and strain tolerance capability and behaves as a most reliable, trusted and committed worker.

x. The boss may not take any drastic action against the subordinate even when the latter commits major misconduct.

xi. The boss may not witness any situation/incident when the subordinate stands in the way for implementation of any plan issue. The activities of the boss for task accomplishment may go uninterrupted, undisturbed and unhindered.

xii. The boss may change his perceptions about the subordinate and may look to his subordinate as a 'facilitator', not as problem-creator.

xiii. After a thorough review and objective analysis the boss may observe the positivity in the action process, behavioural attitude and deliberation of the subordinate.

xiv. The subordinate may not feel it advisable or appropriate to run into confrontation with his boss on any matter as he notices that the boss remains on the right track. The subordinate may develop a positive image about his boss and may change his mindset accordingly.

From the above discussion it is transparent that the corporate objectives as also the union/association objectives which constitute the objectives of the individuals/subordinates bring a lot of attitudinal changes amongst the partners (that is the boss and subordinates) in the organization. This may result in the creation of a conducive and congenial environment for the establishment of a healthy and harmonious relationship between the boss and the subordinate, when the objectives of the union/association are similar or akin to the corporate objectives

In the evolutive process of attitudinal changes both the subordinate and the boss perceive each other as positive personalities and subsequently they develop a clear mindset to interact in a desired manner. The boss gives positive stimuli to the subordinate and responds to stimuli given by the subordinate in an appropriate way so that the subordinate may offer positive stimuli to the boss and may respond to the boss to make complimentary transactions. Once the complimentary transaction starts, there is every likelihood that it will continue, till such a period as either of the two persons express activities contrary to the implied understanding formed through the interaction process. Prolongation of complimentary transactions enhances the positive thought processes of the subordinate and the boss in a congenial milieu and may build up good rapport and confidence in each other.

But in a situation when the objectives of the union/association are not similar to or are contrary to the objectives of the corporate management, inter-personal relations between boss and subordinate may not develop. In such case both subordinate and boss may have requisite qualitative traits to form complimentary transactions but they may not be effective to carry on a cordial interaction process (complimentary transactions) for a long period as lack of a congenial milieu which crops up due to differences in objectives may stand in the way of making smooth and unhindered transactions.

If the objectives of the union/association or individual subordinate objectives differ largely from those of corporate objectives, the management (boss) style of functioning changes. The boss may become harsh and unreasonable. He may resort to autocratic processes to get anything done by the subordinate. He may give close supervision and use negative strokes to the subordinate to deliver the goods. The boss remains unhappy and may not get the desired level of productivity in the usual course of activity. The boss may need to exert authority to compel his subordinate to perform the assigned task. Nothing appears to be achieved smoothly without application of stringent measures.

The subordinate may feel unhappy and discontented as management is averse to fulfilling his requirements. The expectation and aspiration as envisaged in subordinate's framework are not given importance. The subordinate perceives the boss as a 'stranger' who normally remains unconcerned and shows a casual approach to any issue relating to the well being of the people.

The subordinate may not have the impetus to regain his strength to deliver to the best of his ability. He experiences a situation which lacks a comfortable atmosphere to work/stay on.

The wide gap of objectives of the union/association from those of corporate objectives may create a situation of mistrust, suspicion and misunderstanding. The subordinate and the boss remain at loggerheads. Both have the feeling of 'I'm not ok, you are not ok' or 'I'm ok, you are not ok'. This feeling keeps them away from establishing healthy human relations. It may be that both the boss and the subordinate have adequate qualitative traits but they may not be effective in making complimentary transactions to develop interpersonal relations.

The reason may be the vast difference in each one's objectives and the boss and subordinate may not feel any urge to establish human relations through the interaction process.

From the above deliberations it becomes clear that the intra-organizational milieu (IOM) may adversely affect the building of healthy human relations between boss and subordinate. It also happens that the extra-organizational milieu (EOM) brings a phenomenal change in the attitudes of subordinate and boss which in some cases takes the place to play the role of deciding factor for the establishment of inter- personal relations.

Extra-Organizational Milieu(EOM)

The extra-organizational milieu arises out of the inter-functionaries approach in the societal system. An organization as a subsystem cannot evade the responsibilities impliedly bestowed for its smooth and effective running according to the needs, requirements and expectations of people, society, government and local bodies. It is, therefore, imperative to look at different perspectives and to take into account all possible relevant aspects to make wide coverage while formulating corporate objectives, policy guidelines and strategic plans of the organization for the prospective period. The following are the probable areas where most organizations may fail to give due importance and weightage due to heterogeneity and variability of problems, situations and conditions.

i. the needs, demands and expectations of the people, factors making people happy or unhappy, satisfied or dissatisfied.
ii. the family system—microscopic or macroscopic, the influence of the family-ties arising out of the family system over the individual's performance, expectations and desires.
iii. the societal system—its rigidity, conservatism or prejudice; enlightened and liberal society.
iv. the societal expectation, the influence of societal taboo on societal members.
v. the role of the society in the educational system, spread of literacy, improvement of living condition, upliftment/well being of the people.
vi. government policy, guidelines, objectives.
vii. government thinking, lines of action, approaches.
viii. the role of government in poverty alleviation, illiteracy eradication, growth and development of the people.
ix. the style and mode of functioning of the government, government strategy.
x. forms of government—autocratic, democratic, progressive, liberal, people-oriented, community-based.
xi. the role of local bodies in the process of growth and development of the people and the society as well.
xii. influence of the local bodies over the activities of the people.
xiii. approach of the trade unions to the development of the society.
xiv. trade unions objectives and relationship of trade unions with the government or governmental agencies.
xv. the role of the non-government organizations for the growth and development of the people, in poverty alleviation, in providing medical benefits, education.

If the above factors are appropriately taken into consideration while preparing organizational objectives, vision and long-term projection, a healthy, comfortable and congenial extra-organizational milieu may appear. Thus the three 'actors' namely, family, society and government (including local bodies) play a preponderant role to bring a change in the extra-organizational environment. If the extra-organizational milieu is positive for the growth and development of the organization, the intra-organizational milieu may appear to be positive in most cases. In such situations the boss with requisite qualitative traits may provide ample opportunities, scope and avenues to the subordinates to respond appropriately to the stimuli to make complimentary transactions with him. The subordinate with adequate qualitative traits may not lose such scope and offers and may utilize them fully to create a better state of mutual understanding through the interaction processes. The subordinate may provide positive stimuli to the boss and may respond to the stimuli offered by the boss to form complimentary transactions. The problem arises only when neither subordinate nor boss have the required positive qualities or both of them do not have the optimum qualitative traits to establish inter-personal relations. This situation may not appear to be prominent when the intra-organizational milieu and the extra-organizational milieu are conducive and congenial for effective functioning of the system activities. Milieu factors may exercise influence to bring about changes in the mental set up of the boss and the subordinate to react in the right directions.

The extra-organizational milieu has a greater role to play in changing the intra-organizational milieu. The favourable and comfortable extra-organizational environment encourages the corporate magnets to formulate organization policies, rules regulations, objectives and action plans for growth and development of the people at work and the organization as well. In the process a healthy and congenial intra-organizational environment develops. It happens that government policies, perceptions, long term and short term projects, role action and objectives affect the establishment of extra-organizational environments according to need and requirement, more than any other factor. A liberal, enlightened and progressive government outlook, approach, policy decisions and objectives may bring about a change in corporate policy guidelines, vision and action plans which may result in positive environment within the system activities. On the contrary, an autocratic and authoritarian approach, outlook and activities of the government not only pollutes the environment outside the organizations in its entirety, but also affects the corporate policy makers to frame organizational policy guidelines, objectives and goals which subsequently contaminate the intra-organizational environment.

In reality it occurs that corporate barons may feel insecure and uncomfortable to carry on organizational activities in a situation where an uncertain state of business climate prevails due to implementation of government policy guidelines, decisions, rules and regulations. To stay with the existing system of activities the organization magnets may frame their own policy, objectives and strategies within the ambit of the extra-organizational environment. It may however, be noteworthy to mention that all organization top hierarchies may not formulate their objectives, action plans, policy guidelines, etc., only keeping in view the situation in the extra-organizational milieu; they may look to the overall organizational perspectives as also their own identities in the sphere of welfare activities. Thus, an adverse extra-organizational environment may not greatly affect the health of the intra-organizational milieu particularly in such organizations where people oriented approach is undertaken as policy objective by the corporate policy makers.

However, in a situation where the extra-organizational milieu is congenial and conducive to the growth and development of organizations, progressive and ameliorative measures may be adopted by the corporate magnets in order to improve the overall conditions of the people at work. A change of attitudes of organization executives towards their subordinates may be noticed. They may perceive their subordinates as 'partners' or 'colleagues' instead of 'subordinates' or 'employees'. They may develop an impression that people are the source for the growth and development of the organizations. Hence with the growth of organizations, people's growth must be there. This area cannot be overlooked or neglected. The subordinates may feel comfortable and happy when they notice changes in the attitudes and behavioural activities of the boss. They may form their mindset afresh with up-to-date information and development. They may see a series of people oriented measures have been introduced by the corporate magnets. All these show a favourable climate existing in the system activities. The subordinates may try to come closer and closer to the boss and develop mutual ties and bonds of understanding and confidence. The boss, on the other hand may like to build up a good rapport with the subordinates and may provide all sorts of opportunities and avenues to the subordinates for establishing good human relations through the interaction process.

CHAPTER 8

Leadership Personalities: The Pre-requisites of Human Relations

From the preceding discussion it is revealed that the intra-organizational and extra-organizational milieu contribute much to mould the mindset of the bosses to manifest the desired level of behavioural activities. The human relations (here the boss-subordinate relations) pattern is decided, inter alia, by factors like thought processes and approaches of corporate management, government thinking and objectives, expectations of the society and the government, contribution of the government for upliftment and well-being of the masses and management directives to deal with issues. The human relations established through the influence of external forces may not have a long lasting effect. The pseudo human relations are likely to continue till the existing system remains active. But it is also noticed that the boss is not likely to surrender or compromise the inherent traits he owns on some ethical/vital aspects over which the whole self-concept is formed. Thus, manifestation of a different pattern of human relations established on the basis of the boss's own thought process, levels of ego patterns and temperamental set-up may not be ruled out. The boss under such circumstances may continue to express his behavioural reactions in his desired manner, either ignoring external directives or manipulating the situation appropriately so that he may not face any sort of difficulties for smooth manifestation.

Role Performance of Boss as a Human-Relations Maker

The boss is the main partner in the joint task of building human relations between him and his subordinate. The subordinate in such processes of interaction activities is only a facilitator to provide the required quantum of stimuli to the boss or to respond to stimuli given by the boss. The whole process is a give and take exercise emanating from perceived thought patterns and level of ego structure of both subordinate and boss. The success of such a joint venture depends mainly upon the maturity level of understanding the boss possesses towards his counterpart and also his intention to carry out complimentary transactions with his subordinate. The likes and dislikes of the boss, perception towards subordinate, expectation levels of the boss and the required standard of traits etc may sometime become the deciding factor in such a process of establishment of human relations. The boss may go ahead with his subordinate for developing understanding and trust on the basis of mutuality, if his mindset already permits the establishment of personal relations (human relations). This is solely an area of the boss to take the lead/initiative to start the process. The subordinate, on the other hand, watches the situation and remains in preparedness to follow the instructions of the boss and acts accordingly as soon as green signal is received. The subordinate acts/reacts positively and appropriately only when he feels that his boss desires and provides such activities. But it is not also a rare occurrence that the subordinate makes complimentary transactions all the time. It happens in some situations that subordinate does not comply with the advice of the boss in toto and reacts in the opposite direction even though the boss gives positive stimuli. Such kinds of subordinates may be few in numbers in the organization. It is a rather common phenomenon to tolerate the situational stress by the subordinate and to overcome the phase-risk through an appropriate response. Under such probability the subordinate obeys the instructions of the boss howsoever harsh they may be, like a good boy, and responds to the stimuli from a child ego, so as to continue with 'parent-child' transactions. A strained and compulsive human relation is established in this situation.

If the subordinate receives negative stimuli from his boss all through the inter-action phases he may not be able to show his tolerance spirit for a long. He may try to find some alternative avenue to switch over and on getting a chance, may get out of the existing system. To take such vital decisions he invariably calculates his losses or gains in terms of material substance as also mental comfort. In most cases where mental torture by the boss is extreme and the subordinate finds it difficult to sustain, he may change his organization or shift to alternative avenues even if his material benefit is much lesser than what he gets. In such situations the subordinate gives more importance to maintenance of mental health than on monetary benefit available.

When the subordinate fixes his mindset about leaving the organization, he generally does not express his anger, hatred or disregard towards his boss. He strives his best to maintain decorum and decency so long he remains with the boss; and he continues to form complementary transactions in the 'parent-child' relationship pattern. The subordinate in such a case may perhaps want the uninterrupted and smooth sailing of his exit plan and to achieve it he may keep himself aloof from any sort of confrontation with the boss or anybody in the staff or line authority. During such a period the subordinate may become unusually docile, sober and obedient and may try to remove the ill-feeling of the boss towards him through manifestation of behavioural activities. The success of such a manipulative task depends on how the boss develops his mindset/impressions about the subordinate as also the limiting factors which may expose the boss's weaknesses. The boss generally does not stand in the way of the going away of the subordinate from the organization if he is not mentally hurt through the activities of the subordinate. He may chalk out the action plan for proper replacement secretly from the day the subordinate hints at his plan for leaving the organization and may keep him away from the attachment of vital or sensitive portfolios. During the interval period the boss may change his attitudes and perceptions toward his subordinate and may show his sympathy, liberal outlook and positive approach in his style of functioning. He may outwardly show his willingness to come close to the subordinate and to establish better human relations in order to gain popularity as a people-oriented person. But in reality it transpires that a negative-minded personality cannot suppress his qualitative-traits as they come out automatically through personal interaction.

The boss is like the 'karta' (head) of the family who instructs the members to move in a specific direction as per his desire. The 'karta' imposes his authoritative power or gives his spontaneous support to perform the assigned task. The attitude, behaviour, way of treatment, mode of expression and style of functioning of the 'karta' indicate what sort of personality he holds. This also evinces the ego pattern and self-concept of the 'karta' which expresses his desire, likes, dislikes, expectations, strengths, weaknesses and qualitative traits as a total man. The family members usually study the mindset of the 'karta' and act/react accordingly in order to achieve a common goal set on common terms and understanding. This way the family may run smoothly and without interruption and may develop harmonious relations amongst all the members of the team. But the smooth running of the family may not last for long if the attitude of the 'karta' is not acceptable (which results from negative attitude) to the members of the family. Under such situations the family members give their utmost efforts to reconcile and create a state of pseudo-harmonious relations. This state of family environment may not continue for an indefinite period; it may collapse at any point of time even on a trifling issue when the tolerance level (under compulsion) by the family members reaches its saturation mark. But in the process of interaction 'karta' may realize his evil deeds/activities. He may, therefore, mould his ego pattern to form a modified mindset and may behave in a positive way to reflect his justified, reasonable and judicious actions taken in the broader interest of the members and the family as well. Such activities on the part of the 'karta' may activate members to establish a unified team to carry on the assigned task as per his direction. The reformed activities of the 'karta' may develop a sense of belonging, a feeling of concern and togetherness and also a 'we-feeling'. The members may accept the job as their own and perform it with seriousness, sincerity and commitment. They do not blame the 'karta' if they cannot achieve, rather they own the responsibility and ask for any sort of punishment. Thus a state of congruent personal relations prevails in the family and complimentary transactions occur all through the interactive process. The family members remain complacent and express their feeling like 'I'm OK, you're OK. The family, therefore, runs in the desired direction. But the family may not run smoothly if some family member happens to be the 'spoiled child'. Tackling of such a member is a hard task as it requires an appropriate psychological boost as well as compensatory behavioural treatment of the 'karta'. The activities of the 'spoiled-child' may affect the carrying out of the assigned task. The relationship between such family members and the 'karta' may become strenuous and uncomfortable. The possibilities of forming cross transactions may not therefore be ruled out.

In an organizational set-up the boss is the prime person to inculcate ethical values, work culture, discipline, essence of loyalty and obedience into the minds of the subordinates. He may get immediate results if he becomes successful as a role performer in the capacity of subordinate. It happens that in the process of discharging the assigned task and responsibilities, the boss may develop a sense of concern and propriety. He expects that the subordinates who work under him should have similar thought patterns and should own the quality of role performances. If the subordinate notices that the boss possesses the intrinsic qualitative traits of leadership he may accept him as his guide, model role-accomplisher and path-pointer. He may soon become the follower of his boss and may act/react according to the need, requirement and desire of the boss. The subordinate subsequently may come close to the boss and develop a sense of understanding and togetherness through the exchange process of giving stimuli and responding to stimuli or vice-versa. This interaction exercise makes a lot of complimentary transactions which indicate the existence of a comfortable state of relationship between boss and subordinate. Both subordinate and boss may develop a feeling of happiness which may emerge out of their life positions like 'I' m OK, you are OK'. This state of life position continues till the period interactions form complimentary transactions. But a change in such exchange processes may occur when a rift in the under-standing-base surfaces. The subordinate, after such an incident, may become cautious and alert and he responds to the stimuli or supplies stimuli in a calculated manner. The subordinate loses his faith, trust and confidence in his boss and re-thinks the situations/circumstances before he makes any vital deal. He erases the portion of the suspected activities of his boss out of his mind after he has confirmed from different sources the role activities of his boss and frames the mindset anew with a modified perceptible impression.

In such a situation when the subordinate starts thinking about the unclear activities of the boss, the following behavioural manifestations may appear in the process of interaction:

i. The subordinate may try to keep himself aloof from his boss to the extent possible and may restrict his personal visit/appearance to his boss.
ii. The subordinate may not disclose the secret information collected from private sources to his boss on the apprehension of getting leaked by him.
iii. He may play a dubious role while discharging the task assigned by the boss.
iv. He may take active part in the 'peer-group' or 'subgroup' activities in order to safeguard his interests.
v. He may develop a fear-psychosis and may consider his boss as a 'punishment imposer' and not a 'well-wisher'.
vi. He may feel that a climate of mistrust and misunderstanding prevails in the organization.
vii. The subordinate may not respond to the stimuli in the direction desired by the boss all the time. He may sometimes indicate to his boss the probable effect of such responses and may give hints about his intention to be initiated in the next course of action.
viii. When the subordinate receives any instructions/directives from his boss, he immediately analyses the inherent cause/purposes of the advice, the intention behind it and the motives of the boss. After thorough perusal and looking at different perspectives the subordinate reacts. The frequency of occasions to come closer to the boss may become less. The chance of developing personal relations may appear to be remote.
ix. The subordinate may form complimentary transactions on the basis of selectivity.
x. The subordinate may experience a bitter feeling of staying with the situation. He may feel the whole gamut of the working environment as unbearable, intolerable and unwarranted.
xi. The subordinate, through role performance, may express his indifference, apathetic and silent activities and may keep himself away from group participation.
xii. The subordinate may make his boss understand that if he does not support his misdeeds/manipulative activities spontaneously and in appropriate time, he may stand in the way to manifest further activities.
xiii. The subordinate may remain under stress and in an uncertain state which may affect his functioning and establishment

of mutual understanding. The subordinate feels that 'employer-employee' relations/'man-management' relations are transformed to 'master-servant' relations where there is no substance of personal touch, human dealing, positive feeling and empathetic approach. The boss remains busy in his career-building avenues and to achieve his goal he undertakes short-term courses of activities for implementation without looking to the need, difficulties, desires and expectations of the subordinates. He does not even feel the need to assess the possibilities of completion of the assigned task with the existing input/infrastructure available. He commands his people to deliver the service in a time frame and creates a noisy and unhealthy scene if the task is not accomplished.

Thus it become apparent that misunderstandings between the boss and the subordinate develop from inter-personal activities. The subordinate may not react appropriately according to the desire of the boss. He may rather react in the opposite direction. Such situations may appear only when the subordinate becomes unhappy and hurt with the behavioural activities of the boss which may be envisaged through the mode and style of his functioning, the kind of leadership approach held and the thought processes conceived for working in some direction. It is noticed that initially most subordinates tolerate the atrocious activities of the boss and they give him sufficient time, scope and opportunities to adjust with the culture, environment and locational situation. The subordinates continue to provide positive stimuli to the boss or respond to the stimuli given by the boss in the desired direction for as long as they consider adequate for the boss to understand the whole perspective. If after such a gestation period, the boss does not evince comfortable behavioural activities, subordinates develop a feeling of insecurity and uneasiness which may result in loss of confidence in the boss. The subordinates may manifest incompatible behaviour and may form as many cross transactions as possible. The inter-personal relations become bitter and harsh. There develops all-round confusion, misunderstanding and mistrust between the boss and subordinates that may stand in the way of smooth functioning in organizational activities. But it may be remembered that not all bosses behave in such a manner. Some bosses are highly positive in their style of functioning and give emphasis on human aspects in order to establish harmonious relations.

Now from the foregoing some questions may arise:

1. Why can the boss not predict the situational climate in the organization to adjust to people at work with his own thought processes, mindset and perceptions in order to achieve the organizational objectives?
2. Why does the boss behave differently with the subordinate in a situation when he gets full cooperation and support to accomplish the assigned job?
3. Why can the boss not develop better human relations with the subordinates?

The answer lies with the ego structure of the boss who prepares his mindset to behave in a particular manner. Ego-patterns set the norms of a person's behavioural activities to carry out his own style of functioning, approach and mode of dealing with people. The boss's leadership traits are greatly influenced by his ego-state. He behaves with his subordinates, develops inter-personal relations, makes transactions as per requirements of the particular kind of leadership style which he possesses. Hence, the establishment of harmonious relations largely depends upon the type of leadership the boss holds. To have a through acquaintances of human relations it becomes essential to discuss the different kinds of leaders generally found in the organizational activities.

Types of Leader

Classification of leaders has been made considering the behavioural activities, dispositional set-up, perceptible effect manifested by the leaders through the inter-active processes while discharging day-to-day activities. They are:

i. Autocratic, whimsical, desperate leader.
ii. Supportive, participative, open leader.
iii. 'So-So' leader.
iv. Surrendering, succumbing, unprincipled leader.

Autocratic, Whimsical, Desperate Leader

This type of leader may not be rare in the organizational set-up. The boss possessing such leadership trait holds the life position 'I am OK, you are not OK'. He considers himself a super-person knowing everything better than anybody in his rank, below or above his rank. Some of his perceptions about subordinates that are manifested through behavioural actions are mentioned below:

1. Subordinates are good for nothing. They do not want to work, nor do they have the ability to deliver quality work.
2. Subordinates are not serious or sincere in their work. They take everything in a casual manner.
3. Subordinates can be made active by keeping them under pressure all the time.
4. They can be put under constant supervision to perform the assigned task.
5. They are non-performers and do not bother about their responsibilities.
6. The only way to make them work is to exercise punitive measures. Resorting to disciplinary action or creating an atmosphere of hire and fire may bring some attitudinal change in the subordinates towards their duties and responsibilities.
7. Subordinates need negative stroking. Even for a trifling mistake they should not be allowed to go free. Action is a must for each and every misdeed.
8. They cannot be shown any leniency in their approach of tackling any problem as it may result in developing an impression in their minds about the strength and weaknesses of the boss.
9. They do not need human treatment as such treatment may make them lazier and more indolent.
10. They are a wasteful lot, and very few amongst them are effective.
11. They have no spontaneous aspirations or demands for a better career path. They want to remain in the same level/strata so long they are in service. They do not mind or do not feel uneasiness whey they receive commands from the boss who is much junior in age and experience.
12. They have no concern about the progress and prosperity of the organization. They come to the office to pass time and get their salary.
13. Barring a few, most subordinates are more rights conscious than duty conscious. They consider themselves as the most

privileged class to avail of the benefits/facilities without shouldering any responsibilities.

The boss develops a self-concept considering his traits, capabilities, style of functioning, grasping power and method of tackling situational problems as excellent. He never takes into account the shortcomings and weaknesses he possesses while framing his mindset. He develops his own feeling, emotion, sentiments and disposition which results in behavioural action. Some of his salient behavioural manifestations are discussed below in order to understand him thoroughly from leadership perspectives:

1. He may hold the impression that there is nobody to challenge his action. He may, therefore, do as he likes. In some cases, he may become so desperate in his activities that he ignores the instructions of his higher authority and sticks to his action.
2. He is not a people-oriented person. He is basically a person having no sympathy and no cooperative attitude towards the people at work.
3. He may show his speed in his activities to create awareness amongst the people around him about the need and necessity of speedy disposal of the cases and also to develop a sense of fear-psychosis amongst the slow and inactive people. It may also happen that outwardly the boss expresses his speed, but in reality he is not so. It is just to create a good image amongst his people.
4. He does not like people nor does he help them at times of need and requirement. But in order to create a better image and impression in the minds of the people, he shows his philanthropic and humanitarian approach extending the benefit/facilities to some persons in unusual ways.
5. He may openly criticize his subordinates and blames them for minor mistakes in the presence of others.
6. He does not consider his subordinates human beings. He does not look to their difficulties or their needs for the performance of their task. On some occasions they are even instructed to do such jobs which are impossible to perform considering infra-structure, time factor and availability of sources.
7. He does not give proper weightage and importance to the

excellent service given by his subordinates. But in case of some subordinates who are average performers but are otherwise close to him, it may be noticed that he is very liberal with them. He issues appreciation letters and expresses his commendable satisfaction over their performance openly in meetings.

8. He is unreasonable, irrational and biased in his decision-making. As he possesses some unverified, unauthenticated impressions about the people around him, he gives his opinions or comments upon the performance of the people on the basis of information available in his data bank.
9. He is very conservative in his outlook and develops his thought patterns accordingly. He does not go according to the demands of the organization in the overall changing scenario.
10. He does not feel to analyse or ascertain the consequences of any decision he takes. He thinks that he is thorough in his area of activities and so his decision is perfect.
11. In general the boss in such an echelon is loyal and obedient to his superior and disciplined. He does not do such sort of activities which displease his boss.
12. He wants his subordinates to flatter and praise him for each and every activity and that they should remain at his disposal.
13. He may have a strong desire to show his importance, power and authority to his subordinates. He may enjoy it when he dresses down his subordinates even in some cases for no fault of theirs.
14. He does not think to derive any material gain from building good rapport and understanding with subordinates. He, therefore, does not come close to his subordinates nor does he allow his subordinates to be close to him.
15. He is moody, arrogant and aggressive in his dealings with people. He is unpredictable and the subordinate may find it difficult to study his mindset.
16. He is never happy with his subordinates nor is he happy with the services his subordinates deliver.
17. He does not believe in the 'team-building' concept for the achievement of group objectives. Rather he wants to fix responsibilities to individuals and to monitor their working through close supervision, threats and strict discipline.

18. He is not acceptable to his subordinates nor are his subordinates acceptable to him. Subordinates pay respect and regard to him under compulsion as a ritualistic measure, not in a natural and spontaneous way. Hence, the relationship as it appears between boss and subordinates is that of a master-servant relationship.
19. He likes to punish the subordinates and gets pleasure when he dismisses his subordinates even for a minor misdeed.
20. He develops set norms to tackle situational problems. He uses devices like coercion, intimidation and fear-psychosis to achieve his goal. These devices give the signal to his subordinates that they should either deliver the goods or quit the organization as there is no other way in between.
21. He does not come forward to help when his subordinates pass through difficult situations and considers them as a helpless lot. This may result in developing a feeling of hatred and bitterness amongst the subordinates towards their boss.
22. In order to satiate inherent desire he may form a 'coterie' with some subordinates to collect information concerning the latest developments, the thought process of other subordinates, their activities and their perceptions about him. The boss may in the process bestow unwritten power to the 'coterie' members who give a better image of the boss to the subordinates and try to make an attitudinal change towards the boss.

This type of leadership, based on autocratic, whimsical and desperate qualitative traits, may bring changes in the organizational milieu through the interactive processes. The leader may be successful in achieving his goal within a short span of time, but continuous use of this therapeutic leadership style as a tool for achievement may not be effective in the long run. Such leadership processes may not show any results even for a short period, particularly in a situation when a new leader takes over the charge from a person having a similar level of leadership traits. The main reason for the failure of this type of leadership for a long period are discussed herein below:-

1. The main factor of production/service in any organization is people who deliver the goods to the satisfaction of others as

per the directives of the leader only when they get better treatment from the boss. If the leader ignores people and does not consider them human beings, people at work may not respond appropriately as per the desire of the boss. Initially during the observation period (that is the 'cushion' period given to the boss for adjustment with the new work climate/culture), subordinates comply with the instructions of the boss without looking to the nature and type of instructions and they make complimentary transactions in order to develop harmonious human relations. But they may not continue with the same helping mindset/behavioural pattern, after the 'gestation period'/'cushion period' is over.

2. The subordinates expect justice, equity and reasonableness from the boss while dealing with the problems. They develop a feeling of aloofness when the boss settles issues in a biased and whimsical manner. Repetitive application of such a mindset by the boss in the decision-making process may bring a compulsive state of non-compliance which may result in cross transactions after a certain period of time.
3. The subordinates want that the boss should accept them as members of the team, should take them into confidence and should consult them before he takes decisions pertaining to them. This they feel may develop a sense of 'we-feeling', cohesiveness and togetherness amongst them which may facilitate the establishment of cordial understanding and mutual ties on solid foundation. But the absence of initiative on the part of the boss or the apathetic attitude of the boss may create ill-feeling, bitterness and insecurity in the minds of the subordinates. The subordinates dislike their boss and at the opportune time they manifest their aggression against the boss through non-observance of rules, non-compliance of instructions and expressions of disregard.
4. Stroking is a psychological impetus needed to motivate the people for the growth and development of the 'selves' and the organization as well. Every human being needs strokes, particularly positive strokes for a job well done.

   Likewise, the subordinates aspire for positive stroke from their boss for their excellent performance. Positive stroking given to the right person for right performance at the right point of time may bring a change in the attitude of the 'positive-stroke taker' which may result in increase in production, productivity and quality as also an improved state of human relations pattern.

The subordinates develop good rapport, understanding and confidence when they receive positive strokes as a token of recognition for their excellent performance. This situation leads to complementary transactions in the interactive process. But non-accordance of positive strokes by the boss for outstanding performance of the subordinates not only demotivates them to excel in their performance but also forms biased, selfish subordinates and those who hate the boss. Such a situation tends to form a life position of the subordinate 'I am not OK, you are not OK' or 'I am not OK, you are OK.' Hence dealing with the boss may take a crucial turn to make 'crossed transactions' all the time. The subordinates may not find a congenial atmosphere to work with the boss comfortably. A state of cold relationship between the subordinates and the boss may appear to be prevalent in the organizational climate which, if it continues for long, may have a perilous effect on the effective functioning of the system.

5. The subordinates may notice a situation where much importance is given to the affiliation/link made to the boss by the people at work who seem to be close more because of their belonging to the 'coterie' group than because of their performance. These people in the 'coterie' group are nurtured for specific purposes by the boss and their image is placed before the higher-ups in such manner that they are the only people who deliver the goods and they are very indispensable for the effective functioning of the organizational activities. The boss is exposed to the system for his biased motivated, ill-designed frame of work through such people in the group who excel more in feeding information to the boss than in performing the assigned/allotted task. The hobnobbing of the boss with the people in the 'coterie' group, who are basically non-performers, creates a negative perception about the boss in the minds of almost all the subordinates. In such situations the subordinates may experience their workplace as uncomfortable and suffocating and they want to get rid of

this state and climate of organization. Prolongation of such a work milieu may badly affect the quality of service, productivity and production. The image and stature of the organization may appear to be at stake if timely corrective measures are not taken.

6. The boss wants immediate delivery of the goods from his subordinates without giving due regard to the need, necessities, infrastructure and other requirements of the subordinates for performing in a time frame of schedule. It may happen that some of the subordinates despite their honest and sincere effort may not achieve their target. The main reason for non-achievement of goals is the non-supply/non-providing of infrastructure/support to the subordinates. When the subordinates draw the attention of the boss to provide the necessary support in order to complete the assigned task in scheduled time with perfection, the boss either remains mum or expresses his apathetic attitude towards their requirement. But, at the same time when the boss comes to know that some subordinates lag behind the target and are not capable of reaching the goal, he immediately jumps upon them and shows his utmost displeasure for non-performance. In some cases the boss starts groundwork and prepares records to initiate appropriate measures against the subordinates for non-achievement of targets. The boss may go to the extreme level of taking disciplinary action against the non-performing subordinates as he believes in the 'hire and fire' philosophy.

The subordinates may feel the situation as very cumbersome as on the one hand they are not given required support for effective functioning and on the other hand they become the victims of non-performance. The attitudes, behaviour and activities of the boss make the subordinates unhappy and the subordinates wait for the opportune time to express their grievances. They develop a feeling of oppression, anger, retaliation and intend to remain away from the organizational climate. However, such a situation cannot run for a long period without remedial measures.

The foregoing discussion depicts the perceptions and behavioural manifestations of the leader towards his subordinates. Such a leader whose adult ego suffers from the contamination of the critical parent is exclusively an autocratic, a whimsical and desperate type of leader based on the philosophy of Mc Gregor's Theory X. He is a workaholic person and does not compromise on work with any of his subordinates barring a few ones who happen to be the persons of his own group. He normally as a matter of principle as also for his existing unbalanced ego pattern does not want to be close to his subordinates nor does he allow subordinates to come close to him in order to establish a congenial and happy state of human relations. He considers subordinates as subordinates only, not anything more than they are in the cadre. He does not feel the necessity of affording any amount of human touch to their issues or problems. Hence in reality the relationship in whatever form emanates is that of master-servant relationship, though outwardly the leader may manifest his activities as that of a liberal leader through his exposure to some calculated benevolent act in order to create an image as role performer.

The above type of leader may bring an unhealthy state of organizational climate after his consecutive successes as this leadership style cannot work effectively for a long period in any organizational set-up except the system activity where by virtue of its structural pattern and objectives superior command cannot be questioned.

Supportive, Participative, Open Leader

This type of leader is more or less opposite to the autocratic type of leader as discussed above, with regard to the style of functioning, behavioural activities, leadership approach and objectives. He is very cooperative, accommodating and helpful to the subordinates. He considers his subordinates as his own men belonging to the same family. His perceptions, thought-process and mindset about subordinates are briefly discussed hereunder:

1. The subordinates are the source of his power, authority, stature and image. They are part and parcel of the system activity as their absence brings a halt in the running of the activity and team objectives vis-à-vis organizational objectives cannot be achieved without their participation.
2. They are a useful lot and an important organ of the system. They are very effective, sincere and serious to their

assignments. They are committed to the institution, devoted to their duties and loyal to the boss.

3. They have needs, aspirations and expectations and they want to go up in the ladder. To satiate their needs they work hard. They want to shoulder higher responsibilities and they want to lead and not to be led all through.
4. They are human beings. They deserve human treatment from the boss.
5. They expect that their problems are reasonably and judiciously sorted out with human touch.
6. They attach topmost importance to the progress and prosperity of the organization to which they belong in the process of discharging their duties. They think that their existence depends upon the existence of the organization. If the organization grows, they grow; if the organization dies, they die. They give their best effort to show results.
7. They have a desire for positive strokes for the job well done by them. They want that recognition of excellent performance be given publicly and immediately after the performance is done. This works as an effective tool to motivate the working lot to further their activities.
8. They are sensible people. They can understand the situation. They can study the behavioural pattern of the boss. They cannot tolerate unusual situations created intentionally by the boss in order to put them into a trap. They want free and frank discussion.
9. They do not like the constant and close supervision of the superior. They want freedom to discharge of their duties as they think they are capable of performing the assigned task independently.
10. They do not remain happy just by fulfilling their bio-physiological needs. They want something else like power, respect, recognition, authority, status and good treatment by higher authorities as blue-eyed persons. Thus their happiness depends on the level of satisfaction they get towards non-bio-physiological needs.
11. They are sentimental, emotional and moody in their dispositional orbit. Tackling their issues requires application of mind, justice and thorough overhauling of the situation. During the course of interaction, it may be essential to notice that in no way should their sentiment be hurt.

12. They are in general peace-lovers, obedient, disciplined and believers in the philosophy 'work and let others work'. They develop concepts that rights and authority come through diligence and discipline.

The supportive/participative leader establishes a set of norms about his subordinates to prepare his overall thought processes and mind frame and subsequently manifests his behavioural activities during the inter-active process. Such a leader has his own style of functioning, mode of administration and method of tackling situations and all these he acquires through the qualitative traits he possesses. Some salient behavioural manifestations of the participative leader are briefly discussed in order to know his mindset, his perception about his subordinates and his own emotional set-up and activities:

1. The leader is co-operative, open, free, frank and helpful to the subordinates. He does not mind taking pain for the benefit of others.
2. He works in a team and gives full support and freedom to the team members to express their views and give their suggestions without fear or favour. For any mistake made by any team member unintentionally, he does not make the team member responsible; the team leader himself owns the responsibility.
3. He believes in the philosophy of 'openness, participation, motivation and solutions through discussion/negotiation'. He never undermines the capacity, potentiality and efficacy of the subordinates. Rather he keeps high hope in his subordinates.
4. He never goes into confrontation with his team members on any issue without having a threadbare discussion with them. He likes to settle issues through a participative process.
5. He wants his people to come close to him and to develop human relations/personal relations and this is possible only when mutual understanding, mutual trust and confidence are established. He thinks that sound human relations create a healthy climate of industrial relations which facilitate to increase the productivity, profit and profitability of the organization.
6. He develops a family culture in the organization through his interactive process and creates a sense of 'we-feeling'

'togetherness' and 'belonging'. In such an organizational climate subordinates treat their boss as their own family head and they place their demands, requirements, wants, problems and grievances before him with the expectation that the principles of equity, justice and rationality will be adhered to while solving the issues. The subordinates accept the verdict of the leader spontaneously as they are certain that the decision of their boss can never be wrong and unfair. Such a situation appears due to the application of a selfless, people oriented approach by the boss.

7. He has no biased feelings or hatred towards any subordinate. He does not give special favours/treatment to anybody which might tend to indicate his activities towards nepotism, favouritism and opportunism.
8. He is not vindictive and harmful to his people at work. During the course of discharging duties if any 'spoiled child' (erring subordinate in the team) shows his disregard to the boss and does not comply with the instructions, the boss makes an honest effort to bring him in line with the other obedient lot. He does not initially think to use negative devices to set him right. He applies psychological techniques to ascertain the real cause of maladies and thereafter through the inter-active processes in a congenial climate he tries to form complimentary transactions. When all possible means fail to correct his behavioural activities the boss may go for negative action.
9. The boss possesses the life position 'I am OK, you are OK'. He keeps himself in a happy and jolly mood and seldom shows bitterness in talking or an aggressive attitude to his subordinates. Rather he calls his subordinates to sort out problems in a conducive atmosphere through discussions in a team spirit.
10. He thinks that the organization is not his own property; it is a joint venture with equal share of each and every individual in the family. Hence, the subordinates should be included in the decision-making process and their suggestions should be given due weightage.
11. The boss does not believe in the 'authoritarian approach' based on the 'carrot and stick' philosophy. He considers the people as sensible human beings who have high aspirations and expectations to go up in the hierarchy. They want to

satisfy their psychological needs in a systematic and well-designed framework. They may not tolerate the autocratic behaviour of the superior for a long period. They are outstanding performers of the assigned tasks.

12. He is fast in decision-making and wants to complete the task immediately. He analyses the situation, discusses the matter with team members, studies the pros and cons and thereafter comes to conclusions. He provides material and moral support to the team members and gives adequate infrastructure to complete the job in scheduled time.
13. He is basically a people cum task-oriented leader. He gives positive strokes for excellent performance. He does not mind providing extra benefits/concessions to his subordinates who are outstanding performers, violating laid down norms as a special case without precedent in future. For this if he needs to place the matter before higher management for approval he does so in a convincing way, narrating circumstantial factors which necessitate the granting of such concession/relaxation to them.
14. He is a great motivator to making attitudinal change in the subordinates. He creates a clean image in the minds of subordinates about his unblemished and honest records through manifestation of his model role activities. The subordinates accept his leadership traits in a situation when they observe his positive qualities beneficial to their interests and consider him as leader of the team.
15. Initially he does not take such decisions which throw any subordinate away from the organization resulting in putting him under an intolerable situation. As a motivating leader he does not believe in the 'hire and fire' philosophy. In an extreme situation when no extenuating factor is available, he may have no other alternative but to resort to such drastic measure as removing the subordinate from the present assignment. This too, he does it in the greater interest of the institution and the subordinates as well.
16. He does not use any such language during the course of interaction which may hurt any body belonging to some caste, creed, religion and community. He holds frank discussions with his subordinates but does not use slang words while discussing. He always maintains official decorum in his behaviour and action. This creates a

decent behavioural culture in the organization which not only increases the moral value of the subordinates but also makes the subordinates more disciplined.

17. He is well accepted by the people at work for his temperament, disposition, behavioural activities and style of functioning. His subordinates pay respect, show their positive attitude and sincere effort to achieve team targets and express loyalty to the leader and the institution as well. The boss accepts his subordinates as his own men and develops healthy human relations with them. He makes complementary transactions through the interaction processes.
18. He is a believer in the 'human approach'. He thinks that when an individual is in trouble or faces problems 'human treatment'/'personal touch' may bring relief in his mental state. He may feel relaxed and he may have sufficient time and scope to think over his problems for solutions. In this way, the boss may solve the problems of his subordinates through his personal touch therapy. The boss feels that human treatment should be considered as the main tool for solving subordinates' problems; it may bring confidence and trust amongst subordinates and they may express their whole-hearted support, cooperation and assistance to their boss. The subordinates may consider their boss as their own man. They may feel the organizational climate as very comfortable and conducive to work. This may bring both subordinate and boss close to each other and provides ample opportunities to establish mutual understanding, mutual ties and faith.

From the above deliberation it becomes clear that such a leader is a model role performer through manifestation of his behavioural activities. Unlike the autocratic leader, he does not believe in the philosophy of achieving goals through a creation of a state of fear psychosis amongst the subordinates. He thinks that all time achievement is possible only when team members are made to understand that their problems and grievances are given top priority for solution and that their boss is a leader for the well-being of the people at work and also for task performance. He has the perception that negative discipline may bring short term results in a conditioned situation and in a specific activity. But a long lasting result will come through positive discipline and human treatment which the leader believes is exercised by a 'people oriented cum task performance' approach.

The supportive, participative and open leader brings a lot of change in the organizational work climate through the process of his functioning and performance. Some of the vital changes are mentioned below:

1. Changes in thought patterns, attitudes and behaviour of the people at work in the organization are observed. People do not stand in the way of introducing a new techniques, devices and methods in the system for achieving greater productivity, profitability, production and also for sustaining their position against the stiff competition in the market.
2. A state of happiness, comfort, a homely environment and a climate free from fear, threat and intimidation amongst the team members may become prevalent in the organization.
3. Mutual ties, understanding and adjustment are established between the people of different strata. Everybody enjoys the feeling of 'joint venture', 'team effort' and 'collective assignment'. The people at work develop a sense of belonging, 'we-feeling' and togetherness. This situation subsequently tends to establish congenial human relations between subordinate and boss and also healthy interpersonal relations between subordinates and superiors.
4. The industrial relations climate appears to be very conducive for joint consultation/negotiations on all issues including problematic issues. Such environment helps all sections of people to discharge their assigned task and to achieve goals set by the superiors. This makes for all round development and growth of the organization in the systematic manner.
5. A remarkable change in the working pattern may be noticed. The subordinates take extra-initiatives to complete the assigned tasks. In case of need, they may get peer-support and assistance to perform their function. The services of the colleagues and line personnel are readily available. Though each person has an allotted task, nobody has any difficulty completing the job in a time frame schedule. Others volunteer to extend services in emergent situations.

6. People in the organization may experience a tension-free environment as no encroachment in the functional jurisdiction is made by the boss normally. The boss gives liberty to the subordinates to tackle the situation by themselves within the laid down norms. He provides moral support and necessary infrastructure to complete the job.
7. The subordinates may feel a sensitive charm to work under the supportive leader who inspires and motivates them to accept higher responsibilities. The boss may help the subordinates to reframe their mindsets through his behavioural actions and manifestation. He creates a change in the mental set-up of the subordinates which subsequently leads them towards alienation to a changed pattern of mental disposition.
8. The boss gives cognisance to the higher value of ethical activities through his actions and style of functioning. The subordinates feel satisfied with their role performance. They succeed to achieve their target and win over the situation. They feel praised and proud of being the members of the team. All these boost up their morale which tends to increase productivity, production and profitability.

So-so/Indifferent Leader

In the foregoing deliberation behavioural manifestations of two types of leaders (autocratic and participative) with opposite mindsets were discussed in order to assess their role performance towards establishment of human relations between boss and subordinates. The above categories of leaders fall in the extremes of the pole, one is for no concern of the subordinates and other is for high concern of the subordinates. Apart from such two types of leaders another kind of leadership personality may be noticed in the organization whose perception, mindset, ego pattern and self-concept are not the same as those of the leaders mentioned earlier. This leader is a 'so-so' or indifferent leader with no sincere and honest effort to make headway in his area of action. He has a mixed perception about subordinates. Some of the perceptible areas about his subordinates are discussed below in order to have a broad idea about his feeling, emotion, thinking and attitudes towards the subordinates:

1. He thinks subordinates are average people and most of them want to stay with the existing system without disturbing the structure, pattern and activities. But, if the situation warrants a change in the system of activity for their survival, subordinates do not hesitate to go for a change.
2. Subordinates as people are basically good. In normal circumstances they do not like to create any situation which may put the boss in awkward position. They are loyal, obedient and follow the instructions of the leader without hesitation.
3. The subordinates usually do routine work and do not take extra initiatives to complete the assigned task. But it is not rare that subordinates give whole-hearted support, cooperation and commitment to achieve the team target.
4. The boss perceives that the subordinates have inner feeling, emotions and desires to shoulder higher responsibilities. But they generally do not expose their need or aspirations before the boss/superiors probably thinking that their expectations/demands may not be given due weightage, importance and cognisance.
5. The boss feels that the subordinates need motivation to bring them on the right track for higher performance. It may create an environment of self-involvement in the process of team performance.
6. He thinks that the subordinates do not like close supervision or a continuous and persistent watch on their job by the superior. They want the liberty to perform their job under the guidance of the boss. Some subordinates may not like excessive interference by the boss in the area of their operation as they feel competent to complete the assigned task.
7. Most subordinates are 'yes man' who promptly respond to the situational action of the boss in the desired manner. They do not see the pros and cons of their reactions.
8. The subordinates in general do not have stress tolerance. They are easily amenable. They cannot stand for a long in odd situations and they surrender after one or two jolts they receive for their actions.
9. Barring a few, most subordinates are more conscious about benefits, privileges, rights and concessions than their responsibilities and duties. They want to remain within the boundary of their area of performance.

This type of leader may own some qualitative traits which are noticeable during the process of interactions with the people at work. The leader may have some characteristic qualities which other types of leaders may not possess thereby creating a distinct separate entity from that of the other type of leader. Some of the salient qualitative traits of a so-so/ indifferent leader are discussed below in order to have a broad idea of their mindset, emotion, feeling, thought patterns, attitude and state of mental disposition and temperament.

1. The leader may not be energetic or dynamic in the area of his functioning. He does not take extra initiative for the achievement of his goal.
2. On most occasions he remains busy with stereotyped activities. He does not intend to make a change in his role-behaviour.
3. He feels contented with the existing system and is averse to change in the methods, procedure and practice.
4. He is calm, cool and sober in disposition. He does not like to be involved in office politics. He wants to complete his tenure without disturbing the existing system.
5. He is an opportunist and likes to enjoy the benefit of a congenial state of situation. He hardly takes the risk of creating a new environment to develop a better work-culture. He keeps himself away from the situation where the possibility of assigning him a sensitive job role exists.
6. He is neither a believer of the 'employee-oriented' concept nor a believer of the 'job-oriented' philosophy. He does not apply a particular concept all through his role activities. He is not consistent in his approach.
7. He lacks the skill, expertise and tact to motivate the people at work. In some cases he appreciates his subordinates for excellent performance while in other cases, he remains silent. He is haphazard in his method of tackling.
8. He is not keen to develop rapport with subordinates. If in the normal process of work personal relation are established, he may not discourage the subordinates. He does not take any initiative to develop mutual understanding, ties and confidence with his subordinates.
9. He is indifferent towards his subordinates. He has no clear perception about the people at work. He generally does not apply his analytical skill and ability to reach to a

solution for the problems placed by his subordinates. He takes the matter casually and sorts it out through the 'patch-up' process to ease the problem temporarily.

10. He is not straightforward in his activities. He is not liberal, enlightened and positive in his approach. Neither is he harsh or vindictive towards his subordinates.
11. He does not believe in 'hire and fire'. He does not like to give capital punishment to his subordinates for any sort of misdeed. He intends to avoid taking disciplinary action against his subordinates.
12. He lacks administrative traits and the ability to impose discipline amongst the subordinates. He himself fails to strictly adhere to the norms of discipline
13. He does not give weightage to the human concept while he deals with personnel problems. He lays no special emphasis on human considerations in the decision making process. He takes decisions within the framework of norms and rules. He strictly goes by laid down policies and regulations without looking to the merit, rationality, natural justice and situation of the case.
14. He has no required trait and skill to motivate his subordinates for achievement of goals. He is not successful as a team leader for the accomplishment of team tasks.
15. He may have a life position 'I am not OK, you are not OK', or I am not OK, you are OK'. Such a boss may feel unhappiness as he thinks of himself not very effective in the area of his jurisdiction. He considers himself a man with mediocre traits and may not find any outstanding ingredients in himself to make him a dynamic leader for excellent performance. He may develop a mixed perception about his subordinates. Sometimes he feels that his subordinates have a happy state of life, but on some other occasions, he may not see any bright state of life position of his subordinates. This sort of feeling may emerge out of his unsuccessful activities and non-satiation of desired aspirations.
16. He is timid, cowardly and passive in his activities. He is not a courageous enthusiastic person to give the lead to people to achieve the organization goals. He has no confidence in his activities and most of the time he depends on his subordinates for completion of the assigned tasks. He cannot take decisions on any matter

without consulting his subordinates. It is not that he consults his people as a measure of the participative approach; he discusses matters with his subordinates because he is not fully aware of the matter.

17. He is loyal, obedient to his superiors and never goes into confrontations with them. Most of the leaders of such type are 'yes-men' to their bosses and they remain at their beck and call to show their regard and faith in them.
18. He does not go to the depths of the problem. He collects superficial information, analyses the situation without doing much to trace out the genesis of the issue and settles things without looking to pros and cons of the situation.

From the foregoing deliberation it becomes apparent that such type of leader is not effective for the growth and development of the organization as he lacks dynamism and enthusiasm to take the risk of confrontation for achieving target. His leadership may create altogether a different state of industrial climate through his style of functioning, method of tackling issues and manifestation of behavioural activities. The health of the organization vis-à-vis the organizational milieu which appears under such leadership are discussed in brief herein below:

1. A climate of 'ad-hocism' in administration may be prevalent. It seems that a change in the leadership is overdue and at any moment it is likely to occur. People at work may feel the need for such change probably because no noticeable improvement in administration is made.
2. The leader has no interest in the growth of the organization. He does not take initiatives to go for aggressive marketing to fulfil corporate requirements. Most such leaders are passive in their activities; their thought patterns, mindsets and perception about the subordinates and higher ups are not conducive for the smooth running of the organization. It appears that the organization is nobody's concern.
3. The leader passes his tenure without disturbing the system. The institutional development which comes through competition and challenging assignment remains at a halting state. A deteriorating condition of organizational health may be observed. The leader hardly takes corrective steps to keep pace with the prevalent situation. A state of uncertainty exists within the system.

4. An environment of mutual understanding, mutual ties and mutual trust between team leader and team members does not exist in the organization. The leader does not give much importance to the establishment of better human relations. The leader shows a casual approach towards needs and requirements of the subordinates. He does not consider them as the most vital factor of production. Their problems and issues are not settled properly and at the right time.
5. The subordinates working under such a leader feel helpless, uneasiness and unhappy and they want to get rid of the leader. They consider their leader unproductive, ineffective and impotent. They feel that the health of the organization will go down if the leader continues his service for a long period.
6. The indifferent, apathetic and passive attitude of the leader towards the developmental aspect of the organization creates a firm impression in the minds of the people at work that his presence may jeopardise their interests and his stay with the organization for a long period may push the organization to the state of irreparable damage.
7. Such a leader neither believes in 'hire and fire' as an exclusive measure for improving discipline, nor does he think the participative approach as the only device to improve industrial relations. He has no faith on the above two concepts. But it is interesting to mention that the leader on some occasions uses the 'hire and fire' technique when he feels it is appropriate. The motivating (participating) approach is also sometimes applied by the leader to make the subordinates know that he is a people oriented person. The haphazard and whimsical application of the concepts may not bring any positive change in the attitudes of the subordinates. The leader remains an unacceptable boss to the subordinates who spontaneously do not want to remain under his direct supervision. The boss-subordinate relation, therefore, gets affected.

Surrendering/Succumbing/Unprincipled Leader

This type of leader is different to those of the leaders mentioned in the foregoing discussion. Such a leader is unconcerned with the organization. He has no leadership quality to work with the people as a successful team leader. He cannot take decisions on his own. He talks to his own people, takes their opinion and gives decisions. If he gets pressure from any corner to withdraw decisions or to keep them in abeyance, he may do so as he does not have the requisite traits of stress tolerance. He cannot exercise his adult ego properly due to its contamination by the child ego/nurturing parent ego. He may have a life position like 'I am not OK, you are not OK', or 'I am not OK, you are OK'. He never feels a satisfied, happy person. He thinks of his weaknesses and limitations and considers himself ineffective for accomplishment of any major task. As a leader he is unsuccessful at achieving the team goal. He lacks the ability to exert his thinking and decisions on subordinates.

In order to know much more about the leader's qualitative traits, perceptions and mindsets, it may be expedient to ascertain what such a leader thinks about the people working under him. Some of the main areas of perception about subordinates are discussed below:

1. Subordinates are stubborn, emotional and unconvincing. They want the thing immediately without looking to the eligibility, rationality and genuineness of their demand.
2. Subordinates are aggressive and hostile. They are much more conscious about their rights than their duties.
3. They are unproductive, indiscipline, disobedient and disloyal. They are not concerned for the growth and development of the organization. They are concerned about how they can gain maximum through application of pressure tactics. They do not consider themselves as members/partners of the organization to which they are associated.
4. Subordinates are more passive than active with regard to completion of team objectives. They spend too much time on wasteful work.
5. They do not bother anybody for anything. They think they are supreme and that the management is powerless.
6. Subordinates are supremely egoistical. They sometimes forget their boundaries of action and interfere in management activities. They pretend to be the main power for manipulative work.
7. They are casual in their approach and activities. They do not take organizational work seriously. They remain busy with their personal work or their own union work.

It becomes obvious from the above discussion that the surrendering type of leader does not hold a good impression about his subordinates. According to such a leader, subordinates are more liabilities than assets. He wants to get rid of the people working under him. He becomes exhausted, disturbed and fed-up at the constant intervention by his subordinates on each and every issue irrespective of its magnitude and gravity and he cannot perform his assigned task under such environmental conditions.

This type of leader has some qualitative traits which are different in some aspects from the traits of other types of leaders. The most salient traits are discussed herein below in order to find out the level of mindset and disposition the leader holds to establish human relations vis-à-vis industrial relations.

1. The leader suffers from an inferiority complex and he feels that he does not have the requisite ability and skill to work with the people as a team leader to achieve the team goal. Maybe he is wrong in gauging his limitations and weaknesses but he prepares his mindset in such form to perceive that other colleagues/peers are superior to him in every area of activities.
2. He is not strong in administration. He lacks the ability to convince his boss with regard to the actions taken by him. He sometimes shows his casual approach in dealing with personnel problems. He is flexible in his decisions. He cannot stick to his own decisions.
3. He has no stress tolerance ability to confront any challenge which may provide a big jolt to him. He keeps himself away from the situation so that he is not exposed to an unpleasant environment.
4. He does not believe any specific philosophical management approach or style of functioning. He is an opportunist and takes full advantage of the situation. He changes his leadership style of functioning at the opportune time.
5. He is timid, cool, calm and quiet. He does not like to be involved in any complicated activities. He is afraid of group behavioural action. He cannot sustain group pressure. He has no principles as such to follow for work accomplishment.
6. He is weak at decision-making. He cannot take any decisions on his own. He has no clear knowledge about his

own job role. He lacks the ability to study the situation in depth and to analyse it in a broader perspective.

7. He is a person who wants to keep the boss happy. He therefore does not take any decision or does not create any issue which may cause worries, anxiety and unhappiness to his boss.
8. He has no self-entity or individuality of his own. He has no moral, ethical values to honour. He wants to become the 'blue-eyed boy' of the boss. He, therefore, does not mind surrendering any of his qualitative traits to appease his boss. He remains in preparedness to serve his boss as and when required.
9. He lacks dynamism; he shirks responsibilities and passes them on to others. He does not believe his subordinates. He always suspects his subordinates/colleagues are forming a new group to move against him. He fails to develop mutual ties, understanding and mutual faith between himself and subordinates.
10. He is a person who never feels happy, satisfied and contented. He thinks that others may be happy. He holds his life position as 'I am not OK, you are OK' or 'I am not OK, you are not OK'.
11. He is not a firm believer in the human approach or positive stroking as a measure of increasing productivity as also to create congenial atmosphere for improving industrial relations. He takes casually the problems whenever referred to him for solution and does not give much weightage to the human aspect/human touch of the problems for settlement.

From the earlier discussion it is now clear that establishment of human relations depends mainly on the kind of leadership approach/style of function the boss resorts to. Basically, an employee-oriented approach brings the people close to the boss, thereby making room for exchange of views, to develop understanding between the boss and subordinates. Under such circumstances a climate of cooperation, reciprocity, mutuality and cohesiveness exists which manifests itself through behavioural action in the interactive process. The boss gains recognition, acceptability and support from the subordinates as leader of the team. In the process human relations are developed with the objective of running the business activities smoothly and effectively to achieve the targeted goals.

Now it becomes essential to ascertain and analyse the type of leaders/bosses who have an employee-oriented approach and those who lack such an approach. Evaluation of thought patterns and behavioural manifestation of the leaders who are much more concerned about the well-being of the subordinates may give an indication of the magnitude and extent of human relations developed between boss and subordinates.

The supportive, participative, open type of leader is much more liberal, enlightened and employee-concerned than any other type of leader prevalent in the organizational set-up. This type of leader puts his best effort to sort out the personnel issues through human-therapy. He treats his subordinates as his own family members and considers their difficulties, sufferings and problems as his own concern. He looks to each and every issue concerning subordinates with due care, weightage and importance and he never ignores even a trifling issue placed before him. He is free and frank to the subordinates and shows his eagerness, willingness and seriousness to help them at the time of need.

He encourages his subordinates to work without fear and favour and he gives them support and assistance for the accomplishment of their tasks.

He breaks the official barrier of communication with the subordinates and creates a climate of openness and accessibility by introducing a 'direct contact culture' at the work place.

He is non-vindictive, a well-wisher, a path-pointer and a counsellor to the subordinates. He makes them understand his thought processes and perceptions about them, the qualitative traits he possesses, his objectives and action plan through interface discussion, interactions in deliberations, group conferences and manifestation of behavioural activities.

He gives liberty to subordinates to work independently and delegates required authority to complete the assignment effectively and smoothly. In the process of discharging functions, if any subordinate faces any problem or comes to such a situation, the participative leader comes forward, clears the 'path' of the subordinate to go ahead and takes the responsibilities and risks on his own. He makes the subordinates feel that he is always available to help them in performance of their functions and in receiving their due share in the organization.

The participative leader brings a change in the organizational environment through the process of his 'work-style', mode of approach and behavioural action with the objective of achievement of goals with and through the participants. The subordinates feel work-satisfaction, leadership-role contentment and satiation at being members in the organization. It is the leader who transforms the mindset of the subordinates suitably according to the needs and demands of the organization to fulfil individual goals vis-à-vis team goals.

The participative leader provides all support, assistance, help, advice and guidance to the subordinates to function smoothly and effectively and to make their own room in the organizational activities. Such a leader gives a standing green signal to his subordinates to take his help, if needed, without hesitation. The broad mentality, perceptible dispositional patterns and positive employee-oriented thought process of the leader touch the sensitive areas of the subordinates who virtually act as the toys of the leader.

The subordinates become so impressed with the leadership role for employee oriented activities that they consider him as a 'guru'. The leader earns acceptance and creates a 'win-win' situation in the organizational set-up.

The aforementioned qualitative traits of the leader facilitate attitudinal changes of the subordinates which bring confidence and trust in the leader. The subordinate puts his best effort for coming close to the leader in order to develop mutual understanding. The following are some cases of situations which help subordinates to establish human relations between themselves and their boss.

1. Subordinates do not feel any psychological barriers to place their matters before the leader for consideration on merit. They do not have any doubt about the integrity of the leader or about his seriousness about solving the problems. The subordinates always consider their leader as a guide, friend and well-wisher.
2. The positive strokes given by the leader change the attitudes of the subordinates to respond in a similar pattern. The subordinates give as much response as possible to the stimuli received by them to create complimentary transactions. Usually, positive stimulus begets positive responses in a situation where ego patterns of both the stimulus provider and response giver are more or less the same.

3. The subordinates find a conducive situation for interaction between them and their leader. The working climate lets the subordinates to come near their leader and build up strong understanding and rapport between them through interactive processes and interface discussions.
4. The subordinates notice that the leader takes the initiative to look to their interests and puts in his best effort to solve their problems. They also find that the intention of the leader is to help them and to accept them as his own people. Such positive thinking and action plans of the leader creates an awareness amongst the subordinates to think that they are part of the organization and that they have an important role to play for the achievement of the team goal. The subordinates start forming their mindsets afresh, looking to the attitudes, behavioural patterns and activities of the leader. They consider their leader as their own man, like the guardian of the family. The mindset so formed, the perception pattern and thought processes of subordinates give them extra courage to come nearer to the leader and to interact with him.
5. The subordinates analyse and evaluate the activities of the leader manifested in different situations in order to ascertain his perception, thinking pattern and attitude towards them. If after thorough overhauling, cross-verification and study of the situational phenomena, no negative or adverse approach or attitude is noticed, the subordinates become confident about the boss's employee-oriented activities. After this, they become much more loyal and obedient to the leader and show positive behavioural activities while interacting with him. Thus, within a short period they win the leader's heart and make a room in the appropriate place.
6. When the subordinates observe that the leader's soft attitude towards them is genuine and spontaneous and the leader honestly and sincerely works for a better position and amelioration of their condition, they pay extra regard to him. The subordinates may change their mindset and make themselves first line soldiers of the leader to deliver the goods as per his requirements. The subordinates get ample scope to have direct communication with the leader to form as many complimentary transactions as possible.

The aforementioned situational manifestation may facilitate subordinates and the boss to know each other in a broader perspective and thereby to develop mutual ties, understanding and bonds. There may appear a conducive climate of creating mutual trust and confidence between subordinates and their leader. In this potential and congenial environment the subordinates and the leader develop a sense of agreement in different spheres activities as a solid unit. A sense of belonging to the team, a feeling of pride in being members of the team and a feeling of 'we-ness' and togetherness are developed. Better human relations in the organizational set up are established as an important device to achieve team goals vis-à-vis organizational goals. But it is worthwhile to mention that a slight symptom of adverse attitude by the leader on any employee, even on a trifling issue, may cause a consequential affect on the activities of the subordinates. They may then start rethinking on the leader's role with suspicion which may create a rift in mutual ties.

It is transparently clear that human relations are better established in a situation where the leader is supportive, participative or open in his style of functioning and approach. Thus, the more participative, employee oriented and supportive the leader is, the more solid is the foundation of human relations.

The participative/supportive leader brings a change in the organizational climate to work in a joint effort for the achievement of goals by providing encouragement, security and support to the subordinates. The leader gives them recognition and respect, raises their morale, builds up good rapport with them and accepts them as his own, reliable and dependable people. This situation makes the subordinates committed, loyal and trusting of the organization to achieve the desired target. Then subordinates give their all out efforts and use their expertise and abilities to fulfil the expectations of the leader. All these indicate a high degree of understanding between the subordinates and the leader tending towards developing better personal relations/human relations through 'open-communications'.

From the foregoing discussion it is clear that the leader with an enlightened, liberal and employee-oriented approach may be effective in building up better mutual ties to establish comfortable human relations with his subordinates. But there may not be any grounds to think that the other type of leaders do not establish human relations. The basic difference between the participative and the non-participative leader in matters of building up of human relation is that the former establishes permanent, natural, spontaneous human relations through application of a persistent human approach in a congenial, agreeable atmosphere whereas the latter forces the people to agree to his terms to establish human relations, which is temporary and artificial in nature. The non-participative leader, i.e., the autocratic, so-so or surrendering type) creates a situation to compel the subordinates to accept the dictated terms and develops pseudo-personal relations with them. Such a leader exploits the situational advantage through his personal involvement in ritualistic forum and creates an environment which may apparently evince his 'kind-hearted personality' towards the well being of his people. He generally does not miss the opportunities available to him to express his sense of 'we-feeling', togetherness, gregariousness and co-operation with the people at the appropriate time with the malafide objective of projecting his individuality as a leader with an employee-oriented approach. He tries to win the hearts of the people through manifestation of his fake activities. With this he may make some room in the perceptible areas of his people to form a positive mindset towards him. This sort of perception about the so-called participative leader does not last long and is washed away as soon as the subordinates come to know the real activities and thought processes of the leader.

It transpires that the leaders other than the participative leader may develop relations with their subordinates by concealing their real leadership approach and restricting their behavioural activities temporarily in order to achieve their vested goal. They pretend to be the well wishers, guides and 'kartas' (heads) of the organizational team as family and offer their helping hand to serve them in case of need. These leaders do not want to build up relations with their subordinates as they do not accept the subordinates as their own men. So whatever positive approach the leaders show to their subordinates to establish human relations, it is unnatural, forced and artificial. This relation is not long lasting as the truth (that is the real behavioural approach of the non-participative leaders) cannot remain suppressed for long. During the course of the interaction and exchange of views the leader's real ego pattern and mindset about the subordinates are exposed. The subordinates express an apathetic attitude and feeling of hatred towards the leader for his dual activities. They drive away the artificial benevolent act of the leader from their innocent mental faculty and form a new mindset to perceive the leader's role and to react and interact accordingly. The leader loses credibility, worthiness and acceptability for his behavioural activities and he is considered a person with inhuman qualitative traits.

Hence human relations can be established only when leader treats his subordinates as his own men, behaves humanly, feels their problems as his own, gives the human touch in each and every matter pertaining to the subordinates, shares their suffering and needs, protects them when they are in trouble and likes from his heart. All these behavioural activities are manifested in a situation where the leader functions as a participative/employee cum task oriented leader.

Human relation develops a 'team entity' and facilitates work in a collaborative and joint effort to achieve the team target. Under such situations the relationship between leader and subordinates becomes easy, informal, cordial and comfortable which tends to develop mutual ties and understanding. This helps to reach to an agreement on any issue which crops up in the organization. The decision making process and functioning of the system becomes smooth and effective. A climate of cohesiveness and a joint spirit becomes prevalent. This indicates better industrial relations in the organization and helps to increase productivity, profit and profitability.

It transpires from the foregoing discussion that human relations are necessary to get the work done by the leader with and through the subordinates as it provides a harmonious climate of work culture through the participative process. Human relations create a positive ethos to work together and thus prepare the groundwork for the leader and team members to perform. Human relations are the means not the end to achieve the team target. It works as a device to drive the people to the destination. Now, a question arises as to what is needed to achieve the individual vis-à-vis team/organizational goals, or in other words what act as keys to success. This area which provides the ultimate objective of any individual, team or organization will be discussed in detail in the next chapter.

CHAPTER 9

Key to Success: Evaluative Approach of Attributing Factors

Every organization be it a club, hospital, society, educational institution or family has its own objectives for functioning with and through its members. The individual belonging to the organization as aforementioned sets his own goals in line with the team or organizational goal and puts his best efforts to achieve those goals. Better human relations provide a congenial atmosphere and the necessary input to the individual to undertake the job for completion. Such a situational environment helps the individual to proceed uninterruptedly for the achievement of the set-target. But it should be noteworthy to mention that better human relations are not the device to achieve the goal, but the effective facilitator to reach the goal. It is very difficult to fulfil one's desire to win, to achieve and to reach the destination in a situation where no congenial or conducive environment exists.

QUALITATIVE TRAITS

Now, one needs to know the attributing factors which bring success in fulfilling one's expectations to achieve goals. In a situation where better human relations already exist, the individual either as a member of the team, as a team leader or as an independent person should have the following qualities to achieve the target:

1. Self-determination
2. Ability to remain firm to follow the set procedures to achieve the objectives.

3. Tolerance
4. Positive thinking of goal achievement
5. Ability to take corrective step to streamline action plan
6. Ability to exploit the situational scope and facilities for his own gain.

Detailed deliberations of the above qualitative traits are presented herein below:

1. Self-determination

It is the most vital quality an individual should possess to achieve his goal. It acts as a driving force to push the individual on the right track to fulfil his desire.

A self-determined person gets extra power, courage and firmness to accept any sort of challenging assignment. He puts his best effort to perform his work and shows his effectiveness and efficacy in the whole process of his delivery of service.

Self-determination is not an imposed activity, it is a spontaneous act derived from the earnest desire of the individual. A person may develop a state of self-determination and may frame his mindset accordingly through the process of different activities as discussed below:

i. The sincere and strenuous effort of the person may remove the hurdles that stand in the way of the smooth functioning of the assigned activities. Repetitive attempts and constant follow-up to perform the job may bring success in the area of job accomplishment. Seriousness, sincerity and willingness to do the job allotted to him not only pushes the person to go ahead with the assignment for successful completion but also provides mental strength to sustain any sort of untoward trauma caused in the process of discharging activities. The person may be exposed to the vagaries of a situation and environmental conditions while working in a systematic way. But he finds pleasure and enjoys the feeling of contentment when each and every step of activity passes through successful operations. The sincere and strenuous effort to deliver the goods with the objective of achieving the goal may bring some changes in the attitude of the person as mentioned below:

a. It may enhance the will-power of the person to complete the assigned task. The person may look to the situation in its entirety and may foresee the possibility of reaching the target.

b. Persistent effort to win creates a mindset afresh to perceive the surrounding people, environment and obstacles that stand in the way of his performing the allotted job, and to take remedial measures to deal with the situation in its proper perspective.
c. The person feels that he is competent to overcome the situational hurdles and he is sure to succeed.
d. In the process of continuous effort to perform, he forgets his past activities, shortcomings, weaknesses and limitations. He may rather observe his strength, plus factors, positive symptoms and favourable milieu to achieve his set-goal.
e. He may initially be exposed to suffering, hardships and odd situations while carrying out the assigned task. But subsequent non-stop efforts bring a drastic change in his mental set-up which provides him with the courage, ability and energy to perform the job as assigned to him in the context of achieving the goal.
f. He may feel highly satisfied with regard to his activities and may develop the confidence to perform the task effectively. He may hold an impression that nothing is impossible to achieve if the proper goal-setting is made. In the process of giving in the best effort he may develop a feeling of 'must win'. All this makes him strong to fulfil his desire.

ii. *Devotion to the Job*

This activity makes the person a 'workaholic' as he completely surrenders himself to fulfilling his mission. He has no thinking other than the target which he is set to achieve. He accepts the assignment as a great challenge and shows his 'leeching activities' to serve the purpose.

Devotion to the job brings a lot of changes in the behavioural activities as well as mental set-up of the person. Such probable changes are discussed below:

a. It increases the 'will-force' of the person to facilitate achievement of goals.
b. The devotion in its totality may create an environment of the 'work-world' in the perceptible area of the person

which may enhance the mental strength to achieve the set goal.

c. Continuous engagement in work activity with the objective of getting some results may develop intuition to win the race. He accordingly chalks out his activity plan and proceeds as per schedule in order to perform his task.
d. The person may feel committed to work and may find pleasure only when he thinks that he has contributed considerably. Commitment to work increases the stature of the person. It makes him happy. It gives him extra energy, support and impetus to perform his job.
e. Devotion to the job brings some specific interest for its completion and the person leaves no stone unturned to reach the desired goal. The person experiences a different type of feeling when he achieves his goals one after another. With this he establishes his effectiveness, competency and ability to perform the assigned task. He earns recognition as a 'goal-reacher' and an all-time winner. All this satiates the person's esteem which elevates the ethical value and strengthens the power of self-determination.
f. A completely devoted person may not have time to keep track of the activities which he feels are unimportant other than the job assigned to him. He remains actively engaged to systematize his activities and take recourse to suitable measures in order to reach the target. He considers himself to be instrumental for the achievement of the goal. He finds his task not difficult to accomplish in a time frame situation. This sort of feeling develops confidence to accept any type of challenging job which can be performed effectively by the person.
g. The person may develop a paradigmal concept with the feeling 'must win', 'must achieve', must get' 'must do', 'must succeed' and so on with other positive thinking. This boosts the level of mental strength as also the will power of the person.
h. Devotion to the job makes the person much more job conscious. He gets well acquainted with the objectivity of the job methodology and application of techniques to achieve the objective, the obstacles and shortcoming

inherent in the system and the level of strength and support required to win the desired objective.

Thus, job-oriented activity of the person brings success in achievement of objectives.

This develops a feeling of indispensability which strengthens the moral base of the performer.

iii. *Hard Labour*

Hard labour has no substitute for achievement of one's goal. It is the activity which makes the road smooth to go ahead with the mission. The situational variables which initially appear to stand in the way of performing the task subsequently disappear. Hard labour strengthens the driving force to form a strong determination to succeed. It brings some changes in the perception scenario of the person as manifested in his behavioural pattern and functioning. Salient changes as occurred are mentioned herein below:

a. Hard labour keeps the person in a happy and jolly mood. The person finds pleasure in his activities, specially when he crosses the barriers of his success one after another. He becomes mentally strong and his commitment to his achievement appears to be transparent.
b. The person may not consider any barrier/obstacle as a threat to the smooth functioning of his activities. He has the excellence and expertise to drive away obstacles through diligence and establishes dominance over such situational obstacles. Thus he develops his mindset to perceive the surrounding objects, persons and situation afresh in order to succeed in his activities.
c. In the process of performance through hard labour when the results of success start coming he may experience a sea-change in the behavioural manifestation of the people connected directly or indirectly with his activities. This increases the will-power and mental strength of the person and gives him the impetus to carry on to achieve the target.
d. Hard work makes the assignment very simple. The person may not find any difficulty reaching his destination. He may develop thought processes to search out ways and means of achieving the goal.

e. The person may earn recognition, respect, appreciation and esteem through his hard labour. He may develop a feeling of achievement which brings strong determination to do job by hook or by crook.
f. The person may find pleasure in the process of task accomplishment especially when he completes the task after putting in hard labour for it. He may get extra energy and power to do much more work for achievement. He may thus keep himself engaged in the activities of performing the job and subsequently he succeeds.
g. With hard labour the person can go to any extent to fulfil his desire. He does not look to his past activities limitations and weaknesses; he always looks forward to go ahead with the objectives already set. Through hard work he develops confidence and a mental state of 'sure to win' as well which in fact brings success in the area of his functioning.

iv. *Holding the Idea to Win*

The person may develop a feeling of winning the race in the process of his functioning. If he prepares his mindset with convincing belief that he is sure to win the battle of task accomplishment he takes appropriate measures to achieve the target. The person who carries the impression of getting the results may find it a congenial environment in which to perform his assigned task. Some changes in his behavioural activities may be noticed which are discussed below:

a. A strong will power remains active to fulfil the desire of the person. The person with enthusiasm and zeal proceeds step by step to complete the assigned job. He gets extra-ordinary energy in the process of his performing the task and he keeps himself exclusively engaged in the job so that the set-target is achieved.
b. The person holding the idea to win commensurate with his capability and skill may develop the confidence to perform the assigned job. He draws out an activities-plan, gives his whole energy and effort to accomplish the job, takes corrective steps when required and achieves the target.
c. Such a person feels a sense of satisfaction when he succeeds at activities one after another. This makes the

person mentally strong to remain in preparedness to face the challenges to achieve the target.

d. The person remains firm in his mission to win. He becomes committed to the job. He develops an urge and interest in completing the task. He entirely dedicates himself to the achievement of his goal. All this brings a feeling of self determination which satiates his need to achieve.

Self-determination bring success in the work activities undertaken by the person. There is rare incident where self-determination does not work to fulfil a person's desire to achieve. It may happen that the person may not succeed in his effort to win if the target/goal set for achievement is much higher than his capabilities, the infrastructure provided and because of other factors than what should be in the normal course. In this instance, self-determination may not bring fruitful results to achieve the target but it may make sure that there is no lack of initiative, effort and attempt noticed on the part of the person to reach the goal, and the performance level is not appallingly low.

There are lots of success stories of achievers who have been able to fulfil their desires to reach the goal exclusive through self-determination. Two such cases are deliberated to give an idea as to how only the trait of self-determination brought success to two persons in all their efforts and activities undertaken by them.

Case Story I

Mr. Victory hailed from a downtrodden family of a remote village where no educational facilities (other than primary education) were available for the growth and development of the children. For further education, the children of the village were to come to the town which was 3-4 KM away from their village. The education was not so costly as it was in cities and towns. But at the same time it was not cheap or easily affordable by the poor families.

Mr. Victory was born and nurtured in a family comprising 5 brothers, one sister and his mother. He lost his father in his formative childhood and had no occasion to record any incident of his father's activities in his memory tape which he could replay and utilize to give support to any decision making process. He could not even remember his father's physique, appearance or incidents of offering affection to him. He was practically brought up by his mother as a nurturing parent. His mother gave him support and protection to grow in a normal manner. She filled the vacuum caused due to the non-presence of his father with love, affection and active participation in day to day activities. She also gave him the treatment of a critical parent when needed for his growth and development.

Mr. Victory spent his childhood in deprivation and destitution. After completion of primary education at his village he was admitted in a school of the nearby town. He had no money to pay the monthly tuition fees of the school, no standing means to procure proper clothing and to meet the other necessities of life. His family health at that time was in a broke and tattered state. He felt pressure to discontinue his studies. The family milieu too was uncongenial and inconducive to carry on studies. He had no active supporter or well wisher other than his mother who always had been with him as his guide, path-pointer and counsellor. When Mr. Victory had to pass through different phases of turmoil in his childhood to decide the course of action to be taken, he suddenly discovered a mindset already framed with a strong self-determination to continue study at whatever cost, to get excellent results and to establish himself in life. He developed an entirely different state of mental-set up with a dire urge to stand on his own feet. He made up his mind to go ahead with the action-plan chalked out to complete the course of study with outstanding performance. He had in his mind to occupy the top ranking position in the Evaluation Tests of the school. He kept his aspirations and expectations high all the time in his childhood. He had strong will power which enabled him to achieve his desired target. The attributing factors that facilitated the development of his self-determination were as follows:

i. The helpless, miserable and intolerable condition through which Mr. Victory had to pass developed a feeling to face the challenges to grow and to establish himself in life. Such sense of feeling drove him to take firm decisions to achieve his goal.
ii. The solitary state of Mr. Victory prompted him to have self determination to win and to achieve.
iii. The situation either to die or to survive through struggle brought a dramatic change in the mindset of Mr. Victory.

During a short span of child-hood Mr. victory experienced unbearable suffering, inhuman mental torture and a series of obstacles that stood in the way of smooth and effective discharging of his work. The only way he felt for his survival was to have a strong determination to face the challenges and to overcome them to bring success in his work.

iv. When it was very difficult for Mr. Victory to prepare his career due to poverty and unfavourable circumstances he had to face, he did not give up hope. He put in his best effort and gave hard labour to do better in the Examinations in which he appeared. His will-force to succeed, his hard labour to achieve and his strenuous efforts to were appreciated by most people known to him. The recognition of his diligence and effort brought a change in his behavioural pattern which accelerated his will power to form a mindset with strong determination to win.

Mr. Victory had to struggle a lot for keeping his existence. No other person came forward to help him except his mother who gave him moral support, assured him of his achievement and motivated him to carry on. his assigned task through her love, affection, counselling and advice.

Mr. Victory remained unaltered to his determination to succeed in his efforts and activities.

Since Mr. Victory had no ancestral property or source of income to meet the expenses to carry on his studies, he had to arrange for money at a young age when he was in standard VI or VII. With his strong self-determination to do ('must do'. he found the avenue to earn money by giving tuitions to little children.

He gave some part of his available time for coaching little ones and continued to remain engaged in such activities till he completed his studies.

Mr. Victory crossed the target of his studies at school, college and university smoothly through hard labour, sincere and strenuous effort, commitment, devotion and holding the idea to win all the time.

He never thought that his course of studies would not be completed. He had a robust will power which always worked for successful completion of his activities.

Mr. Victory had never been a pessimist. At the age of twelve or thirteen when most of his classmates were busy enjoying their childhood with their parents and relatives, Mr. Victory kept engaged to earn something for meeting his educational expenses through coaching activities. He also enjoyed himself such activities because he got the pecuniary support through such activities to fulfil his desire to continue his studies. He had always an optimistic outlook. He had a feeling that he could perform the task undertaken by him successfully. He had developed the impression that if others could do the job, he could easily do it too and even if other could not do the job, he could do it. The strong determination of Mr. Victory never disappointed him. It brought success to him in each and every activity. He won the battle for his growth and development, he achieved all the goals set by him.

Mr. Victory excelled in all areas of activities he had undertaken. He demonstrated his performance in the academic field as per his expectations, got the highest distinction in the university and secured a good job through stiff competition. All these had been possible due to his having firm self-determination.

The success story of Mr. Victory gives an indication that even in an odd situation where no infrastructure, resources or assistance are available, where an uncongenial, inconducive and unhealthy environment exists and where achievement of anything appears to be an act of impossibility, a person can become successful in his mission to achieve if he develops a strong self-determination and prepares his mindset with the feeling of 'must do', 'must achieve' and 'must win'. This sense of feeling makes suitable changes in his perception framework which facilitates the smooth functioning of his activities. It is essential to mention that the person may have to face a series of obstacles and hindrances in the process of carrying out his activities. These obstacles may seem to be very strong to give jolts to stop his work-activities and may create situations so that he cannot perform his job role effectively. It is noteworthy to remember that nothing is unachievable if self-determination exists. If the person wants to succeed, he should not look to the obstacles from a negative angle and should not feel that the task is difficult to accomplish, he should not measure his level of competency and strength to fight against obstacles, he should not look to his areas of weaknesses, he should not think that he has nothing to surmount. What the person needs is to have a strong base of self-determination. He should develop aggressive feelings to fight against hindrances. He should take a pledge to cross the boundary of obstacles and to reach the destination. He should stick to his decision to win. He should be courageous, strong and stubborn to face any sort of challenges. He should keep himself in high profile with regard to achieving the target. He should give hard labour and a sincere and strenuous effort and devotion with the sole objective to complete the job undertaken by him. He should make his will power strong with determination to achieve by any means and to remain in preparedness to pay any cost for that.

The above example of Mr. Victory highlights how a person can become successful in his mission when he remains in a difficult situation. In this case study it is evinced that the quality of self-determination alone can bring success in the work-activities of a person, when a person hails from a broken family. Thus members of every organization, whether it is a club, family, hospital, educational institution, factory or any sort of organization which runs to fulfil some objectives, may become successful in their mission through strong self-determined effort even if a congenial atmosphere of human relations or a conducive environment does not exist. The self-determination trait that arises out of the spontaneous urge to achieve something makes a lot of changes in the person's behavioural pattern and activities. Commitment, devotion and diligence to work are the sequel to the self-determined outlook of the person.

Case Story 2

This is a success story of a lady who fulfilled her desire and expectations through self-determination. She had to struggle a lot to succeed in her mission to achieve.

The lady Ms Saver was born and nurtured in a low middle class family of a remote village. Besides her parents, she had three brothers in the family. The family had no income from ancestral property. Ms. Saver's father had to put in hard labour to run the family. The societal clan to which her family belonged was conservative and superstitious. The clan believed in the early marriage of girls and had no moral or religious sanction to allow the girls to have a school or college education.

Ms Saver's parents were different from the societal group. They were very liberal, enlightened and progressive with regard to children's education (including the education of their daughter), career path and establishment in life. They gave her the liberty to carry on studies. They had high hopes on Ms Saver. They wanted Ms Saver to go for higher education and did not bother about the societal boundary framed against girls' education.

In the village where Ms Saver spent her child-hood period there was only one school for girls' education. That was a Middle High School. The number of girl students in the school was very little. All the girl children of the village were not sent to the school for education. Only the parents who were liberal and who had positive thinking about their daughters' education allowed them to carry on their studies in the school. Ms. Saver's parents were amongst them. It is noteworthy to mention that mostly all the girl students except Ms Saver came from affluent families and they did not feel the dearth of money or anything which they wished to get. For showing better results in class performance as also in the annual evaluation tests they had their own private coaching arrangements. Ms Saver's parents had no money to afford expenses towards private tuition or coaching which she realized even during her formative years. Ms Saver noticed that her classmates who had private coaching used to discuss study topics amongst themselves and stopped discussions immediately on seeing her. Ms Saver had also observed that such groups of students used to consult, during recess period, the study notes given by the private teachers in the classroom for preparation of home tasks, and closed their study notes as soon as she came to them. They created a filthy environment in the school and made her know that a poor student like her had no place in the school for studies. They even went to the extent of lodging a false complaint against her before the school authority. All this they did with the calculated move to demoralize her so that she could not perform well in the class examination.

Ms Saver observed that most of her classmates who came from solvent families could not tolerate her because (i) her family had no precuniary status in the society (ii) she was good in her studies and was excelling in her performance even though she did not take help from anybody (iii) she was loved by the teachers for her sincerity, brilliance and commendable performance in class as also for her being good in conduct and behaviour (iv) her name was cited as an example of the ideal girl during discussions on related topics by the villagers.

At the critical juncture when Ms Saver's classmates who made themselves enemies to her, had been trying to get better results in the class Tests by way of taking private coaching on different subjects, Ms Saver developed a strong self-determination to compete with her classmates at any cost. She took a pledge on her own to do excellent performances in class Tests in school. She also determined to study in college and university and to show her performance in undergraduate and post-graduate examinations. Ms Saver knew that her parents had no financial strength to support her educational expenses. Yet she took her decision to achieve. She remained unaltered to her decision till she became successful in her mission.

Ms. Saver prepared her mindset appropriately during her formative years to teach a befitting lesson to her classmates. She then decided to give hard and strenuous labour and sincere efforts to yield results. She was very hopeful in her activities. With her diligence and untiring effort arising out of her self-determination she scored outstanding results in class examinations of the school which had classes up to standard eight.

Since the village school could not provide further education to the girl students beyond class eight, the educational career of most girl students ended halfway. But Ms Saver was adamant and stubborn to carry on further studies and she decided to appear in the School Final Examination as a private candidate if the continuance of her studies as regular student was not possible. Ms Saver's firm determination to do made it possible to complete the School Final Course as a private student.

Ms Saver had a great desire to have college and university education which was available in the nearby town (thirty to forty kilometres away from her village). Her village was not well-connected with the nearby town through bus or railway services. Thus, to commute from her village to the town to attend college was a rare possibility. It was also not possible for her to get a college education as she had no capacity to afford the expenses of staying in hostel for the continuation of her studies. She noticed that a lot of obstacles stood in the way for carrying on further studies. In her family too there had not been unanimity of opinion amongst the family members including near relations with regard to allowing her to continue studies. But her parents had been with her all the time.

Ms Saver made up her mind with strong self-determination (must do, must win, must achieve) and remained prepared to face any challenge in the process of satiating her desire to pursue further studies. She developed her mindset with positive and unaltered thought patterns. She always held an impression that it was not difficult for a person to overcome societal barriers and financial hardship if he/she had a strong and spontaneous will.

Ms Saver met the expenses needed for completion of her undergraduate and post-graduate studies from the earnings she had through the delivery of coaching services to some school children of the town. The time spent for coaching services was compensated by putting extra effort in her studies so that the level of performance was not effected. She completed her studies in college and university with the desired result. She did her PhD work with a fellowship. She established an outstanding academic record through hard labour, sincere effort, commitment, and devotion to work arising out of her spontaneous determination to achieve. She was successful in all her activities.

From the foregoing discussion it becomes clear that self-determination is the most essential quality a person should have to achieve his goal. But it is noteworthy to mention that this qualitative trait alone cannot bring success in work. Other factors and qualitative traits have also a role to contribute. Such traits are discussed in short.

2. Ability to remain firm to follow the set procedures to achieve the objective

The person should not be fickle minded, he should not fluctuate in his decision. He must be strong mentally to cope with any situational occurrence that may arise out of his decision. It is possible to succeed in his role assignment if with other qualitative traits, he is capable of remaining firm to follow the procedure already set for achievement of the objectives.

The person, to be successful and to strictly follow the goal setting Objective, needs to have the following qualities:

i. He is a discipline-oriented person and is firm to enforce discipline in every system of activities. The person never violates any norms of discipline. He manifests his activities as a model-role player to indicate others to follow in the same line of activities.

ii. The person is sincere, diligent and systematic in the accomplishment of his task.
Such a person may prepare his projection to follow the goal-achieving path and may show his worth and ability to succeed.

iii. The person is honest and clean in the development of his mental strength to win. Such a person gains acceptability from the people. He develops a congenial atmosphere to work through his activities based on realities, reasonableness and rationalities. He earns a reputation, recognition and societal honour as an unbiased and honest personality.
To remaining on the right track, the person requires enormous power, energy and courage to stick to his decision to follow the set objectives.

iv. The person has a clear perception about the people surrounding him as also the objective set for achievement of individual or team goals. Such a person with clear perception makes his mindset appropriately to suit the work-environment and gives his effort to follow the action-plan already set to reach the target.

v. The person is ethical, morally high, tough and strong in his mental state. He may be much more 'conscious of work' than of any other factor. He never shows his negative approach to perform his job.
Such a person never goes back from his initially set goal and keeps himself firm to sustain any sort of pressure in order to follow the set-objective.

vi. The person has the ability to analyse the situational circumstances under which goal is set and the rationality/reasonableness of such setting. The person is also judicious, witty, prudent and has extra-ordinary skill, tact and exposure to justify the stand taken for remaining firm to achieve the targeted goal. The person with such qualitative traits may experience some sort of feeling which gives impetus, courage and mental strength to win.

The person possessing the aforementioned qualitative traits gets the appropriate mental strength to remain firm to follow the set procedure and to crush the barriers that stand in the way of achieving his goal. The mental power and strength of such a person is so solid, the question of making deviation from the originally set goal is absurd and out of the way. The firmness to stay with the decision and to achieve any set goal is essentially the most important quality of the goal setter/decision maker or the person implementing the decision. It should be mentioned that when the goal is set (or when the decision is taken on any matter) care is taken on each and every aspect which is directly or indirectly connected with the goal-setting/achievement so that the goal set/decision made is rational, reasonable and within the reach considering the efficacy and competence of the goal achiever, situational variables prevalent in the system and availability of infrastructure. However, the person may not be successful in achieving the goal if the same is set without considering the factors as mentioned above.

3. Tolerance capability

The person should have the ability to tolerate the situational hazards that may crop up in the process of achieving the target. It does not happen in all cases that the target is achieved without experiencing any odd circumstantial occurrences. It may be that in some cases the person succeeds comfortably without facing any trouble.

The person wishing to achieve the goal may experience hardships due to various factors some of which are deliberated below:

i. The environment under which the person passes through may not be congenial to help him to continue with the job. The person may not get the necessary infrastructure for completion of the assigned task. On the contrary, he may find situations which create barriers for him. The non-receipt of the required infrastructure may cripple the person to perform the job effectively as in most cases it makes the person incompetent and incapable of completing the job. The person becomes the victim of the situation and in order to succeed in his effort he prepares his mindset appropriately to tolerate the jolt received by him. He does not take the matter lightly. He studies the situation in an overall perspective and keeps it in his mind to give an adequate reply at the proper time.

ii. The person may not get immediate results of his labour. He may have to put in continuous effort till he reaches his target. For getting his result he may have to pass through the mental exercise of keeping patient, cool and calm. This is another quality of tolerance of time. The person perceives the whole thing in the proper manner and strengthens his mental set-up to sustain the effect of the repetitive nature of activities.

iii. If the goal is set by the individual and he himself is to achieve the goal, he may face a lot of pressure (both external and internal) that creates obstacles in the way of his moving forward to achieve the target. Besides he may experience mental pressure for not getting results. If the goal is set and the persons in the team are required to achieve the goal, the pressure comes from different quarters to perform or not to perform the job. Someone outside the team may try to halt the activities of goal achievement or may exert pressure to expedite the process of reaching the goal and may express concern for any delay. The team members themselves are exposed to a heavy mental load for their incapacitation of performing job. All this creates an unbearable state of mental set-up of the team members causing anxiety, stress, worries for non-achievement of the target. The person with the quality of stress tolerance can survive and show results. Such persons remain firm in their activities and may not experience adverse effects of the pressure on their mindset because of the stress tolerance quality they possess.

iv. It may happen that the activities of the person may not prove to be effective in the result-orientation programme. All his attempts, endeavours and actions may fail at some stages to bring the desired result. A climate of uncertainty for reaching the destination may prevail. No sort of encouragement, impetus, strokes might be available to roll the person's activities towards their goal. This situation may arise when the target fixed is more than the capacity level of the performer, or when the available resources are not adequate to fight the shortcomings, barriers and hindrances standing in the way of moving towards the achievement of the goal. To overcome such situation the person with a cool and calm temperament, as also one having excellence in stress tolerance may be useful.

Stress tolerance capabilities may be found amongst the following category of persons:

i. The person is strong in his decision making processes and is not amenable to any situation. He sometimes shows his autocratic style of functioning in order to make others know that his decisions remain unaltered. Such a person gets confident in his work and proceeds to complete his task fearlessly. Tension, anxiety and stress cannot drive him away from his activities.

ii. The person who is honest in his activities and does not hold any malafide intention to have undue gain from his action, can set an example of clean functioning. He proves his credit-worthiness through his model role playing and gets extra energy and initiative to go ahead with the action-plan to achieve in a time-frame schedule. Such a person earns sufficient power to sustain a tense situation.

iii. The person with dynamism and a people cum job-oriented approach may earn the acceptability of the people. Whatever he does he gets the support of the people. The people develop an impression about such a person as their well wisher, well doer and path-pointer. They are quite sure that he cannot do any harm to them. Rather he helps them to move forward for fulfilment of their desires. Such a person has the quality to bear with any situational stress caused in the process of his functioning.

iv. The person who is stubborn, rigid to his decision and decides to do things without looking to the consequences may have the capability of stress tolerance. It is noticed in most cases that the ego pattern of such a person is not in a balanced state. His adult ego is contaminated by the critical parent and his life position is 'I am OK, you are not OK'. He may feel happy in his present state of life position considering his qualitative traits are superb to tolerate and kind of stress that occurs in the process of his discharging duties.

v. The person who accepts the assignment as a challenging one and mentally remains in preparedness to boldly face an odd situation may develop his mindset afresh to move forward to achieve the desired goal. The energetic, enthusiastic and fearless mood like 'do or die' of the person makes him a completely different person who does not pay heed to the difficulties and runs after the achievement of goals successively one after another. His mental strength and power at a particular point of time is immensely capable of sustaining any stress caused due to his actions.

4. Positive thinking of goal achievement

For the achievement of goals it is one of the prerequisites that the person should have positive thinking about the objectives and targets set and the processes to move forward to reach the targets. Such a person develops his mindset according to his need and requirement and makes a clear perception about the people surrounding him, the objectives set and the hurdles to be faced in the process of his working. The following are the qualities such a person generally possesses:

i. He is optimistic in nature. He never thinks about the non-achievement of anything. Even in case of failure on one or two occasions he never loses his spirit and zeal to achieve. He keeps his mind strong and will-force high to succeed in next attempts.
ii. He has a strong attitude to win as if he is born to achieve and to get anything and everything he wants. He proceeds to perform his assigned task without fear or favour. He never goes back if any hurdle appears to stay in his way of working. He takes the challenge, removes the obstacle and goes further to fulfil his desire.
iii. He is hardworking, sincere and tenacious. He gives his all-out effort to complete the job assigned to him. He is a workaholic and finds pleasure through work performance.
iv. He is disciplined, obedient and loyal to the boss. He does not go against the desire of his boss. He remains happy and keeps his boss happy through his activities. He keeps his boss informed of the time to time development of the actions taken to achieve the goal.
v. He is dynamic in his activities. His style of functioning often brings a change in the work-climate to motivate the people to put in their best efforts for successful completion of the job

assigned to them. He believes in work completion. He has a great perception that the accomplishment of a task is possible if a person works hard and takes the risk of facing odd situations that may crop up in the process of work performance.

vi. He is prompt in decision making. He thinks that the importance of the decision gets lost if a timely decision is not taken. He gives immediate decisions in order to get quick results. He wants quick delivery of goods and services to ensure the smooth running of the process for work achievement.

vii. He has transparency in work activities. He has a clear conception of his job role. His aspiration is much more than the target set for his achievement. He keeps his mindset in high profile and makes his thought -processes accordingly in order to succeed in his attempt to achieve the goal. He sets his mental pattern like 'never to lose', 'always to win'.

viii. He is courageous, adventurous, and likes to take tough assignments to show his efficacy and competency in completion of his job. He is rigid in his decision making and sticks to his decisions particularly in the area of work-performance.

ix. He is committed to the job assigned to him and keeps himself engaged to achieve the target within a time bound programme. He makes a lot of sacrifices and is devoted to fulfilling his desire for achievement.

x. He is achievement-hungry and searches for new avenues to reach the destination. He develops a sense of doing, achieving, winning and remains busy with work schedules.

xi. He is a good observer of the situation and a silence worker. He has great stress tolerance capabilities. He takes his assignment sincerely with a pledge to perform within a time frame schedule.

xii. He is very conscious about his job-role and territorial area of his activities. He neither goes beyond boundary of his activities unless called for, nor does he allow anybody to encroach on his own area of functioning. He wants to complete the job himself. Such a person has an urge for satiation of self-actualisation needs which he meets through excellence of performance solely by him.

xiii. He is more or less a balanced personality with a moderately cool dispositional temperament. He excels in drawing up actions plan through studying the situational climate and other perspectives keeping in view the needs, requirements, objectives of the goal setting, infrastructural availability, and the time-frame schedule of goal achievement. He takes strategic measures to implement the action plan for achievement of the target.

xiv. He develops a strong determination to succeed and remains in preparedness to drive away the obstacles that stand in the way for achievement of goals. He never bows down to anybody to show his inability to perform. He starts his work on a war footing with the objective of completion of the task as per schedule.

5. Ability to take corrective steps to streamline action plan

The person should have adequate strength to take appropriate measures to monitor the activities. He should be able to adopt corrective steps to streamline his action plan in order to achieve the targeted result. It is very essential to evaluate the performance of all concerned at regular intervals in order to identify the weak areas where support is warranted as also to know the prospect of achievement. This is possible if the person possesses the necessary quality of ascertaining the situation and of taking corrective steps to streamline the action plan. The importance of such a qualitative trait is discussed herein below:

i. The target is fixed after taking into account various aspects in the matter. It is possible that after fixation of targets a lot of changes occur. Under such circumstances the performer may not be able to ascertain his strength and weaknesses and to prognosticate the outcome of his performance if he lacks the ability to judge the situation and to take corrective step as per needs and requirements.

ii. The person, in order to perform his assigned task, prepares action-plans and proceeds accordingly. But after sometime he may feel that his activities do not bring any result. He may, therefore, require to take feedback and to take corrective steps to strengthen his activities. The person with such qualitative trait can excel in this area.

iii. If the evaluation of the performance of the concerned person is made at a short gap or a study is undertaken at regular intervals to see whether activities are carried out as per action-plan, the person may be able to coordinate the activities and may provide necessary input, if required, to succeed in his attempt. Co-ordination work is essential to compensate the deficit areas as also to develop a 'we-feeling' and sense of belonging to the team. Team members may feel that a comfortable state of work-culture is prevalent where participants are treated as family members and are given due importance and human recognition for their work performance. All these may help to function effectively so as to achieve the target.

iv. The person with the ability to take corrective steps may excel in the identification of causative factors for non-performance and also in finding out remedial measures to be applied for effective performance. In order to make the team members effective and to set them in the right order such a person uses his motivational therapy and behavioural techniques to raise their morale to take active part in the target-achievement process.

It is quite natural that target cannot be achieved if after ascertainment of the non-performance area (NPA).
no corrective step is taken to strengthen the areas. It may also happen that the person fails to achieve the target because of not getting proper feedback and for not taking corrective steps to streamline the action-plan.

v. It is only possible in the process of evaluation of performance at some interval to know how much is achieved and how much is yet to be achieved as also to look at the level of the person's strength and resources available as against strength and resources required for moving forward to achieve as per action plan. The person after initiating a feedback process may utilize the opportunity to prepare his mindset afresh to activate his thought-processes and provide the necessary strength and input for achievement of the target.

vi. When the person comes to know the deficit pockets/NPA after thorough overhauling the totality of the assigned task and also the extent of task performed, he may need to make an in depth study for preparation of an action plan to perform the unfinished task . He may also need to pass through the processes of other activities, viz., organizing, motivating and controlling for completion of the task.

It becomes, therefore, transparent that the person should have expertise in all areas of function to take corrective step to streamline the action-plan and the lack of such skill/ability may result in non-achievement of the desired target.

The qualitative traits as aforementioned makes the person strong and firm in his decision making process which keeps him, all the time, in a high profile to achieve the targeted goal. This sort of qualitative trait/ability may be found amongst the persons whose temperamental disposition, behavioural pattern, activities are discussed herein below:

i. The person is stubborn and does not listen to anybody to change his action plan. He may be biased and his adult ego may be influenced and contaminated while he performs.
ii. The person has analytical ability and may excel in assessing the situation, the causative factors and remedial measures for application.
iii. He has the requisite energy, power and capability to sustain any pressure, risk and hazards that may stand in the way of his performing the assigned task.
iv. He is a fearless person and does not succumb to any threat, intimidation and coercion. He does what he desires. When he undertakes the job he proceeds and does not look at the consequences.
v. He may have a job oriented cum people oriented approach. Since he is basically a workaholic, he may sometimes manifest his activities as a believer in and practitioner of theory 'X' which gives less importance (or no importance) to people-welfare activities than work activities. Such a person may not be acceptable to the people as he is not liked by them from the core of their hearts.
vi. He is straightforward and disciplined. He generally does not say 'no' to any task assigned to him. He, therefore, does not like the person who says 'no' for any job. He wants disciplined, obedient and 'yes sir' type of subordinates to work with him.
vii. He is hard working, sincere and loyal to the team. He always wants to be focused in public as a best deliverer of the goods through his performance and service.

viii. He is more or less a person with a hot disposition, whose adult ego is contaminated by the parent ego and particularly the critical parent ego. His life position may be like 'I'm OK, you're not OK'.

6. Ability to exploit the situational scope and facilities for his own gain

This is a unique quality a person requires, if he desires to have perfection and accuracy in the quality of job he delivers. Such a quality helps the person to perform his job and to achieve the goal. In the process of performance the person may be exposed to the vagaries of the work-climate and at the same time he may find a lot of opportunities and facilities available which may facilitate his working. The person with such an ability makes fullest utilization of the scope and facilities for achievement of the goal set for him.

This sort of ability may be found amongst such persons who possess the following qualitative traits:

i. It is very difficult to ascertain whether

   a. situational scope and facilities are useful at that moment
   b. such facilities give any indication of consequences
   c. there is any malafide intention of providing such facilities

   The person with an analytical ability and an aptitude for critical assessment may sort out the problems as mentioned above.

ii. The person has clear perception of his job role as also background knowledge of fixation of the target. He is dutiful and discharges his duties with the intention of setting an example as a model role-player.

iii. He is sincere in his work and is conscious of the need to compensate the deficiency and to utilize the opportunities available in the course of delivery of goods. He knows each and every opportunity that crops up at the time of crisis has a major role to speed up the process of activities. Such facilities/opportunities are short-lived and do not last long. Hence this may necessitate immediate utilization of opportunities to give support for achievement of the desired target. The task of searching out opportunities and its immediate utilization is possible if the person possesses the requisite skill and ability to analyse the situation through application of mind and keeping a constant watch and observation on the change of the situation.

iv. He is an optimist and never thinks of the possible debacle of his action-plan. He goes forward and never looks back. He keeps his morale high. He believes in the concept of hard work, honesty and obedience. He develops his mindset and thought process to perceive that everything is achievable. He may think like 'if someone can do it, I can also do', 'even if some one cannot do, I can do it'.

v. He is the person who is against the principle of surrendering. He does not succumb to pressure or threat. He is witty, keeps a strong vigil on the day-to-day development of the situation. He has a tenacious approach of completing the task and remains unchanged to his vow 'I must achieve'. He has a strong sense of feeling that every man is born to do, to achieve and to succeed.

It is thus transparent that a person should have some six qualitative traits as discussed in the foregoing deliberation, for achievement of his target. Such qualities are found to be very effective in fulfilling the person's desire. But all these qualities may not be required for achievement of each and every target. One type of quality which is always needed is 'self-determination'. This qualitative trait is a must for the success of every mission. One cannot think of getting anything in terms of achievement without his determination to have it. The man can take suitable steps to chalk out action plans, organize activities, coordinate with the people and regulate the activities, only if he is mentally prepared to accept the assignment to achieve. Mental preparedness means a mindset framed to accept the challenge, the driving force of which emanates from a strong base of self-determination.

If a person gets anything without his determination to get it, this can not be termed as achievement. This is simply like a gift, such as an inheritance. For achieving anything the person should have self-determination.

It happens that in some activities success comes more easily and much before the stipulated time. This is possible where obstacles are less or absent while the infrastructure, resources and opportunities are abundantly available to utilize effectively and to implement the action plan. Under such circumstances the person leaves no stone unturned to use the scope, situational benefits and resources to go ahead with the projected activities with the objective to win and to achieve. It is noteworthy to mention that when any assignment is taken, the person should immediately develop his mindset with the framework 'must do' so that base of self-determination is formed. The person can proceed for a successful mission only when his will-power drives him to carry on with the activities undertaken by him for achievement. In the process of his performing activities under an action-plan, if any scope or opportunity is derived, he should immediately explore the genesis, nature and objective of such scope/opportunities and benefits and if, after thorough scrutiny, no malafide objective appears, he should utilize the scope/benefit to implement the action plan prepared for the achievement of his target.

It is pertinent to mention that some people still remain in the world of primitive thinking for achieving any goal without any determination. They think that they may get if it is due to them. Such people form their mindset and develop their vision to succeed their mission with the grace of the super power. They feel it is futile to take initiatives or to form self-determination to reach the goal unless the super power desires. According to them man cannot perform any job, cannot succeed his mission or cannot achieve the goal if the super power does not dictate it. They think that a self-determined person, even when he gives hard labour, puts in serious and strenuous effort with positive thinking to win and devotion to his job, cannot achieve his target if the super power does not want it. The person needs sanction to proceed from such power. It is noteworthy to mention that a person develops confidence, earns intuition and forms a different state of courageous and encouraging mindset when he sincerely and honestly labours hard and makes repetitive attempts to win. Maybe some hidden force stimulates his driving force to engage in such activities which will bring success in his mission. But one thing is clear that the person needs to have strong determination to do, to win, to achieve and to labour if he wants to fulfil his desire. He cannot get the sanction from his super power to achieve without effort and diligence. Achievement does not come without performance while performance does not come without 'willingness to do' and 'determination to perform'. It is just like a dream of a boy of passing the examination without attending classes and studying subjects. In reality the reverse is the situation. The boy should have strongly determined base and labour hard to pass the examinations as the achievement of anything is not automatic. It is good to have faith on the super power as it may enhance the power of the inner person to establish confidence in self which may help to bring success in his mission. But it works when the person sincerely gives labour, prepares his mindset to succeed, to win, to achieve. It is foolish to think about achievement without performances, determination and diligence. Preparation of the mindset and development of self-determination is not a difficult task for a person. What a person needs is to create a sense of urgency and necessity for the thing which he wants to get. If he wants to reach any target set by him, he should develop a feeling that reaching the target is essential. He should think of himself as competent, effective, strong and capable enough to win the mission. He should keep his morale high. He should keep confidence in himself. He should consider the mission as challenging and achievable. With these he can develop his mental power and use his determination to win.

It is seen in some cases that persons gives up hope of winning any activity. They consider themselves weak and unsuitable, unfit for achieving some goals. They think that the given tasks are not meant for them. These are designed for the persons in the society who have skill, expertise, strength, power and resources for achievement. Such persons, suffering from inferiority complexes and weak personalities, are incapable of forming a strong base of self-determination and they are sure to lose the game. They are indolent, archaic, stereotypical persons who lack dynamism, aggressiveness and a competitive disposition. These persons remain happy with trifling jobs.

Thus there is no denying the fact that mindset of a person occupies a pivotal position to drive him to reach the place he desires. It is immaterial whether he is capable of doing it or not. It is only pertinent whether he is mentally prepared to do it, whether he decides to do it and whether he forms his mindset to do it. Doing or not doing has a direct relation with the mental framework. A well built mindset and a strong determination to do and to achieve inspires, motivates and pushes the person to the direction he wants. Practically, the person turns into a slave of the 'mind-force' and he creates and performs the job under the direct control of such a 'mind-force'. Once the person strongly decides to do something and then starts his activities, there is no question of force once the person starts his activities, there is no question of backing out from the activities. So long as the 'mind-force' remains in a commanding position, the person gives his result. If the 'mind-force' (i.e., the base of self-determination) becomes weak during the process of activities due to non-availability or non-supply of certain qualities and infrastructures, he ceases to win. This is observed in a situation when the person working in a team does not get adequate infrastructure to complete the assigned task but receives continuous threats from his boss indicating the consequences he may have to face for non-performance or non-completion of the work. The mindset of the person obtains a great jolt from his boss who underestimates the person's efficacy and passes strictures without ascertaining the realities. The person may lose his confidence and trust in his boss which affects his 'self-determining' power to succeed.

It is thus clear that a strong and positive mindset is a pre-requisite for developing self-determination. The more the positive mind-set is framed the greater is the force of self-determination. But due to various reasons the mindset of a person does not form appropriately. Some such reasons are as follows:

1. Uncongenial environment prevalent at the workplace and place of stay may make the situation unsuitable for the growth and development of the person. The person remains unhappy and dissatisfied with the environment. He feels unfortunate for the existing condition. He strives to make a change from the present environment. Under such conditions the mindset of the person remains in a deplorable state.
2. The style of functioning of the boss, expectations towards subordinates, mental dispositions, ego patterns and behavioural manifestations of the boss play a vital role in establishing some kind of boss-subordinate relationship. The positive, open and participative approach of the boss wins over the heart of the subordinate which reflects on the formation of the mindset of the subordinate accordingly. The reverse is the situation in the preparation of the

mindset of the subordinate. The negative, authoritarian and supervisory approach of the boss creates an environment of confusion, uncertainty and inconvenience of the subordinate. The subordinate may not like to stay in such an uncomfortable state of the workplace. All these negative attributes of the boss may affect adversely the formation of the mindset of the subordinate. The parental behaviour, thought processes, expectations and ego state of the parents/parent substitute and the family status and condition may also contribute in framing the mindset of the person appropriately.

3. An unexpected occurrence may change the formation of the mindset of the person. Such incidents may have a positive or negative impact on the mindset depending upon the nature and quality of incidents.
4. A change in the existing practice, system and policy and the introduction of a new method or system in the organization where the person works may bring a change in the mental-set up of the person.

The above factors as deliberated may bring a major change in the mental conditions of the person. The most damaging causative factor is the boss's humiliating attitude towards subordinates. In any work place subordinates may not be able to deliver quality goods or to enhance productivity if they become the victims of continuous threats and lack of appreciation from the boss. Under such an organizational milieu created through the style of functioning of the boss, the subordinate feels suffocated, uneasiness and remains under the pressure of fear-psychosis. He treats his boss as a personality more concerned with faultfinding than giving impetus to boost up productivity. All these factors adversely affect the formation of his mindset. The subordinate with a broken mindset may not be able to form strong determination. He may therefore, find it difficult to achieve his target, to win his mission and to fulfil his desire. It is then rare that the subordinate is able to perform his assigned task. The most pathetic situation occurs when the boss does not show any positive behavioural action for the hard-won performance of the subordinate. Rather, the boss demonstrates his displeasure and apathetic attitude at the activities of the subordinates.

It is thus apparent that the attitude of the boss, his style of functioning, behavioural patterns and perceptions towards subordinates contributes much to the formation process of the mindset of subordinates. All these actions of the boss emanate from his ego-state patterns developed in formative childhood, the input and infrastructure received in subsequent periods (adolescent and adult period), exposure to moulding therapeutically environment, knowledge, skill and experience acquired over a period of years. The ego-state pattern of an individual may be balanced with more or less equal distribution of all three ego states (viz., parent, adult, and child) in the whole ego-state pattern or otherwise. Under such a balanced ego state pattern the 'adult' is not influenced or contaminated either by the 'child' or 'parent' or both. The individual, therefore, can work independently. The boss with a balanced ego-state pattern may not have major problems working with the subordinates or vice-versa as the chances of building good rapport, understanding and confidence between each other very much exist. The formation process of positive and strong mindsets of the subordinates becomes smooth and uninterrupted which facilitates the development of the base of self-determination.

The unbalanced ego-state pattern of an individual may have unequal distribution of the ego-states in the whole ego state pattern. The 'adult' ego is disturbed by the influence of 'parent' or 'child' or by both. Either or both ego states contaminate the 'adult' and interrupt in the process of its effective functioning. The problem, therefore, lies with the boss having an unbalanced ego structure to go along with his subordinates to accomplish the job on common objectives. Both the boss and subordinate fail to come close to each other to develop mutual understanding and rapport between them. The subordinate, under such situations, may not find it a congenial atmosphere to form a solid and proper mindset in order to develop strong grounds of self-determination.

In any organizational system where both boss and subordinate cannot work together purposefully and effectively simply because of the former's unacceptable style of functioning due to his unbalanced ego-state, the initiation of the following measures may help the boss to make some attitudinal changes to work in a joint spirit so that subordinates can form the proper mindset:

1. Participation in a workshop, conference or training programme by the boss on 'personality development', 'motivation', 'human relations', 'human behaviour' and the like, which can give an in-depth idea of probable behavioural manifestations under different situations and the appropriate skill and technique required to overcome the situation in order do develop smooth and on-going human relations with the subordinate.
2. Continuous exposure of the boss to the interaction process with people of different segments, in a training programme designed exclusively for the purpose of understanding each other's ego patterns and finding a solution for amicable adjustment with the people when incompatible situations arise.
3. Arranging frequent meetings of the executives where higher management should emphasize the corporate objectives and vision and the role of the executives for the achievement of goals through a participative system.

   Open and free deliberation by executives on the line of action taken for performance of the assigned task and the difficulties if any faced by them, followed by feedback discussion where higher management should identify the 'blind-area' (generally the biased ego-activities) for taking corrective and remedial measures.
4. Holding short group meetings with the subordinates at regular intervals seeking active participation and involvement in the process of achieving the targets set by the higher management.

   Subordinates may be requested to express their feelings on the work environment, style of functioning etc. and to provide suggestions for better performance, growth and development.
5. Enrichment of knowledge of the boss in the area of Transactional Analysis, Gestalt Therapy, Human Behaviour and the like through discussions, attending ritual-performances, informal get-togethers, making the boss conversant with the latest research on behavioural aspects published in different articles and the participation in related subjects.
6. Arranging as many informal invitations of the subordinates at the residence of the boss as possible in order to ascertain

the ego patterns of subordinates as also the need of the subordinates. Such informal invitations afford ample opportunity to chitchat on different aspects between boss and subordinates which may open up a new era of understanding to build up a mindset afresh with positive thought-processes.

7. Indicating the necessity of stress tolerance quality as one of the most important traits.

   The higher management may convey the message of not making any hasty decisions under pressure and to deal with the situational problems with utmost care, courage and the stress tolerance capability.

   This may give the boss sufficient time to study thoroughly the situation, to enable him to take decisions in a comfortable environment after taking into consideration all aspects. He may get some time to think about the necessity of forming a new mind-set.

8. Re-ascertaining the veracity of the information submitted to the boss against a subordinate.

   It happens that an unbalanced boss collects information in respect of subordinates from his people belonging to the 'coterie' formed by him for his survival and growth. The boss initiates action against his subordinates without assessing the authenticity of the sources of the information. The boss should always keep in mind that in order to appease him, his so-called own people can concoct stories against subordinates.

   It may, therefore, be required that the boss should ascertain, re-ascertain, re-assess and re-check the veracity of the information from different sources. If any source gives information contrary to the information supplied by the coterie group or even if all the sources are okay as to the authenticity of the information, the boss should prepare his mindset afresh with a positive approach and start behaving freely, openly and without bias. He should make his will-force strong, firm and robust to establish harmonious human relations with subordinates. This may help to wipe out the bad impression about the subordinates from his mind and to develop positive thought-process about them.

9. The use of positive body language, posture and motivating words by the boss while talking to his subordinates:

If the boss starts talking to his subordinates ungrudgingly with a smiling face it conveys the green signal to them that a congenial environment exists to carry out transactions with the boss.

The biased boss (with the boss's 'adult' contaminated by the 'critical parent') may initially find it difficult to do so, but with determined spirit and strong will-force to change the mode of talking, expressions and behavioural patterns, the boss may succeed in his mission.

The boss should remember that abusive language, body gestures and postures that hurt the subordinates cause irreparable damage to the formation process of human relations and develops a negative attitude in the mindset of both boss and subordinates.

Chapter 10

HRD Hummings: Facilitating Agents to Change thought Patterns and Behavioural Manifestations for Establishment of Human Relations

In the preceding chapter detailed and thorough deliberations were made on the most essential aspect of human activities. Every human being regardless of caste, creed or religion is born to do something and continues to carry on activities during his lifetime to deliver his goods and services. He therefore searches for potential areas and endeavours to reach those areas for the fulfilment of his desires. Success or failure in his operations to achieve depends on several factors which have already been discussed. In an attempt to deliberate upon such key factors for successful operation in an organizational set-up presumptions have been made that (i) a congenial human relations climate exists (ii) a conducive work culture and work ethic prevails (iii) people do not lack the requisite knowledge, skill and tact for performance (iv) the work-people are average and more or less balanced in their activities. The importance of human relations, work environment, ego patterns and performance skills is emphasised as playing a facilitative role for job accomplishment. Elaborate and in-depth analysis on such topics has also been made in earlier chapters in order to help the people reach to expectation levels of work performance. As a corollary to the foregoing discussion and the concluding observations it is now essential to list out important do's, don'ts, admonitions and limiting/controlling advice for the growth and development of the person. All such suggestive hummings may help to prepare a positive mindset in the person for better and effective utilization of the opportunities, resources, infrastructure and benefits available to him. The person feels the necessity of developing mutual understanding, mutual trust and confidence through interpersonal activities for better work performance and achievement of team goals.

Altogether 200 HRD hummings are mentioned in this chapter with the objective to bring a change in thought patterns, perceptions and the mindset of the person who sincerely complies with and honestly believes in its utility and efficacy) so that he can play a positive role in any situational activity. Such hummings mould the person's ego state largely if not completely, enrich his information or data centre and guide him in the right direction to reach his destination and meet his goal.

HRD HUMMINGS

1. Winning or losing is influenced by the strengths and weakness of a person's driving force.
2. Do not hurt the person, if he is already hurt.
3. Utilize the boss's mood for the well being and upliftment of people.
4. When the boss is in an emotional and moody state, do not expose yourself to an environment which irritates him.
5. Never say 'no' to the boss in a crude form though you may be a hundred percent correct in your proposition.
6. The best way to change the wrongful decisions of the boss is to submit the matter to him when he is in a good and humorous mood.
7. Do not show your anger if your boss says something to you for your non-performance.
8. Take the cream from the boss and throw the waste into the dustbin.
9. When you become emotional, do not take any decisions.
10. Show your honesty and sincerity through your performance.
11. If you love the job, people surrounding the job will love you.
12. A person cannot be a good performer if he does not like the job that he does.
13. A person can learn the job better if he makes mistakes.

14. Keep yourself aloof from coteries if they are formed by the people who are in opposition to the boss.
15. Bring transparency to jobs you do before the boss.
16. Keep the boss informed of situational developments occurring in his absence.
17. A strong will drives the person to the place of his destination.
18. An honest effort never goes waste if properly utilized.
19. Self-determination is the key to success.
20. Always set a goal before you proceed to perform.
21. Draw up an action plan to achieve the target.
22. Do not be frustrated if you cannot win in the first few attempts.
23. Always keep your expectations high.
24. Never look back when you proceed further. Your vision should be forward, not backward.
25. Do not think about results but simply put in your best effort.
26. Everybody is born to achieve.
27. Prepare your mindset to win, not to lose.
28. Be alert, keep your ears open, observe the situation and do not pass any comment.
29. Do not be hasty while taking decisions.
30. Do not make mistakes knowingly.
31. A helping attitude is always good but action should not be made at the cost of other.
32. A person's image is built-up when he manifests his behavioural actions.
33. Behave decently, it does not cost but pays.
34. Behaviour is the cause of discipline and indiscipline.
35. It is preferable to have spontaneous discipline than imposed discipline.
36. Imposed discipline is short-lived while spontaneous discipline lasts long.
37. Hard labour brings success if done systematically.
38. Do not hate the person, hate his actions.
39. Devotion to one's job has no substitute.
40. Hard labour brings a sea change in the behavioural manifestation of other persons who are directly or indirectly connected with the activities.
41. Hard labour enhances the will force of the person to complete the job within a time frame schedule.

42. You may find transparency in work if you put in hard labour.
43. Hard labour brings confidence and develops a mental state of 'sure to win'.
44. Be alert when you interact with your moody boss.
45. Take calculated steps when the issue is touchy and sensitive.
46. It is better not to react when the boss shows his anger.
47. Do not go against the boss on any matter. Remember, the boss is supreme, he can do a lot against you.
48. It is easy for the boss to harm you if he wants.
49. Enhance your will power through hard labour.
50. Always accept a task easily. Do not think of not doing it, always think of doing it.
51. Self-esteem comes through hard labour; maintain it.
52. Every activity has its objective. Some objectives are exposed and some are hidden.
53. Self-determination makes the road smooth to go ahead.
54. Self-determination may come through diligence, sincere effort, devotion and perception to win.
55. Avoid doing what the boss is reluctant to do.
56. Be alert, follow the steps cautiously if your boss is unpredictable.
57. Move in a calculated way, if your boss does not like you.
58. Keep your interaction with your boss restricted if you sense an adverse climate.
59. If you are hurt by a management decision, tolerate it; do not go into confrontation with the decision maker against the decision.
60. The boss may not succeed in his mission if he fails to win the subordinate.
61. If you are affected by any action of the management, accept the action sportingly, console yourself, do not show any sign of discomfort.
62. When you deal with human problems, use the human touch.
63. Man has a iot of problems. When you deal with the problem do it with an empathetical approach.
64. Bosses may not be equal in all parameters, but in one area all bosses are equal; they intend to get work from the subordinates. So be a performer, show your worthiness.
65. Be positive in your approach, attitude and style of functioning. Mind it, a person with negative attributes rarely succeeds.

66. Treat the people working with you as your own men. Consider them as members of your family.
67. Be rational and neutral when you deal with any issue. Remember, all people are your own people. Misjudgement on any issue may have repercussions on hundreds of issues.
68. Be open with people so that others do not get a chance to misjudge you.
69. Man can win over any situation through honesty and hard labour.
70. Keep yourself happy. Happiness begets happiness.
71. If you feel happy, you become happy.
72. If you are not happy at the action of some person working with you, call him alone and counsel him to improve. Do not dress down a person in the presence of others. Praise people in public but do not give negative strokes publicly.
73. Do not pass comments without a thorough study and verification of the incidents.
74. Try to regulate emotions through a diversion of the topic. It is possible when you are confident about your mental strength and power.
75. Human beings in general do not like criticism. They want appreciation and praise in public. Do avoid criticism.
76. Develop confidence in the boss, you will enjoy working with him.
77. Be assertive. Convince the boss with logic and facts.
78. Everybody is born to achieve, so do not be a pessimist about achieving goals.
79. It is not that all things are easily available, you will have to work hard to have them.
80. It is easy to make the subordinate disciplined in a situation when the boss is disciplined.
81. It is unwise to expect discipline from subordinates if the boss himself breaches discipline.
82. Man is a sensitive animal. Be careful when you deal with the sensitive issues of the people.
83. Man is emotional. It is easy to get anything done when he is in a state of emotion. Do not exploit such situations for your own gain and benefit.
84. Do not be emotional. Control your emotions. Remember, emotion does a lot of harm to a person, if not controlled in time.

85. Structure your time, give priority to the job to be performed and then proceed.
86. If you are overqualified, knowledgeable and expert in your field of operation and your boss suffers from an inferiority complex, make him comfortable through manifestation of your behavioural activities and observance of norms of discipline, etiquette and official decorum.
87. If you see that the target given by your boss is unachievable, never express your negative outlook regarding acceptance. Take guidance and suggestions to facilitate achievement.
88. Do not be impatient or intolerant of any decision of your boss. Take it easy and obey accordingly.
89. Do the job as the boss wants, leave out that which the boss does not want.
90. Keep your mindset always in high profile to achieve the goal. Mind it, once you start thinking of your weaknesses, you lose to gain.
91. Be transparent in your work-activities. It is you who have to show results.
92. Be assertive. Advocate your opinion with facts and figures. Never get biased.
93. Learn to give. Remember everything is recorded.
94. Commitment, sacrifice and devotion are three essential parts of work achievement.
95. Draw up your action-plan before you commence your work. A haphazard way of work will not bring the desired result.
96. Keep your will power strong to perform any work. Remember, weak will power makes your performance weak.
97. Be calm and quiet when you deal with human issues. Do not use slang in the presence of subordinates.
98. Focus your personality as a role model. Others keep a watch on your activities.
99. Do not hold any personal grudges against anybody. If you are hurt by the activities of anybody, do not be vindictive when you are in the commanding position.
100. You are the best judge of your performance. If you are satisfied and happy with your work, the boss is also happy with you.

101. When you achieve the target, give the credit to your subordinates. When you fail to achieve the target take the responsibility as your own.
102. Do not hold any preferential impression about a person. Remember, such biased impression may damage your judgement power.
103. Openness and frankness in any participative system is good.
104. Remember, do not lose your individuality during the deliberative process.
105. If you are new to the situation it is better to listen and keep quiet during deliberations than to ask questions that are unwarranted.
106. Be friendly to all. Make others know through behavioural manifestation that you are with them.
107. Do not be over-smart. Remember, your activities do not go unnoticed.
108. Be polite and docile with your boss. Do not express any behavioural indication that may generate insubordination.
109. Do not think of yourself as super person. Keep on being what you are.
110. Nobody can claim that he excels in all areas and he has nothing to learn. Everybody has something to learn from others.
111. Do not ignore the boss. Mind it, the boss keeps close watch on your activities.
112. Do not judge the situation on the basis of one or two incidents. Take the totality of the circumstances, assess them and make your decision.
113. Keep yourself happy. Happiness makes the person active and effective. It increases productivity and brings an attitudinal change in a person and keeps him on a high profile.
114. Be good to others. Remember, it is more difficult to be good to others than to be bad to them.
115. As you think so will your mindset be. Remember, good thinking does not cost but pays.
116. Don't be biased. A biased person cannot be effective as his decisions are faulty.
117. Whenever any assignment is given, think how best can it be done.

118. Before you take decisions on vital matters, think of the pros and cons, ascertain the organizational gain in the long run and study the effect on other segments.
119. The decision maker should have a clear concept of the issues and of the basis on which the decision is taken.
120. Frequent changes of decision not only weaken the decision making power of the boss but also create an impression in the minds of the subordinate about the boss being indecisive, unpredictable and intolerant.
121. Prioritise your area of activities, structure your time and act accordingly.
122. If you want work from your subordinates, set the example of your work. Remember, a non-performing boss cannot expect better performance from his subordinates.
123. If you are not happy with anybody, do not expose yourself through your activity. It is better you control your emotion for the time being.
124. Human beings are not the same, they function from different perspectives. It is, therefore, natural to have divergent views on issues. You should take into account all these aspects while applying human skills to settle the issues of your subordinates.
125. No one can claim to be omniscient. Every person has something to learn from other. So do not lose it, enrich your knowledge.
126. As soon as you get entry to a new set up or organization, get yourself acquainted with the system, culture and environment.
127. Love the work, love the organization, love the people. It pays.
128. Work sincerely and honestly. Do not wait for the result, it is sure to come.
129. Whenever you evaluate the performance of a person, judge the performance not the man.
130. It is unwise, unethical and detrimental to the health of the institution to evaluate the performance of the subordinate on the basis of relationship criteria.
131. Objective assessment is always better than subjective assessment.
132. Do not be vindictive. Rather be supportive, facilitative and co-operative.

133. Do not compromise on discipline. Mind it, the organization cannot function effectively without discipline.
134. If you want to grow, if you want your organization to grow be disciplined and make others disciplined.
135. For existence and growth discipline is essential. Lack of discipline or indiscipline makes the organization weak and ineffective.
136. Where there is a question of survival and growth, there is discipline. Even nature follows discipline. Our body organs function on discipline. Remember, if any part of the system does not work in a disciplined manner, the whole system gets affected.
137. Human beings are sensitive resources. They are emotional. They need love, affection, recognition and affiliation. Give emphasis on these issues while dealing with human problems.
138. Nobody is perfect in all parameters. The best way to acquire perfection is through perseverance and untiring practice to develop confidence.
139. It is easy to be acceptable to others, if others are acceptable to you.
140. Exploit each and every opportunity available. Lost opportunity never comes back.
141. Do not wait for opportunity to come. Labour hard and put in your best effort to create opportunity.
142. A good performer enjoys recognition in the field of activities while a non-performer is ignored. There is no substitute for good performance.
143. Do not hate the wrongdoer, hate the wrong deeds. Make the opportunity available to the wrong doer to rectify his misdeeds.
144. Assertiveness brings confidence. Be assertive when you put forward your line of thinking in the decision making process.
145. Responsibility and authority are relative nomenclatures. Authority cannot be expected without responsibility.
146. Dynamism is the essential quality of the leader. Dynamism does not mean reckless functioning to show the leader's worth. A haphazard way of functioning makes the situation a mess.

147. Man gets results according to his labour. Labour hard to obtain expected results.
148. It is unwise to pass strictures on any person without ascertaining the realities.
149. It is easy to detect the faults of other but is difficult to rectify one's own faults.
150. Whenever you get the feedback on the performance and qualitative aspects of any person, do not act without verification from different quarters. A decision taken by you on the basis of wrong information may have widespread repercussions unconducive to effective functioning.
151. Before you pass any comment, you should ensure that it is required to justify rationality, reasonableness and necessity.
152. It is very easy to be a critical leader but it is more difficult to be an acceptable leader.
153. A critical leader cannot last long while a participative leader works for a longer duration.
154. You should not carry biased impressions of your subordinates. Remember, the establishment of human relations depends on how you perceive your subordinates.
155. Positive strokes are an essential device to enhance the morale of the achiever while negative strokes demoralize if applied persistently. Negative strokes in some cases bring positive results when they are urgently required.
156. Positive strokes given on time and in the presence of others are more effective than positives stroke given untimely and privately.
157. A few words of appreciation expressed by the boss even before a small gathering may bring a change in the mindset pattern of the subordinate to develop his base of self-determination.
158. Fix your target of expectation far above the level of expectation set by your boss. Mind it, it is not your boss but you who have to achieve the target and this is possible only when the target is set above expectation.
159. A worker of a team is known through his performance while a leader of the team is known through the performance of his team workers.
160. A worker pays respect to his boss from the core of his heart only when he sees that the boss is disciplined,

impartial, honest and non-vindictive. Remember, a worker-boss relation becomes much more compatible when the magnitude of respect expressed by the worker increases.

161. It is good to be humorous but is bad to be an abuser. An abuser cannot develop good rapport and understanding with subordinates.
162. The boss is the guardian of the team; he should not be partial to any team-member. Remember, biased decisions will disrupt the whole process of activities.
163. Each and every activity is important to perform. It is the subordinate who is to prioritise the activity and complete the job in a time-frame schedule.
164. Never get upset and frustrated if you cannot succeed even after a repetitive attempts are made. Success comes after failure.
165. Do not keep any matter pending for tomorrow. Do it immediately. Once you start keeping matters pending, they will pile up.
166. Man can earn confidence in work when he practices again and again. Remember, practising has no substitute.
167. If you find the boss in a bad mood, do not put forward new problems before him. It is better to observe him for a while before placing any issue before him.
168. Be impartial, think impartial, act impartial. Partiality makes enemies, impartiality makes friends.
169. The boss may take suggestions from possible sources before taking any decision, but his decision should not be biased or influenced by anybody. Remember, a biased decision does more harm than good.
170. If you want to do something you can do it, if you do not want to do it, you cannot do it. Your doing or not doing something depends exclusively upon your desire.
171. Nobody has come on the earth knowing everything. It is perseverance, sincerity and labour which make the person a master in the area of his work.
172. If your boss says something which is not correct, you should not argue over the matter; you may place the matter some other way so that he does not take it seriously.
173. If you pay respect, you can expect respect. Mind you, if anybody gives respect without obtaining respect, it is

done under compulsion and is short lived.

174. Never show your anger or dislike to anybody in the presence of others. It may create a bad impression about you besides creating a strain in relations between him and you.
175. You may not know your blind areas. So take it easy if someone points them out. Mind you, the more you know about your blind areas, more chance you have to rectify yourself.
176. No man is free from limitations. They differ from man to man in quality as also in quantity.
177. Do not take any decisions under pressure. Remember, decisions taken under pressure not only affect their quality but also demotivates the concerned people.
178. If you want to succeed in your mission as team leader, build up a family-like relation with the team members instead of a master-servant relation. People become committed to work only when they feel the existence of a conducive family climate in the work place.
179. It is immaterial to subordinates as to who comes as a team leader, but it is material to them when an unconcerned person takes charge of the team.
180. A leader should not develop personal grudges against any team member. If the leader finds there are unethical and unusual activities of any member, he should immediately call him and remove the misunderstanding.
181. The leader can make any team member accountable for any lapse but he cannot absolve himself from overall responsibility as a team leader.
182. A true leader is one who is successful in job accomplishment as per his action plan.
183. Do not compromise your moral value at any cost. Remember, it cannot be regained when once lost.
184. Be honest, sincere, diligent and committed to work, as all these bring a change in mindset to fulfil the level of satisfaction, desire and expectation.
185. It is easy to take decisions but it is not so easy to take the right decision. Remember to honour the decision when taken.
186. Be positive in your approach. Practice saying 'yes', not 'no'.

187. Work hard. The more you work, the more you learn.
188. Keep quiet and remain calm when the boss loses his temper. Do not argue or react.
189. Study your boss accurately and in different situations. Do not give opinions about your boss to others.
190. Your boss may abuse you for your non-performance or less performance, but it does not mean that your boss does not like you.
191. No job is unimportant. Each job has a role to contribute. Do your job with interest, seriousness and sincerity.
192. If a person is not happy with the job he is assigned, he will not be successful in his profession.
193. A person's activities at home may reflect on his activities in a work situation. A person slow in domestic and personal activities may be slow in work activities.
194. If you want to develop a feeling of acceptance and a sense of belonging, love the work, love the people and love the organisation.
195. Treat the people at work as your own family members.
196. Enquire about the health of your subordinates, the health of their families, and significant incidents in their lives. All these help to establish understanding, trust and confidence.
197. Offer a helping hand when your subordinates have family troubles. Assist them in any way you can.
198. Keep your ethical value high all the time. Remember, if it is eroded, it is lost and cannot be restored. A person's acceptance in the society, his reputation and recognition depends largely on the ethical values he holds.
199. An unethical person always carries a stigma which is not removed even after his disappearance.
200. Keep control of all of your senses.

Bibliography

Abraham H. Maslow, *New Knowledge in Human Values,* (Scranton, Pa.: Harper & Row, 1959).

—, *Motivation and Personality* (New York: Harper & Row, 1954).

—, *Towards a Psychology of Being* (Princeton, NJ: D. Van Nostrand & Co., Inc., 1962).

Aggarwal, R.D. (ed.), *Dynamics of Labour Relations in India: A Book of Readings* (Bombay: Tata McGraw-Hill, 1972).

Akkins, W.E. and Labswell, H.D., *Labour Attitudes and Problems* (Pitman and London, 1924).

Alexander, F., *Fundamentals of Psychoanalysis* (New York: Norton, 1948).

Ankalikar, S M., *Labour Management: Its Theory and Practice* (Bombay: New Book Co., 1945).

Anthony Storr, *The Integrity of the Personality* (Maryland: Penguin Books 1966).

Argyris, Chris, *Personality and Organization* (New York: Harper & Row, Publishers, 1951).

Anthony G., and Robert E., Coffey, *Behaviour in Organizations: A Multidimensional View,* (Englewood Cliffs, NJ, Prentice-Hall, Inc., 1968).

Bandura, A., *Principles of Behaviour Modification* (New York: Holt, Rinchart and Ninston, 1969).

Banerjee, R.N., *Industrial Awards and Industrial Relations in* India (Calcutta: New Age Publishers Private Limited, 1963).

Barnard, Chester I., *The Functions of the Executives* (Cambridge: Harvard University Press, 1938).

Bass, Bernard M., *Leadership, Psychology and Organizational Behavior* (New York: Harper & Row, 1960).

Bartley, S.H., *Principles of Perception* (New York: Harper & Row, 1958).

Beach, Dale S., *Personnel: The Management of People at Work,* New York, 1965.

Bendix, R., *Work and Authority in Industry* (New York: John Wiley & Sons, Inc., 1956).

Berelson, Bernard and Gary, A. Steiner, *Human Behavior: An Inventory of Scientific Findings* (New York: Harcourt, Brace and World, Inc., 1964)

Berne, Eric, *Games People Play* (New York: Grove Press, 1964).

—, *Principles of Group Treatment* (New York: Oxford University Press 1964).

—, *Transactional Analysis in Psychotherapy* (New York: Grove Press, Souvenir Press of London, 1961).

Bloom, G.E. and Blum, Milton L. (ed.), *Industrial Psychology and Its Social Foundations: Under the Editorship of Gardner Murphy Rev.,* New York, 1956.

Bolles, Robert C., *Theory of Motivation* (New York: Harper & Row 1967).

Bonnet, C.E., *Labour-Management Relations,* New York, 1959.

Broadbent, D.E., *Perception and Communication* (New York: Pergamon Press, 1958).

Brown, James and Alexander Campbell, *The Social Psychology of Industry: Human Relations in the Factory,* Harmondsworth, 1962.

Chamberlain, N.W., *Union Challenge to Management Control,* New York, 1948.

Chambers, Eric Gordon, *Psychology and the Industrial Worker* (Cambridge: the University Press, 1951).

Cofer, C.N. (ed.), *Problems and Processes in Verbal Behavior and Learning* (New York: McGraw-Hill 1963).

— and Appley M.H., *Motivation: Theory and Research* (New York: Wiley, 1964).

Cooley, C.H., *Social Organization* (New York: Scribner 1909).

Cyert Richard M., and James G. March, *A Behavioral Theory of the Firm* (Englewood Cliffs, NJ: Prentice-Hall, Inc., 1963).

Dahrendorf, Ralf, *Class and Class conflict in the Industrial Society*: tr. from the German, Rev. and expanded by the author (London: Routledge & Kegan Paul, 1959).

Dale, Ernest, *The Great Organizers* (New York: McGraw-Hill Book Company, 1960).

Dalton, M., *Men who Manage* (New York: John Wiley & sons, Inc., 1959).

Davis, Keith, *Human Relations at Work: the Dynamics of Organizational Behavior* (Bombay: Tata McGraw-Hill, 1967).

—, *Human Relations on Business* (New York: McGraw-Hill, 1957).

De Bono, Edward, *New Think* (New York: Basic Books, Inc. 1968).

Dember, W.N., *The Psychology of Perception* (New York: Holt, 1960).

Deutsch, J.A., *The Structural Basis of behavior* (London: Cambridge, 1960).

Doody, F.S., *Readings in Labour Economics*, Cambridge, 1956.

Draver, James , *The Psychology of Industry* (London: Metheun & Co., 1947).

Drucker, Peter F., *Effective Executive* (New York: Harper & Row, Publishers, 1967).

—, *The Practice of Management* (New York, Harper & Row, Publishers, 1954).

Dufty, N.P., *Industrial Relations in India* (Bombay, Allied Publishers, 1964).

Dunlop, J.T., *Industrial Relations Systems* (Henry Holt and Company, New York, 1958).

Erich Fromm, *The Revolution of Hope* (New York, Bantam, 1968).

—, *The Art of Loving* (New York, Harper & Row, 1956).

Eriksen, C.W. (ed.), F.J. Roethlisberger, and W.J. Dickson, *Behavioural and Awareness* (Durham, NC: Duke, 1962).

—, *Management and the Worker* (Cambridge, Mass: Harvard University Press, 1939).

Fayol Henry, *Industrial and General Administration* (Paris, Dunod, 1925).

Fiedler, Fred E., *Leader Attitudes and Group Effectiveness* (Urbana: University of Illinois Press, 1958).

Fisher, Waldo F., *The Role and Functions of Industrial Relations in the Business Organization*, California, 1961.

Franks, C.M., *Behavior Therapy: Appraisal and Status* (New York: McGraw-Hill Book Company, 1969).

Freud Sigmund, *The Ego and the Id* (London: Hogarth Press, 1927).

—, *New Introductory Lectures on Psychoanalysis* (New York: WW Norton & Company, Inc, 1933).

Fraser, John Munro, *Industrial Psychology* (Oxford, Pergamon Press, 1962).

Frederick S. Perls, *Gestalt Therapy Verbatim* (Lafayette, Calif: Real People Press, 1969).

Gardner, L., *Human Relations in Industry*, London, 1961.

Gellerman, Saul, W., *Leadership Style and Employee Morale* (New York: General Electric Company, Public and Employee Relations Services, 1959).

—, *Management by Motivation* (New York: American Management Association, 1968).

—, *Motivation and Productivity* (New York: American Management Association, 1968).

George R. Bach and Peter Hyden, *The Intimate Enemy* (New York: William Morrow, 1962).

Gesell, A., *Studies in Child Development* (New York: Harper & Row, 1948).

Ghiselli, E.E. and Brown, C.W., *Personnel and Industrial Psychology* (New York: McGraw-Hill, 1948).

Gilmer, B. Von-Haller, *Industrial Psychology* (New York, Mc Graw-Hill Book Co., 1961).

Godine, M.R., *The Labour Problems in the Public Service*, Cambridge, 1951.

Golden, C.S., and Harold J. Ruttenberg, *The Dynamics of Industrial Democracy*, New York, 1942

Gordon, T., *Group-Centred Leadership* (Boston: Houghton Mifflin Company, 1956).

Gore, William J., *Administrative Decision-Making* (New York: John Wiley & Sons, Inc. 1964).

Gross, N., W.S. Mason, and A. McEachern, *Explorations in Role Analysis* (New York: John Wiley & Sons, Inc., 1958).

Guest, Robert H., *Organizational Change: The Effect of Successful Leadership* (Homewood, Ill: Dorsey Press and Richard D. Irwin, Inc., 1964).

Gulick, C., *History and Theories of Working Class Movements*, California, 1951.

Hackler, L.M., *New Industrial Relations*, New York, 1948.

Haim G. Ginott, *Between Parent and Child* (Yew York: Macmillan, 1967).

Haire, Mason, *Psychology in Management* (New York, McGraw-Hill Book Co., 1956).

Hampton, David R., *Behavioral Concepts in Management* (Belmont Calif: Dickinson Publishing Co., Inc, 1968).

Harbison, F.H. and Dubin, R., *Patterns of Union-Management Relations*, Science Research Associates, Chicago, 1947.

Harris, Thomas, *I'm OK -You' re OK: A Practical Guide to Transactional Analysis* (New York: Harper & Row Publishes, 1969).

Helson, H. (ed.), *Contemporary Approaches to Psychology* (Princeton, NJ: Van Nostrand).

Herbert, A.T., *Dynamics of Groups at Work*, Chicago, 1954.

Hersey, Paul and Blanchard, K.H., *Management of Organizational Behaviour*, Utilising Human Resources, New Delhi, 1972.

Herzberg, Frederick, *Work and the Nature of Man* (New York: World Publishing Co., 1966).

—, B. Mausner and Barbara Snyderman, *The Motivation to Work*, second edition (New York: John Wiley & Sons, Inc, 1959).

Hoppock, R., *Job Satisfaction* (New York: Harper & Brothers, Publishers, 1935).

Hoxic, R.F., *Scientific Management and Labour*, New York, 1966.

Hughes, Everett C., *Men and their Work* (New York: The Free Press, 1958).

Hugh-Jones E.M. (ed.), *Human Relations and Modern Management* (North-Holland Pub.,1958).

James, Muriel and Dorothy Jongeward, *Born to Win: Reading*, (Mass: Addison-Wesley publishing Company, 1971.

James William, *The Principles of Psychology*, vol. I (London: Macmillan & Co., Ltd. 1890).

Jongeward, Dorothy, *Everybody Wins: Transactional Analysis Applied to Organization: Reading* (Mass: Addison-Wesley Publishing Company, 1974).

Kepner, C. H., and B.B. Tregoe, *The Rational Manager* (New York: McGraw-Hill Book Company, 1965).

Knowles Henry P., and Borje O. Saxberg, *Personality and Leadership Behavior: Reading* (Mass: Addison-Wesley Publishing Co.,1970).

Kobb, David A., Irwin M. Rubin and James M. McIntyre, *Organizational Psychology: A Book of Reading* (Englewood Cliffs NJ: Prentice-Hall Inc., 1971).

Koontz, Harold, and Cyril O'Donnell, *Principles of Management*, fourth edition (New York: McGraw-Hill Book Company, 1968).

Kornhanser, A.W., *Mental Health of the Industrial worker, a Detroit Study*, New York, 1965.

Lawrence, Paul and Jay Lorsch, *Organization and Environment: Managing Differentiation and Integration* (Boston: Harvard University, Graduate School of Business Administration, Division of Research, 1961).

Lazarus,. Richard S., *Psychological Stress and the Coping Process* (New York: McGraw-Hill. 1966.)

Leavit, H.J., *Managerial Psychology* (Chicago: University of Chicago Press, 1958).

Lee K. Frankel and Alexander Fleisher, *The Human Factor in Industry* (New York: The Macmillan Company, 1920).

Lester, R.A., *Labour and Industrial Relations: A General Analysis,* New York, 1953.

Lever E.J. and Goodell, F., *Labour-Management Co-operation .and How to Achieve It,* New York, 1948.

Likert, Rensis, *The Human Organization* (New York: McGraw-Hill Book Company, 1967).

—, *New patterns of Management* (New York: McGraw-Hill Book Company, 1961).

Lyman W. Porter, Edward E. Lawler III and J. Richard Hackman, *Behavior in Organizations* (New York: McGraw-Hill Book Company, 1975).

Maier, Norman R.F., *Psychology in Industry,* second edition (New York: Houghton Mifflin Company, 1955).

March, J.G., and H.A. Simon, *Organizations* (New York: John Wiley & Sons, Inc., 1958).

Marrow, Alfred J., *Behind the Executive Mask* (New York: American Management Association, 1965).

—, D.G. Bowers and S.E., *Strategies of Organizational Change,* New Seashore, eds. (New York: Harper & Row, Publishers, 1967.

Mayo, Elton, *The Social Problems of an Industrial Civilization* (Boston: Harvard Business School, 1945).

—, *Human Problems of an Industrial Civilization* (Cambridge. Mass: Harvard University Press, 1933).

McClelland, David C., et al., *The Achievement Motive* (New York: Appleton-Century Crofts, 1953).

—, et al., *The Achieving Society* (Princeton, NJ: D. Van Nostrand Co., Inc., 1961).

McGregor, Douglas, *The Human Side of Enterprise* (New York. McGraw-Hill Book Company, 1960).

—, *Professional Manager* (New York: McGraw-Hill Book Company, 1967).

Morris, Charles, *Signs, Language and Behavior* (Englewood Cliffs NJ: Prentice-Hall, 1946).

Mussen, Paul Henry, (ed.), *Handbook of Research Methods in Child Development* (New York: Wiley, 1960).

Myers, C.A., *Labour Problems in the Industrialization of India*, Cambridge, 1958..

—, *Industrial Relations in Sweden: Some Comparison with American Experience*, Cambridge, 1958.

Newcomb, T.M., *Social Psychology* (New York: Holt, Rinehart & Winston, Inc., 1950).

Newman, William H.,Charles E. Summer and E. Kirby Warren, *The Process of Management*, second edition (Englewood Cliffs, NJ: Prentice-Hall, Inc., 1967).

Northcoot, C.H., *Personnel Management: Principles and Practice*, London, 1960.

Odiorne, George S., *Management by Objectives* (New York: Pitman Publishing Corp. 1965).

Owens, Robert G., *Organizational Behavior in Schools* (Englewood Clifs, NJ: Prentice-Hall Inc., 1970).

Packard, Vance, *The Status Seekers* (New York: David McKay Co., Inc., 1959).

Perrow, Charles, *Organizational Analysis: A Sociological View* (Belmont, Calif: Wadsworth Publishing Co., Inc., 1970).

Peter and Barbara Wyden, *Growing up Straight* (New York: Stein and Day, 1968).

Porter, Donald E., and Phillip B. Applewhile, *Studies in Organizational Behavior and Management* (Scranton Pa: International Text Book Company, 1964).

Potter, S., *Theory and Practice of Gamesmanship* (Rupert Hart-Davis, 1947).

Reddin, William J., *Managerial Effectiveness* (New York: McGraw-Hill Book Company, 1970).

Reisman, David, *The Lonely Crowd* (New Haven, Conn.: Yale University Press, 1950).

Rice, A.K., *Productivity and Social organization* (London: Tavistock Publications, 1958).

Reynolds, L.G., *Labour Economics and Labour Relations*, London, 1954.

Richardson, J.H., *An Introduction to the Study of Industrial Relations*, London, 1954.

Roberts, B.C., *Industrial Relations*, London, 1962.

Roethlisberger, F.J., *Management and Morale* (Cambridge: Harvard University Press 1941).

—, and Dickson, W.J., *Management and the worker*, Massachusetts, 1939.

Rour, David Knox., *Industrial Relations Management for Profit and Growth*, New York, 1971.

Rubenstein, Albert H., and Chadwick J, Haberstroh, *Some Theories of Organization* (Homewood, Ill. Richard D. Irwin, Inc., 1960).

Sanford, Fillmore H., *Authoritarianism and Leadership* (Philadelphia Institute for Research in Human Relations, 1950).

Schachter, Stanley, *The Psychology of Affiliation* (Stanford, Calif; Stanford University Press, 1959).

Schein, Edgar H., *Organisational Psychology* (Englewood Cliffs, NJ Prentice-Hall, Inc., 1965.

—, and Warren G. Bennis, *Personal and Organizational change through Group Methods* (New York: John Wiley & Sons Inc., 1965).

Schleh E.C., *Management by Results* (New York: McGraw-Hill Book Company, 1961).

Schults, Duane P., *Psychology and Industry*, New York, 1973.

Seiler, John A., *Systems Analysis in Organizational Behavior* (Homewood, Ill: Richard D. Irwin, Inc., 1956).

Shartle, C.L., *Effective Performance and Leadership* (Englewood Cliffs, NJ: Prentice-Hall Inc. 1956).

Sheldon, W.H., *Varieties of temperament* (New York: Harper & Row, 1942).

—, Harvey, O.J., White, B.J., Hood, W.R., and Sherif, C., *Intergroup Conflict and Co-operation* (Norman, Okla.: Institute of Group Relations, University of Oklahoma).

Sidney M. Jourard, *Disclosing Man to Himself* (New York: Van Nostrand Reinhold, 1968).

Simon, H.A., *Administrative Behavior* (New York: The Macmillan Company. 1947).

—, *Models of Man, Social and Rational* (New York: John Wiley & Sons, Inc., 1957).

Skinner, B.F., *Science and Human behavior* (New York: The Macmillan Company, 1953).

—, *Verbal Behavior* (New York: Appleton-Century-Crofts).

—, *Analysis of Behavior* (New York. McGraw-Hill Book Company, 1961).

Slichter, Summer H., *Union Policies and Industrial Management*, Washington, 1941.

—, *The Challenge of Industrial Relations; Trade Unions Management, and the Public Interest.* Cornell University

Smith, May, *An Introduction to the Industrial Psychology*, London, 1945.

Solley, C.M. and Murphy. G., *Development of the Perceptual World* (New York: Basic Books, Inc., 1960).

Stogdill, R.M., *Individual Behavior and Group Achievement* (New York: Oxford University Press 1959).

Strauss, George and Sayles, Leonard R., *Personnel: The Human Problems of Management* (Prentice-Hall, 1962).

Suojanen, Waino W., *The Dynamics of Management* (New York: Holt, Rinchart & Winston, Inc., 1966).

Sutermeister, Robert A, *People and Productivity* (New York: McGraw-Hill Book Company, 1963).

Taylor, Frederick W., *The Principles of Scientific Management* (New York: Harper & Bros., 1911).

Terman, L.M., and Oden, M.H., *The Gifted Child Grows up* (Standford, Calif: Stanford,1947).

Terry, George R., *Principles of Management,* third edition (Homewood, Ill.: Richard D. Irwin, Inc.,1960.)

Thelen H.A., *Dynamics of Groups at Work* (Chicago: University of Chicago Press 1954).

Thomas Szasz, *The Myth of Mental illness* (New York: Dell Publishing. 1961).

Thompson Victor A., *Modern Organization* (New York: Alfred A. Knopf, Inc., 1970).

Thorndike, E.L., *Educational Psychology,* vol. 2. *The Psychology of Learning* (New York: Columbia, 1913).

Townsend, Robert C., *Up the Organization* (New York: Alfred A. Knopf, Inc., 1970).

Trist, E.L. et al., *Organizational Choice* (London: Tavistock Publications, 1963).

Ullman, L.P. and Krasner, L., *Case Studies in Behavior Modification* (New York: Holt,1945).

Uric Bronfenbrenner, *Two Worlds of Childhood, US and USSR* (New York: Russell Sage Foundation, 1970).

Urwick, Lyndall F., *The Theory of Organization* (New York. American Management Association, 1952).

Vernon, M.D., *A Further Study of Visual Perception* (New York: Cambridge, 1952).

Vernon, Philip E., *The Structure of Human Abilities,* Rev. ed. (London: Methuen, 1960).

Vinacke, W.E., *The Psychology of Thinking* (New York: McGraw-Hill, 1952).

Virginia Satir, *Conjoint Family Therapy* (Palo Alto: Science and Behavior Books, 1964).
Viteles, M.S., *Motivation and Morale in Industry* (New York: W.W, Norton & Company Inc., 1953).
Vroom, V. H., *Some Personality Determinants of the Effects of Participation* (Englewood Cliffs, NJ: Prentice-Hall, Inc., 1960).
—, and Philip Yetton, *Leadership and Decision Making* (Pittsburgh, Pa: University of Pittsburgh Press, 1973).
Warner, W. Lloyd, *Social Class in America* (New York: Harper & Row, Publishers, 1960).
—, and Norman H. Martin, eds., *Industrial Man* (New York. Harper & Brothers, 1959).
Watson, J.B., *Psychology from the Standpoint of a Behaviorist,* second edition (Philadelphia: Lippincott 1924).
Webber, Ross A, *Management: Basic Elements of Managing Organizations* (Homewood, Ill: Richard D. Irwin, Inc., 1975).
Wertheimer M, *Productive thinking* (New York: Harper & Row, 1945).
Westerlund, G., *Group Leadership and Field Experiment* (Stockholm; Nordisk Rotogravyr, 1952).
White, Robert W., and R. Lippitt, *Autocracy and Democracy: An Experimental Inquiry* (New York: Harper & Row, Publishers, 1960).
Whitehead, T.N., *The Industrial Worker,* 2 vols. (Cambridge: Harvard University Press; 1939).
Whiting J.W.M., and Child I.L., *Child training and personality* (New Haven, Conn.: Yale 1953).
Whyte, W.F., *Man and Organization* (Homewood, Ill.: Richard D. Irwin Inc., 1959).
—, (ed.), *Industry and Society,* New York, 1946.
—, (ed.), *Money & Motivation,* (New York: Harper & Row Publishers, 1955).
Whyte, W.F. (ed), *Pattern for Industrial Peace,* New York, 1951.
Whyte, W.H., Jr., *The Organization Man* (New York: Simon and Schuster, Inc., 1956).
Woods, *Industrial Conflict and Dispute Settlement,* Montreal 1955.
Woytinsky, W.S., *Three Aspects of Labour Dynamics,* Washington, 1942,
Yoder, Dale, *Personnel Management and Industrial Relations,* New York 1948.

Yoder, Dale, Heneman H.G. Turnbull John G. and Stone C. Harold, *Handbook of Personnel Management and Labour Relations*, New York, 1958.

Young D.M., *Understanding Labour Problems*, London, 1959

Zaleznik, A., *Worker Satisfaction and Development* (Boston: Harvard Business School, 1956).

Zweig, F, *Worker in Affluent Society*, New York, 1962.

REPORTS, DOCUMENTS, YEAR BOOKS ETC.

Central Board for workers' Education, India: Industrial Welfare, Delhi, Grievance Procedure, Delhi.

Central Statistics Organization, New Delhi: Annual Survey of Industries, 1959-68.

Division of Industrial Relations, Stanford University: Industrial Relations Papers, No. 2. January, 1949.

Division of Labour Statistics and Research, Japan: Year Book of Labour Statistics, 1960-65.

Government of India: First Five Year Plan; Second Five Year Plan; Third Five Year Plan; Report of the Labour Investigation Committee, 1946; Report of the Royal Commission on Labour in India 1931; Report of Second Seminar on Labour-Management Co-operation, 1960; Report of the Study group on Workers' Participation in Management, 1957; and Report on Workers' Education, 1957.

International Labour Office: The Worker's Standard of Living, 1938; Industrial Labour in India, 1938; Job Evaluation, Geneva, 1961; and Industry and Labour, Geneva, 1960; The Trade Union Situation in the U.K., Geneva, 1961; The Trade Union Situation in the U.S., Geneva, 1960; International Labour Code 1951, Geneva, 1962; Workers' Nutrition and Social Policy, 1936; Social Security: Principles and Problems arising out of the war, 1944; Problems of Social Security, New Delhi, 1947; Practical Methods of Increasing Productivity in Manufacturing Industries, Geneva, 1953; International Society Policy, Geneva, 1956; Worker Education Manual, Geneva, 1962; Standard of Labour Statistics, Geneva, 1962; Payment by Results, Geneva, 1961; Collective Agreement Series A (Industrial Relations), no. 39, Geneva, 1936; Industrial

Relations; Report VIII 31st Session, San Francisco, 1948; The Role of Government in the Filed of Labour-Management Relations, Canadian Approach, no. 1, Geneva, 1957; and Some aspects of labour-Management Relations in Asia, no. 5, Geneva, 1958.

Labour Bureau: Family Living Survey among Industrial Workers, 1958-59, General Report, 1970; Digest of Indian Labour Statistics, 1960-68.

Labour Investigation Committee, Government of India: Main Report, 1946 (Rage Committee).

Ministry of Labour,India: Towards a Welfare State Delhi, 1954.

Ministry of Labour and Employment, India: Report on the Working of Joint Management of Councils, Simla, 1965; Tripartite Conclusions, 1942-62, Delhi; and Problems of Indian Labour-A Symposium, New Delhi, 1947.

Ministry of Labour and Employment, India: Trade Unions, (1960-61, 1963-64); Consultative Machinery in Labour Field, New Delhi; and Current Problems of Labour in India, New Delhi, 1960.

National Commission on Labour, India: Analysis of Replies to Commissions Questionnaire, Delhi 1969; Indian Worker: A Changing Profile, 1947-67, Delhi, 1969; and Report of the National Commission on Labour, 1966, Delhi, 1969.

United Nations (U.N.): Economic Survey for Asia and the Far East 1961, Bangkok, 1962.

JOURNALS, OFFICIALS AND OTHER PUBLICATIONS

Academy of Management Journal, 1967, 1970-75.

Administrative Science Quarterly, 1956-65, 1971, 1975.

American Economic Review, 1960-65.

American Journal of Sociology, 1965-68.

American Sociological Review, 1948, 1954, 1957, 1960-62, 1970-73.

Applied Anthropology, no. 2 (1942)

Applied Economic Papers, September, 1969.

Asian Labour, New Delhi, 1960-65.

Asian Worker, Calcutta, 1968.

Bombay Labour Journal, 1967.

British Journal of Sociology, 1965, 1970-75.

Commerce, Bombay, Annual Number, 1968.

Eastern Economist, New Delhi, V 51 (3), 19th July, 1968.
Econ, Howrah (WB) May-June, 1974.
Economic Journal, London, 1965-66.
Economic Review, New Delhi, 1968.
Economic Times, Bombay, 28th September, 1967.
Economic Weekly, Bombay, March, 20, 1969.
Financial Express, Bombay, 1968.
Harvard Business Review, 1955, 1964-69.
Hindustan Standard, Calcutta, 10th May, 1971.
Human Relations, London, 1951, 1960, 1968.
Indian Economic Journal, Bombay 1965.
Indian Industries, 1964.
Indian Journal of Commerce, December, 1970.
Indian Journal of Labour Economics, Lucknow, October, 1969. and January, 1969.
Indian Labour Journal, June, 1969.
Indian Potter, Calcutta, 1985-92.
Indian Worker, New Delhi, 29th May, 1967, August 31, 1970.
Industrial Relations, Calcutta, 1970-71.
Journal of Abnormal Social Psychology, 1955-60, 1965-68.
Journal of Applied Psychology, 1956-60, 1962-65, 1970-75.
Journal of Psychology, 1959.
Journal of Social Issues, 1956-60.
Management Review, New York, 1960.
Monthly Labour Review, U.S., 1960-62.
New Sketch, 26th January, 1966.
Oxford Economic Papers, London 1965-68.
Personnel, 1955, 1958, 1970-75
Personnel Psychology 1960-63, 1970-75.
Psychological Review, 1957-59.
Psychological Today, 1968, 1972, 1975.
Public Administration, 1965.
Quarterly Journal of Industrial Relations, California, 1960-65.
Review of Economic Studies, Edinburgh, 1960-66.
Statistics of Labour-Management Relations, California, 1955-60.
Transactional Analysis Bulletin 1967-71.
Transactional Analysis Journal 1970-73.

Index